The War Against the Bible: Ishmael, Esau and Israel at the End Times
Copyright © 2024 by Israel365

All rights reserved.

This book, or any portion of it, may not be reproduced or transmitted electronically, mechanically, or by any other means including but not limited to photocopying, scanning, downloading, etc., without prior written permission of the author.

For sales inquiries, contact: store@israel365.com

Written by Rabbi Elie Mischel
Cover by Yehudit Weingarten
Interior design by Chani Gordon

ISBN: 978-1-957109-52-7, *hardcover* • ISBN: 978-1-957109-53-4, *paperback*

First Edition 2024

www.israel365.com

IN HONOR OF

Rabbi Mordechai Feuerstein ybl"ch

Rabbi Emeritus of Congregation Suburban Torah

With heartfelt appreciation for his many years of
dedication to the Livingston community.

IN MEMORY OF

Rebbetzin Shayndel Feuerstein z"l

May her memory be a blessing to her family and
the Livingston community.

IN MEMORY OF

Rabbi Moshe Kasinetz z"l

Founding Rabbi of Congregation Suburban Torah

May his memory be a blessing to the Kasinetz family
and the Livingston community.

IN HONOR OF

Rebbetzin Sarah Kasinetz tbl"ch

Founding Rebbetzin of Congregation Suburban Torah

With gratitude for decades of love and service
to the Livingston community.

TABLE OF CONTENTS

Acknowledgments		6
Part I: The War Against the Bible — An Introduction		11
Chapter 1:	The World War Against the Bible	12
Chapter 2:	The Hebrew Bible: A Great Voice That Does Not Cease	23
Part II: Biblical Beginnings		38
Chapter 3:	The Fourth Kingdom: Edom and Ishmael Unite	39
Chapter 4:	Ishmael: The Wild Donkey	51
Chapter 5:	Esau: The Deceptive Pig	64
Chapter 6:	From Jacob to Israel: The Secret Power of the Moon	81
Part III: Prophecies of Today — Ishmael		99
ISHMAEL		100
Chapter 7:	Prisoners of Hope: Zechariah's Prophecy of October 7	101

| Chapter 8: | Are we Living the Gog of Magog War? | 110 |
| Chapter 9: | Ishmael's Resentment:
The Al-Aqsa Flood | 120 |

EDOM — 130

| Chapter 10: | Obadiah's Warning to the West | 131 |
| Chapter 11: | Dividing God's Land: The Valley of
Jehoshaphat and the Two-State Solution | 139 |

ISRAEL — 146

Chapter 12:	Pain, Hope and Promise	147
Chapter 13:	Step by Step: A Redemption that Cannot be Rushed	159
Chapter 14:	Jews and Israelis: Labor Pains on the Way to Redemption	174
Chapter 15:	Fight Like David: The Biblical Response to Terror	184
Chapter 16:	Jews Who Refuse to See: From Nazi Germany to Gaza	190
Chapter 17:	Saul's Failure and Bibi's Decision: The Future of Gaza	198
Chapter 18:	Zephaniah's Cry: Don't Rely on America!	206
Chapter 19:	A Religious Revival? Mordecai, Esther and the Lion Within	216

Part IV: Conclusion — **229**

| Chapter 20: | Soon, Soon, Soon:
From War to Redemption | 230 |

Endnotes — **244**

ACKNOWLEDGMENTS

The poet Yehoshua November writes of professors who "long for eternal truths and to be published."[1] Fortunately, I'm no professor (most of whom today work for Hamas, Inc.), but I do, on occasion, long for eternal truths. And yes, I can't deny that I also have an insatiable longing to be published.

John Adams, the underrated second President of the United States, hit the nail on the head when he said that "of all the passions and propensities of man, none is more essential, or more remarkable, than the passion for distinction… A desire to be observed, considered, esteemed, praised, beloved, and admired by his fellows, is one of the earliest, as well as keenest dispositions discovered in the heart of man."[2] Most of us, deep down, need to be noticed - and I am no exception!

This isn't something I'm proud of. Rabbi Nachman of Bresolv once rebuked a Jew, saying: "You don't even know how to recite the Grace After Meals in truth. Because in all that you do, you feel the need to make sure your actions are viewed positively by other people, and you cannot perform even one simple commandment for God's sake alone!"[3] Ultimately, we will all stand before God, and I suspect that whether we were "noticed" in bookstores or on social media won't matter much then.

While acknowledging my baser motivations for writing this book, I'll rely on the broad shoulders of the great light of Israel, Rabbi Abraham Isaac Kook: "It is foolish to refrain from writing words of Torah because of the concern that pride is a motivating factor. We must go forward with all good things and try to elevate our thoughts and intentions. And the pride? Either it will be overcome or sanctified and uplifted to its proper source."[4] Regardless of my own flaws, there is a chance this book may lead some of God's people to return to the wisdom of God's Book. I hope and pray that Rabbi Kook's faith in me, among all the other would-be authors in Israel, was not misplaced.

Having given my own ego its due, I want to thank the special people without whom I could never have published this modest book.

Rabbi Tuly Weisz and Robbie Frohlinger, the founder and CEO, respectively, of Israel365, for leading the rare organization that is unafraid to take an unpopular stand and to stand up for what they believe in. It is a true honor to work together with you and the rest of the extraordinary team. We are making history together.

Yehudit Weingarten and Mordi Levi, for their creativity and hard work in designing this cover.

Shira Schechter, for carefully and patiently editing this book and saving me from embarrassment multiple times.

Avi Borgen, for reviewing and editing this book. Sometimes the most "normal" people are the true revolutionaries.

Michael Chapman, for helping to make this idea a reality. Don't forget - Ozzy can root for the Mets from the holy land too.

Corey and Kristi Ingram, for thinking of my kids almost as much as I do.

Rabbi Pesach Wolicki, for reminding me to write for the good, normal people - and never for the academics.

Rabbi Shlomo Katz, for inviting me to your meal of redemption, a meal that never ends at Shirat David. May Uriel and I merit to wash your hands (and feet?) in the rebuilt Temple.

Rabbi Herschel Reichman, the Rebbe we all desperately needed, who lifted us up when our enemies brought us down.

Dan B, Dan K, Eli, Baruch, Ari and Steve, Jews in their 40s, for never giving up on the revolution.

The amazing Efrat community, for studying the Bible together with me over the last three years. Much of this book is the fruit of our study together and the back and forth that brings our learning to life.

My beloved Suburban Torah community of Livingston, New Jersey, for joyously celebrating our *Aliyah* and for supporting me in bringing this book to publication.

Rabbi Abraham Isaac Kook, zt"l, the light of Israel, and Rabbi Hanan Porat, zt"l, the hero of our time, whose teachings made it impossible for our family to remain in exile. Their Torah is not only the inspiration behind this book, but is the light I strive to live by.

Nachshon, Aharon and Yosef, for protecting us and all of Israel.

Grandma Faye, for teaching me to always say it like it is.

My parents, Howie and Terry Mischel, for teaching us to be proud and unapologetic Jews - and to call out the antisemites when we see them.

My in-laws, Lenny and Mushy Fuld, for convincing Rebecca to marry me when she wasn't all that sure. I hope I never make you regret it!

Judah, for guiding me every step of the way and making this dream a reality.

Judah & Ora, Sarah & Ari, Ariel & Yosef, Ari & Talia, Jessie & Daniel, for being the supportive siblings everyone hopes for but few are lucky enough to have.

Klilah, for the afikomen. You win!

Klilah, Emunah, Aderet and Uriel, our amazing kids who left their comfortable life in New Jersey to become "obstacle to peace" settlers in Judea. It isn't always easy, but you guys are warriors!

And most of all, Rebecca, for *everything*.

Joseph Epstein, America's greatest essayist and the only celebrity to whom I've ever written a fan letter, once penned a disclaimer that he believed ought to appear at the beginning of every book. Mr. Epstein - I'm not sure how many writers have followed your advice. I highly doubt they could do much better.

"I wrote this book in the hope of making a persuasive argument, while giving pleasure to myself in forming my thoughts into sentences, paragraphs, and chapters. Whether I shall give anything resembling an equivalent pleasure to my readers is highly doubtful, I realize, but an author retains his slender hopes. I wish my book were better than it is, but I fear that it is quite the best that I have had the skill and patience to make. If any justification for this book is needed, it is that the book seeks, in its stuttering way, to take a very small part in a conversation which has been going on for a very long while now. For myself, I hope to be able to read it ten years hence without shame or regret."[5]

And let us say, amen.

The earth sways like a drunken man, and it sways like a lodge, and its transgression shall weigh down upon it, and it shall fall and not continue to rise. And it shall come to pass on that day, that the Lord shall visit punishment upon the host of heaven on high and upon the kings of the earth on the earth.

ISAIAH 24:20-21

PART I:

THE WAR AGAINST THE BIBLE

An Introduction

CHAPTER 1:

THE WORLD WAR AGAINST THE BIBLE

October 7, 2023. For the Jewish people, this day - the final day of the Sukkot[1] festival, known as *Simchat Torah,* "The Joy of the Bible" - will forever be etched in our memory. It is traditionally a day of extraordinary joy, when Jews dance for hours to thank God for the gift of the Bible. But never again, until the final redemption comes and the tears are wiped from our faces, will we be able to dance and celebrate on this day with a full heart. The brutal slaughter of over 1,200 innocent men, women, children and babies by Hamas terrorists on October 7, the worst massacre of Jews since the Holocaust, means our *Simchat Torah* joy will always be accompanied with tears for the precious souls taken from us on that day. Though much of the world turns a blind eye to Hamas' war crimes - the rape, assault and mutilation of Jewish women, the murder and burning of over 40 Jewish babies, the slaughter of children and the elderly in front of their loved ones, the taking of over 240 hostages - *we* will never forget. And we will not forgive.

Even as Israelis were still identifying and burying the dead, millions of people took to the streets of major cities across the world to scream their support for Hamas and the destruction of Israel. Over 300,000 people marched through London on November 11, calling for Israel's destruction - and protests are ongoing. Throughout the United States, protestors violently voiced their hatred of Israel, Jews and America, beating Jews, attacking Jewish businesses and threatening Jewish communities. Though a majority of Americans still support Israel, 51 percent of Americans between the ages of 18-24 believe that Hamas' slaughter of Israeli civilians "can be justified."[2] Universities throughout America and across the world have become hotbeds of antisemitism, where Jewish students are verbally and physically assaulted.

Sadly, none of this is surprising. Antisemitism has long been on the rise: those who refused to stick their heads in the sand have predicted for years that the simmering Jew-hatred on college campuses would soon spill over onto American streets. But most did not foresee the targeting of Christians by pro-Hamas activists. After the Hamas massacre of October 7, rioters violently disrupted the iconic Rockefeller Center Christmas tree lighting, chanting "From the River to the Sea" and shoving, punching and kicking police officers.[3] Agitators ruined holiday celebrations across the United States and Canada, drowning out children's choirs and screaming "no Christmas as usual."

If attacks on Christmas seem like mere collateral damage from the Israel-Hamas war, think again. On older Palestinian flags, a sentence is written in Arabic that is cited by Hamas leaders to this day: "*yawm alsabt niqtal alyahudu. fi 'ayaam al'ahada. sawf niqtal almasihiiyn,*" which translates to: "On Saturdays, we will murder the Jews. On Sundays, we will murder the Christians."[4]

Why are pro-Hamas protestors attacking Christians? Why do Islamic leaders plan to first kill Jews in Israel and then Christians in America and throughout the world? What does any of this have to do with the conflict in Gaza?

An Unholy Alliance

Incredibly, jihadists have plenty of friends in the West. Millions of self-described "woke progressives" have allied themselves to Hamas and its goal of wiping the Jewish state off the map. Within two days of the October 7 attack, Chicago's Black Lives Matter chapter celebrated the Hamas massacre on social media, publishing an image of a terrorist paragliding with a Palestinian flag on his parachute with "I stand with Palestine" written underneath. In violent protests on city streets and campuses across the country, young progressives are serving as Hamas' foot soldiers. At Cooper Union in Manhattan, Jewish students were forced to hide in the library as a mob of antisemitic students pounded on the door, threatening to kill them. At Harvard, over 30 student groups signed a petition that blamed Israeli victims for their own deaths, asserting that they "hold the Israeli regime entirely responsible for all unfolding violence," while its president refused to say that calls on campus for the genocide of Jews would violate the school's conduct policy.

If it wasn't so frightening, it would be comical. Thousands of gay and lesbian protestors who wouldn't survive for one day in Hamas-led Gaza have taken to the streets under the banner of "Queers for Palestine." It's jarring to see, as Bari Weiss writes, how "hip, young people with pronouns in their bios are not just chanting the slogans of a genocidal death cult. They are tearing down the photographs of women and children who are currently being held hostage in the tunnels that run under the Gaza Strip. They do so with pleasure. They laugh. They mock the 9-month-old baby who was stolen from his parents."[5] Social justice warriors bend over backwards to explain how Hamas' rape of Jewish women was "resistance" and "liberation."

What is behind this strange and unholy alliance between secular woke progressives and the Islamic jihadists of Hamas? Why do they support a radical religious movement that despises them? The answer, as always, is in the Bible.

The Rebellion Against God

"For behold, Your enemies stir, and those who hate You raise their heads. Against Your people they plot cunningly, and they take counsel against Your protected ones. They said, 'Come, let us destroy them from [being] a nation, and the name of Israel will no longer be remembered.' For they have taken counsel with one accord; against You they form a pact. The tents of Edom[6] and the Ishmaelites…" (Psalm 83:3-7)

This psalm is not merely history, and it is far more than a prayer. It is *prophecy*.

The Psalmist tells us that the day will come when arch-enemies Edom and Ishmael will set aside their differences and stand together in battle against the people of Israel. The spiritual descendants of Esau and the pagan Roman Empire will join together with the children of Ishmael, the radical Muslims who have waited for millennia to avenge the honor of their forefather against Isaac's descendants, the people of Israel. Nations will join together in a deceitful plot against Israel, to destroy them as an independent nation in the land of Israel.[7]

Ultimately, the war against Israel is not about land, power or geopolitics, or even the people of Israel. It is a war against God Himself. "For they have taken counsel with one accord; against *You* they form a pact" (Psalm 83:6). This pact is against "You," God, in order to cause His name to be forgotten. Since He is called the God of Israel, if Israel is forgotten His great name will no longer be remembered.[8] Edom, Ishmael and their allies are driven by a hatred for the nation that represents the God of Abraham, Isaac and Jacob. "So it was, whenever the ark set out, Moses would say, 'Arise, O Lord, may Your enemies be scattered and may those who hate You flee from You'" (Numbers 35:10). Who are the nations that hate God? These are the nations who hate Israel, for anyone who hates Israel hates the One Who spoke and brought the world into being.[9]

The second chapter of Psalms also describes the final war against Israel, in which the nations will "take counsel against the Lord" and seek to throw off the "cords" of God's law. "Why have nations gathered and [why do] kingdoms think vain things? Kings of a land stand up, and nobles take counsel together against the Lord and against His anointed? 'Let us break their bands and cast off their cords from us'" (Psalm 2:1-3).

The sages ask: "Why is the second Psalm, about the Gog of Magog war, immediately followed by 'A song of David, when he fled from Absalom his son' (Psalm 3:1)? So that if one should say to you, is it possible that a slave should rebel against his master, [i.e. that the nations will rebel against God,] you can reply to him: Is it possible that a son should rebel against his father? Yet that happened, and so this too will happen."[10]

Why do Edom and Ishmael hate Israel? God chose Israel to bring His word, the Divine law of the Bible, to all of mankind, as it says, "You shall be to Me a kingdom of priests and a holy nation" (Exodus 19:6). Ever since that awesome moment at Mount Sinai, it has been Israel's holy mission to carry the banner of the God of morality and restraint. "You shall not murder. You shall not commit adultery. You shall not steal. You shall not bear false witness against your neighbor. You shall not covet your neighbor's house. You shall not covet your neighbor's wife…" (Exodus 20:13-14).

The enemies of Israel yearn to be free of these restrictions: "Let us break their bands and cast off their cords from us." Their primary goal in attacking Israel is their hatred for Israel's faith in God, the Bible and the commandments that they wish to destroy.[11] More than any other, this verse captures the strange bond shared by the descendants of Ishmael and Esau. Despite their radically different world views, woke progressives and Islamic jihadists are united by their common hatred of the Bible, Judeo-Christian values and the people who live by God's word.

Marriage only between a man and a woman? The sanctity of life, including the unborn? Woke Edomites hold the Bible responsible for these "backward" ideas. They understand that the God of the Jews and His "outdated" book stand in the way of their agenda to revolutionize society and remake it in their own image. They chafe against the restrictions of morality - a morality rooted in the Bible.

Most progressives view the Bible as a "primitive, immoral [and] superstitious screed"[12] that is the primary roadblock preventing them from fully implementing their secular worldview. Nothing else can explain their hysterical reaction to Christian Congressman Mike Johnson's ascension to Speaker of the House in October 2023. The sharp attacks on his religious faith and biblical worldview by progressive members of Congress were revealing. "Welcome to the Republican Era of not even pretending they aren't forcing their religion on Congress and the American people. This is a slippery, dangerous slope to theocracy."[13] "Speaker Mike Johnson? Anti-choice, anti-LGBTQ, anti-gun safety, anti-democracy. This is what theocracy looks like."[14]

Even Bill Maher, usually the voice of sanity on the progressive left, went so far as to compare Johnson and his biblical worldview to a mass shooter who killed 13 people at a bowling alley in Maine. "When you're this much of a religious fanatic, there is no room for real democracy. That's not what you believe in. He said it today. 'Look in the Bible. That's my worldview.' And I was reading about this horrible shooting in Maine. And, you know, we don't know much about the guy yet, but apparently he heard voices and I thought 'Is he that different than Mike Johnson?' I mean, degree? Yes. But it's thinner than you'd think."[15]

For very similar reasons, woke progressives also share a disdain for the United States Constitution. Much like the Bible, the authors of this extraordinary document were primarily concerned with creating processes that would restrain those who occupy positions of power and grant citizens the ability to remove these leaders when they see fit. Constitutional freedoms are a roadblock preventing woke Edomites from realizing their pagan ambitions.[16]

Muslims share the progressives' contempt for the Bible. From the very beginning of Islam, Muslims referred to Jews and Christians disparagingly as the "People of the Book," the people who believe in a corrupted Bible. "Indeed, those [Jews and Christians] who disbelieve, from the People of the Book... will be in the Fire of Hell, to stay there forever. They are the worst of all beings."[17] Even so, the Koran appropriates many stories from the Bible, while "correcting" many of its key details.

Islamic jihadists believe in God, but it is a God of their own making. They reject the God of the Bible, the God of morality and restraint, for the violent God of the Koran - a God they use to justify their atrocities. "And He brought down those of the People of the Book who supported them from their fortresses and cast terror in their hearts; some you slew, some you made captive. And He bequeathed upon you their lands, their habitations, and their possessions, and a land you never trod. God is powerful over everything."[18] "And kill them wherever you find them … kill them. Such is the recompense of the disbelievers."[19] Jihadists murder, torture and rape innocent Jews and Christians *in the name* of Allah!

Since Hamas terrorists brutally murdered 1,200 Israelis on October 7, specifically choosing the festival of the "Joy of the Bible" for their attack, millions of Muslims and progressives across the world - including people living thousands of miles away from Israel who have never met a Jew in their lives - have rallied on behalf of Hamas for one fundamental reason. As Rabbi David Kimche wrote in his commentary to Psalms 83:6, "[This is why] nations that are far from one another, scattered across the globe, some physically close to Israel and others very distant… will join together with one heart and one purpose: their jealousy and hatred of Israel and the God of Israel."

Why are Hamas protestors attacking Christmas tree lightings throughout the US? Why do they declare war on Christianity by saying "On Saturdays, we will murder the Jews. On Sundays, we will murder the Christians"?

Hamas' attack was not about Gaza, a territory Hamas has ruled since 2006, nor was it about Jewish towns in Judea and Samaria built on supposedly "occupied" Arab land. The attack on Israel was merely a first step in their plan to rule all of humanity through a worldwide caliphate - to finally and permanently defeat the God of Israel and those who believe in Him. Israel is first, but Europe and America are next.

In December 2022, Hamas official Mahmoud al-Zahar spelled out Hamas' long-term plan: "We believe in what our Prophet Muhammad said: 'Allah drew the ends of the world near one another for my sake, and I have seen its eastern and western ends. The dominion of my nation would reach those ends that have been drawn near me.' The entire 510 million square kilometers of Planet Earth will come under [a system] where there is no injustice, no oppression, no Zionism, no treacherous Christianity and no killings and crimes like those being committed against the Palestinians, and against the Arabs in all the Arab countries, in Lebanon, Syria, Iraq and other countries. The entire planet will be under our law, there will be no more Jews or Christian traitors."[20] As Dutch politician Geert Wilders stated clearly, "If Jerusalem falls into the hands of the Muslims, Athens and Rome will be next."[21]

In other words, we are not only in a world war - we are in a world war over the Bible itself. On one side are the jihadists and progressives, the "anti-Bible people" who detest the God of Israel and the demands He makes upon humanity and who willingly justify mass slaughter and rape to defeat Him.

On the other side are believing Jews and Christians, the "Bible people" who pledge allegiance to the God of Israel.

War brings clarity. The war Israel is fighting today, the great war before redemption, has forced people everywhere to choose a side. Every human being, from one end of the earth to the other, must decide if they will stand for or against the people of Israel, the God of Israel, and the Bible of Israel. There is no middle ground.

A Time to Stand Together

To put it gently, the relationship between Jews and Christians over the past 1,900 years has been "complex." Many books have been written on the history of Christian antisemitism, and every Christian reader is advised to study the history, painful as it is, to better understand the hesitance many Jews have concerning working together with Christians. Despite this painful history, many Christians still actively evangelize "to the Jew first,"[22] which badly damages the Christian-Jewish alliance and is deeply insulting to any self-respecting Jew.[23]

Nevertheless, despite all the challenges, much has changed. Over the last 100 years, Christians have gone from being the Jewish people's greatest oppressors to becoming their greatest friends in America and around the world. Little by little, Christians and Jews are recognizing that, as Dennis Prager said, "In the history of humanity, only two religions share a holy book - Jews and Christians." If in the past we clashed over our different interpretations of the Bible, today we recognize that it is the Hebrew Bible that binds us together and which can and must serve as the basis for our friendship.

People of faith, both Jews and Christians alike, are under siege in the modern world - and they are turning to Israel for strength and inspiration. "In a striking way, a Jewish capital in the Middle East has become a capital for those still clinging to the Judeo-Christian tradition in the West."[24] As Eric Cohen writes, Israel is bringing Jews and Christians together. "Jerusalem, forever the Jews' city of hope and once again the West's, is now the emblem of our shared purpose: to work with faith, political will, and moral resolve to rescue and defend our shared heritage from destruction and decay."[25] Israel is proof that God is active in history, that miracles occur and that prophecy is true.

We are under attack, and it is only a matter of time before the war against Israel expands to America and Europe. Jews and Christians no longer have the luxury of arguing with one another about the Bible. When the final redemption arrives, everything will become clear. Until then, we must stand united with mutual respect, and fight, side by side, against the unholy alliance of jihadists and secular progressives who are waging war against Israel, God and the Bible.

Let Him Come, and May We Be Worthy

Why did I write this book?

Jewish tradition records a poignant conversation among the sages about the Messiah. The majority of the sages agreed: "Let him come, but let me not see him," for they feared the birth pangs that the prophets said would precede the arrival of the Messiah. But one sage, Rabbi Joseph, disagreed. He said, "Let him come, and may I be worthy of sitting in the shadow of his donkey's dung."[26]

The fears and yearnings of the sages are our reality. The frightening prophecies of Isaiah, Ezekiel, and Zechariah are playing out in our daily news cycle, and no mortal can know when the process will be complete. Every time we hear of another brave young soldier murdered by a terrorist, we understand the sages who said of the Messiah, "Let him come, but let me not see him." The sages also feared the spiritual degradation of the messianic age, when the masses would turn away from the Bible and embrace the shallow materialism of pagan and secular culture.

Yet God has chosen us to be the generation of the birth pangs of redemption. The only sage who can give us strength today is Rabbi Joseph, who understood that even the lowliest and most painful aspects of redemption - the "donkey's dung" - will one day bring us great light. Bring on the birthpangs of the Messiah, and may we prove ourselves worthy to be the generation in which he comes, no matter how painful it might be.

The enemy is strong and dangerous, but the God of Abraham, Isaac and Jacob is more powerful than man. He will never abandon His people nor those who stand with them. "The Lord is my light and my salvation; whom shall I fear? The Lord is the stronghold of my life; from whom shall I be frightened? When evildoers draw near to me to devour my flesh, my adversaries and my enemies against me - they stumbled and fell. If a camp encamps against me, my heart shall not fear; if a war should rise up against me, in this I trust" (Psalm 27:1-3).

We must rely on God - but God also makes demands of us. Five days before the Israelites left Egypt, God commanded them to bring a lamb offering as a Passover sacrifice. "On the tenth of this month, let each one take a lamb… for each household" (Exodus 12:3). This was no small test, for Egyptian society worshiped sheep as gods. In sacrificing lambs to the God of Israel, the Israelites were guilty of slaughtering the gods of Egypt - which was precisely the point. When the Egyptians saw the Israelites taking the lambs and setting them aside for slaughter, they asked "Why are you taking these lambs?" The Israelites answered, "To slaughter them as a sacrifice as God commanded us."[27]

This was no small act of defiance. The Israelites had lived their entire lives as slaves to the Egyptians. Before they could be redeemed and set free, God demanded that they look their former slave masters in the eyes and speak the truth. "Your gods, the foundation of your society, are corrupt and empty!" Today, God demands the same defiance of us. Before we can be redeemed, we must overcome our fears and find the courage to speak truth to the modern Ishmaelites and Edomites that surround and threaten to destroy us.

American Jews and Christians stand at a crossroads. Will the people of the Bible reject the passivity and defeatism that has plagued America's faithful for decades? Will they continue to sigh over the bloodshed, stick their heads in the sand, and remain bystanders in the great drama of redemption? Will they live lives of quiet fear, afraid to challenge the prevailing consensus, to speak out and say the truth? Or will they stand up and enlist in God's army – not for one day or one week, but for the months and years to come – and fight for the body and soul of Israel and America?

Rabbi Isaac Reines, one of the great early Religious Zionist leaders, deeply loved the people of Israel. When other Jews were persecuted by antisemites, Rabbi Reines felt physical pain; his face became flushed, his body shook, and he would repeat, over and over again: "we must do something!" At times he would gather his family together and say in bitterness: "We must act, we can't sit on our hands! So-called 'important rabbis' sin by remaining passive and not crying out!" Living at a time when Jews were powerless and unable to fight back, Rabbi Reines frequently didn't know what to do - but he felt passionately that he must do *something*.[28]

Traditionally, Jews responded to antisemitism by crying out the first word of the Book of Lamentations: "*Eicha*," "How could it be?" Again and again, we asked ourselves, we asked each other and turned our eyes upwards and asked God: "How can it be? How can our people suffer this way? How can our land, our holy city, lie abandoned and alone?" Living in fear and powerless to stop the pogroms and massacres that cast a constant shadow over our people, all we could do was lament and sigh, "How could it be?"

The time has come to change our attitude towards antisemitism. "The call of 'bring us back to You and renew our days of old' at the end of the Book of Lamentations has burst forth throughout the diaspora. Our land no longer sits alone and abandoned. And so now we must read the first word of this book differently: instead of pronouncing it as *'Eicha,'* 'How could it be?' we must read the word as *'Ayeka,'* 'Where are you?' Every Jew must hear the voice of God calling out to us: 'Where are you? Where are you, son of Israel? It is no longer time to hide! The time has come to leave your hiding places, to go out to battle, united in strength to build up our land... *'Ayeka?'* 'Where are you?'"[29]

It is no longer enough to wring our hands and sigh in sadness when we hear tragic news, and then return to our daily life. "There are millions of Jews who are absorbed in their own personal affairs... Our great struggle, even greater than the struggle against our external enemies, is our struggle against our own people's passivity concerning our national life."[30]

The sages teach that at the end of days, "The wisdom of the learned will degenerate, fearers of sin will be despised, and the truth will be lacking... So upon whom is it for us to rely? Upon our Father Who is in heaven."[31] Rabbi Haim of Volozhin explained that the words "upon whom is it for us to rely? Upon our Father Who is in heaven" is *itself* one of the curses that will plague us at the end of days. The attitude of passivity, the excuse that we can simply rely on God to save us without acting ourselves, is not a solution to our problems but a critical element of the problem itself.[32]

After two millennia of helplessness, the people of Israel are no longer powerless. No foreign nation can stop us from settling our land or from bearing arms to defend ourselves. No law forbids American Jews from protesting the corrupt and evil United Nations in the streets of New York City every day of the year or from marching with pride and strength against Hamas in London.

Meanwhile, Christians are now facing what Bishop Robert Stearns calls the "Bonhoeffer moment." When the Nazis assumed control in Germany, there were 18,000 churches in Germany. Dietrich Bonhoeffer saw the storm clouds approaching and tried to mobilize the churches, believing they could be a bulwark against the evil that Hitler and his henchmen would soon bring down upon Germany and Europe. Incredibly, 3,000 German churches sided with Hitler. 3,000 churches joined Bonhoeffer,[33] but only a handful of these churches actively spoke out against the Nazis. Meanwhile 12,000 churches remained neutral, telling Bonhoeffer that they would not get involved in the struggle against Hitler, as they didn't want to engage in "political matters." The churches that joined Bonhoeffer were a mere 16% of German churches, and they were not strong enough to stem the tide of evil.

Will American churches learn from the failure of German Christianity in the 1930s? Will the American Church rise up and defend Israel and the Jewish people as they are once again threatened with extermination? Though a majority of American Christians say they support Israel, most Christians have thus far remained passive. "We have too many high-sounding words, and too few actions that correspond with them."[34]

The only obstacle, and it is not a small one, is our own passivity. We're busy with our jobs, our children and our local communities. Who has time to march for Israel and protest antisemitism? But as one of my teachers once said, "How can we eat ketchup and ice cream while our brothers' blood is running through the streets?" So long as Israel is under attack, so long as terrorists murder innocents in Israel and hoodlums beat up Jews in the streets of Brooklyn, how can we justify remaining silent? How can any believer, Jew or Christian, remain passive?

Faith precedes action. By studying the Hebrew Bible's teachings for our time, we will find the clarity and purpose we need to act decisively and with strength on behalf of God and His people. "There is nothing more practical than faith."[35] If the biblical teachings in this book inspire even a few believers to arise and fight, that would be enough.

"May it be good in Your eyes to bless Your people Israel at every time, in every hour, with Your peace."[36] For thousands of years, we have yearned for peace, and we will not stop praying for peace until the Messiah comes. But love alone will not stop the jihadists who seek our destruction. The path to peace will not be strewn with roses; it will be forged through faith in God and the fortitude to make our enemies answer for the evil they have inflicted upon us. Let us fight like David, with a sword in one hand and a Bible in the other.

In David's words: "Let the faithful exult… with high praises of God in their throats and two-edged swords in their hands, to execute vengeance upon the nations and punishments upon the peoples… to execute the doom decreed against them. This is the glory of all His faithful. Hallelujah!" (Psalm 149:6-7,9).

CHAPTER 2:

THE HEBREW BIBLE: A GREAT VOICE THAT DOES NOT CEASE

Growing up, I was blessed to receive a strong Jewish education. My parents, who did not grow up with strong Jewish backgrounds, believed it was a priority worth sacrificing for. Throughout my childhood, they ensured I attended Jewish day schools, where I studied classical Jewish texts for hours each day, a gift for which I am eternally grateful. In retrospect, however, there were some surprising gaps in my education - particularly when it came to the Bible.

Christian readers may find this surprising, but it is a remarkable fact that for much of modern history, many books of the Hebrew Bible were simply not taught in most Jewish schools. Most of the day was devoted to the study of the Mishna, Talmud and works of Jewish law. In younger grades, students studied the Five Books of Moses (the "Torah") and the narrative books of the Bible, such as Joshua, Judges, Samuel and Kings, but the later prophets and writings were rarely taught. Though Jewish tradition possesses an extraordinarily rich heritage of brilliant biblical commentaries, these were rarely studied in any formal way. Interested students were left to discover them on their own.

How could the Bible itself, the Jewish people's greatest gift to the world, be largely ignored by Jewish educators? A modern scholar, Professor Pinchas

Polonsky, believes the answer comes down to relevance. After the vast majority of the Jewish community was forced into exile following the destruction of the second Temple, the Torah itself remained relevant. The Torah is the source of the Divine commandments at the heart of Jewish life, and portions of the Torah are read each Sabbath in the synagogue. But what could the rest of the Hebrew Bible offer Jews living as a minority in exile? What relevance did national stories of kings and prophets have for Jews living on foreign soil in small Polish shtetls, bereft of all political power?[1]

For entirely different reasons, many Christians have likewise ignored the Hebrew Bible. At the very beginning of Christian history, the influential heretic Marcion of Pontus taught that the God of the Hebrew Bible was a vindictive god of justice and wrath, while the God of the New Testament was a god of pure grace. In Marcion's view, Christianity had nothing to do with Judaism, and so he proceeded to remove the Hebrew Bible from the Christian canon. Though Marcion was excommunicated from the Church in 144 for his heretical views, the movement he led, known as Marcionism, exerted considerable influence on the Church through modern times.

The Marcionist cause was championed in the 20th century by the German theological liberal, Adolf von Harnack. In his biography of Marcion, Harnack celebrated the ancient heretic, praising him for repudiating the Hebrew Bible and the Jewish elements of Christianity that seemed to bear no resemblance to the benevolent fatherhood of God described in the New Testament. For Harnack, the Old Testament provides historical justification and context for Christianity, but offers little religious value. He concluded that the continued inclusion of the Hebrew Bible in the Christian canon was "the result of a religious and ecclesiastical paralysis."[2]

Within a few years of Harnack's death in 1930, German Christians, the pro-Nazi Christians of the Hitler era, would build on these arguments and declare an open war on the Hebrew Bible. One of their leaders, Georg Schneider, described the entire Hebrew Bible as "a cunning Jewish conspiracy," saying "Into the oven, with the part of the Bible that glorifies the Jews, so eternal flames will consume that which threatens our people."[3] The 1933 Handbook of the German Christians claimed the Hebrew Bible was "the apostasy of the Jews and in that apostasy, their sin."[4] The movement even rewrote parts of the New Testament, cutting out any references to the Hebrew Bible or positive remarks of Jesus about the Jewish people.

Antipathy towards the Hebrew Bible has continued through our own time. In 2018, Andy Stanley, a megachurch pastor in Atlanta, delivered a sermon entitled "Not Difficult," in which he argued that the time had come to "unhitch" Christianity from the Old Testament. Concerned that some

Christians were leaving the faith because of troubling passages in the Old Testament, he declared that "the Old Testament is not the go-to source regarding any behavior for the church" and that Christianity is "not Judaism 2.0."[5]

Though the heresies of Marcion, Harnack and Stanley are rejected by traditional Christians, the Hebrew Bible continues to be marginalized by large segments of mainstream Christianity. R. Kendall Soulen, a professor of systematic theology at Emory University, argues that the standard model of Christian theology tends to view the Hebrew Bible as mere "filler" between the sin of Adam and the redemption of Jesus. The Hebrew Bible, with its extraordinary array of stories and teachings about the people of Israel and their relationship with the nations, is considered background information setting the stage for the truly great drama of Jesus described in the New Testament.[6]

Many Christians go even further and actively disparage the Hebrew Bible. Author Marilynne Robinson explains that "It has been orthodox through most of Christian history to treat the Old Testament as rigid, benighted, greatly inferior to the Gospels. This error has never been truly rectified… It is generally thought of as a tribal epic which includes the compendium of strange laws and fierce prohibitions Jesus of Nazareth put aside when he established the dominion of grace… Christianity has tended to define itself by implied or direct disparagement of the Old Testament."[7] Rabbi Abraham Joshua Heschel summed up this attitude as only he could: "The Hebrew Bible is preparation; the gospel fulfillment. In the first is immaturity, in the second perfection; in the one you find narrow tribalism, in the other all-embracing charity."[8] Given these prevailing attitudes, many Christians unsurprisingly focus on the New Testament while largely ignoring the Hebrew Bible.[9]

As the Church elevated the New Testament over the Hebrew Bible, it also worked to read the Jewish people out of the Hebrew Bible itself through supersessionism, also knows as Replacement Theology. Supersessionism argues that God "replaced" the Jewish people as His chosen nation with Christians because they rejected Jesus as the Messiah. Along these lines, Saint Augustine claimed that the Jewish people are not the legitimate heirs of the Hebrew Bible, but rather an unrepentant remnant rejected by God in favor of the "New Israel" - the Church.[10]

With one fell swoop, supersessionism appropriated all of God's prophecies and promises to Israel in the Hebrew Bible. When reading the Hebrew Bible, Christians were instructed to interpret prophecies about "the people of Israel" as "the Church" and to replace "the land of Israel" with "the world." The Jewish people were no longer God's chosen people, and the land of Israel was like any other country in the world, for the Church would one day inherit the entire world.

The Protestant Reformation and the shattering of the Catholic Church's monopoly on biblical interpretation set significant changes in motion. The reformers' insistence that all believers had the right to interpret the Bible meant that independent-minded Christians would reach widely varying interpretations of the Bible. Inevitably, some Christian leaders questioned and rejected supersessionism, concluding that the prophets of the Hebrew Bible should be read literally and taken at their word. The people of Israel would one day return to the land of Israel! This recognition of God's continued and unbreakable covenant with the people of Israel is the foundation of Christian Zionism.

The prophetic return of the Jewish people to their homeland and the establishment of the State of Israel in 1948 created a theological crisis for supersessionist Christians while affirming the position of Christian Zionists. No longer a scorned religious minority, the Jewish people are once again the vibrant, living and breathing *nation* that God intended us to be, living in the land of the Bible. Proponents of supersessionism struggled to explain how God's "rejected" people had miraculously risen from the ashes in precise fulfillment of dozens of prophecies throughout the Hebrew Bible. It is no accident that the Vatican refused to recognize the State of Israel until 1993, despite its earlier efforts to reject Christian antisemitism. Theologically, the Vatican struggled to make sense of Israel's miraculous rise from the ashes, a reality that undermined almost two thousand years of Catholic theology. Meanwhile, Christians who embraced Israel's continued covenantal role as God's chosen people saw Israel's founding as confirmation of their beliefs and evidence of God's faithfulness to His eternal covenant with Abraham.

The revival of the nation of Israel led to a revival of the study of the Hebrew Bible itself, in both Jewish and Christian circles. The biblical stories of kings and prophets, which seemed so irrelevant to Jews throughout two millennia of exile, are once again essential texts. As the State of Israel confronts difficult internal and external challenges, God's chosen nation is turning to the Bible for guidance. In recent decades, Israel has experienced an exciting renaissance of Hebrew Bible study, with new approaches yielding exciting insights. Meanwhile, increasing numbers of Christians are rediscovering the Hebrew Bible, seeking a deeper understanding of its laws and prophecies concerning the end times.

The Blueprint for Our Time

Still, it's fair to ask: what can we honestly learn from a book as ancient as the Bible? The British novelist L.P. Hartley once wrote that "The past is a foreign country; they do things differently there."[11] Can a book as ancient as the Bible really shed light on modern challenges? Is the Bible merely a collection of outdated stories, moral teachings and laws with little relevance to our time?

This kind of thinking relegates the God of the Bible to a distant past, far from the reality of our own modern world. Prophecies become fairy tales; the possibility that we may be living through their fulfillment doesn't even dawn on those who think this way. By classifying the Bible as ancient history, they are free to ignore the lessons of the Bible and replace them with the popular philosophies of our time. "For they say, 'God does not see us; God has left the earth'" (Ezekiel 8:12).

The sages teach: "Many prophets arose for Israel, double the number of [the Israelites] who came out of Egypt, but only those prophecies which contained a lesson for future generations were written down, while those which did not contain such a lesson were not written."[12]

Jewish tradition believes that every prophecy and every verse contained in the Hebrew Bible was recorded because it is relevant for all generations. This is true even of the narrative books of the prophets - Joshua, Judges, Samuel and Kings - which Christian tradition categorizes as "historical books." Every book in the Bible is meant to serve as a guidebook for all future generations, a template to guide the people of Israel on its long and complicated path to redemption.

In other words, we do not study the Bible to learn the history of the people of Israel, but rather to find guidance for the people of Israel in *our own generation*. As Rabbi Zvi Yehuda Kook wrote, "The word of God was revealed in a particular time and place, but it has a broader value that continues for generations... until the end of time... We must become accustomed to the notion that these books are also relevant for us. The word of God is 'a great voice which did not cease' (Deuteronomy 5:19). It is a great voice which lasts for all time... Therefore it is upon us to reflect and see the value of these things that were said by the prophets for us. We must examine the relevance of Zerubbabel and Joshua, Ezra and Nehemiah, for the atmosphere of our own times. The more we become accustomed to opening our ears to this approach, to absorbing the meaning of the word of God for our generation, so will we merit a truer understanding of the events of our time."[13]

Since the closing of the Biblical canon, we no longer have prophets walking among us. Prophecy will only return in messianic times. "And it shall come to pass *afterwards* that I will pour out My spirit upon all flesh, and your sons and daughters shall prophesy" (Joel 3:1). But in a different sense, prophecy never ended. "'As for Me, this is My covenant with them,' says the Lord. 'My spirit, which is upon you and My words that I have placed in your mouth, shall not move from your mouth or from the mouth of your seed and from the mouth of your seed's seed,' said the Lord, 'from now and to eternity'" (Isaiah 59:21). Isaiah promises that God's word will *never* leave His people - for the Hebrew Bible will continue to speak to Israel and the nations in every generation.

"Ask your father, and he will tell you; your elders, and they will inform you" (Deuteronomy 32:7). "Ask your father" - these are the prophets; "your elders" - these are the sages.[14] Meaning, if we want to understand the events of our time and discern the way God wants us to react, we should not say that we no longer have prophets to guide us. The prophets have already spoken and the sages have already interpreted their words. Our job is simply to "ask" them, to study their words and apply them to the events of our time. "Read in the books of the Torah and they will give it to you, and the books of the prophets and they will speak to you."[15]

As believers, we must accustom ourselves to viewing the events of our time through the prism of the eternal Bible.[16] The stories of the Books of Judges and Samuel, of Deborah, Samson, Hanna, Samuel and David, are far more than stories. They are a blueprint for guiding us through the wars and crises of our generation. In other words, the books of the Bible do far more than predict the future through prophecy. They teach us how to interpret the events of our time.

In a 1936 letter to his brother-in-law, the German pastor Dietrich Bonhoeffer, later hanged by the Nazis, shared a similar perspective. "First of all I will confess quite simply - I believe that the Bible alone is the answer to all our questions, and that we need only to ask repeatedly and a little humbly, in order to receive this answer. One cannot simply *read* the Bible like other books. One must be prepared really to enquire of it. Only thus will it reveal itself. Only if we expect from it the ultimate answer, shall we receive it. That is because in the Bible God speaks to us."[17]

Though the Bible speaks of many nations and to all of mankind, its primary subject is the great drama of the people of Israel, the land of Israel and the God of Israel. Today, as Israel's enemies continue their obsessive quest to destroy God's people and as Israel continues to dominate the headlines of newspapers across the world, it is clearer than ever that Israel's fate - and the fate of the entire world - can only be understood through the prism of God's word. "To the land of Israel you must come with a Hebrew Bible in hand – not only as an ancient book, but as the book of books that is alive and breathing, whose words are words of fire, warming and illuminating with a constant fire, the fire of eternity."[18]

Discerning God's Plan for the End of Days

Traditionally, Jewish thinkers warned the people against speculating about the end of days. Maimonides wrote that "Neither the order of the occurrence of these events nor their precise detail are among the fundamental principles of the faith. A person should not occupy himself with the narratives and homiletics concerning these and similar matters, nor should he consider them as essentials, for study of them will neither bring fear or love of God. Similarly, one should not try to determine the appointed time for the Messiah's arrival… Rather, one should await and believe in the general conception of the matter."[19]

Maimonides, understandably, was deeply concerned about misguided messianic fervor and the disappointment and despair that people inevitably experience when their messianic predictions and calculations do not come to fruition. But this concern must not be exaggerated or taken out of context. "Whoever mourns for Jerusalem will merit to see it in its joy."[20] For Jews, mourning the destruction of the Temple and yearning for redemption is not simply one commandment among many, but rather a litmus test of faith. The degree of pain a Jew feels over the exile of Israel is a sign of his sensitivity - or lack thereof - to God's will. "The harder it is for one to bear the air of exile… this is a sign that one has absorbed more deeply the holiness of the land of Israel."[21]

Rabbi Hanan Porat, founder of Israel's settlement movement in Judea and Samaria, argues that Maimonides' concern no longer applies in our generation. "Out of a belief that we are living in the era of the *'atchalta d'geula*,' the 'beginning of the redemption,' which comes through our efforts here below - and we are called to be a part of it and work together with God to hasten its coming - it is incumbent upon us to deeply understand the times we are living through and to understand which stage of the redemption we are experiencing… Studying and clarifying these matters is the key to making practical decisions, and in light of this study we will mark the way forward."[22] It is critically important to recognize and clearly state that we are living through the beginning of redemption, for doing so is the necessary first step to taking action and speeding its arrival.[23]

Indeed, the 13th century sage Nachmanides ruled that God's command to Israel to conquer and rule the land of Israel applies "in all generations" and that we are all obligated to take steps to fulfill this commandment. How can this command be fulfilled by those who do not serve in the Israeli military? "By moving to Israel and helping to establish Jewish settlement" in the land, but also "by *studying and clarifying the matter of redemption.*"[24]

"But you, O Daniel, shut up the words, and seal the book, even to the time of the end; many shall run to and fro, and knowledge shall be increased" (Daniel 12:4). Because Daniel knew that the redemption was in the very distant future, he said that the "matter of redemption" should be sealed until the end of times. But as the end times draw closer, the uncertainties about the redemption will be clarified little by little. According to Jewish tradition, the redemption must come before the 7th millennium, and so the closer we get to the 7th millennium, the more our knowledge of the redemption will increase.[25]

By the count of the Hebrew calendar, we are currently in the year 5784, only a few hundred years before the 7th millennium. More than any of the generations that came before us, we are blessed to witness God's plan for redemption unfold. If our great-grandparents wondered when and how the promises of the prophets would come true, we no longer need to wonder. We have witnessed the miraculous return of the people of Israel to the Land of Israel. We are watching, in real-time, as God fulfills one prophecy after another, with front-row seats to the redemption of the world. Yes, the Bible speaks to every generation – but it speaks more clearly now than it ever has before.

If we hope to attain true wisdom, we must possess the "courage to represent a unique Torah worldview regarding the revolutionary events of the present and not repeat stereotypical rhetoric from the street."[26] But at the same time, we must possess historical vision, paying close attention to current events and evaluating their significance in the light of the Bible. "Just as yesteryear's primitive fighters would put their ears to the ground to listen for the rumbling caused by the enemy's cavalry, so, too, must we incline our ears to the present to perceive the historical convulsions caused by the almighty winds of Providence... The Master of the Universe is strolling through the garden, and we must hear His footsteps."[27] We can and must apply the words of the prophets to our own time - which means we have an obligation, as believers, to pay close attention to the words of the Bible and to the events of our time.

"Moses said, 'Let me turn now and see this great spectacle; Why does the thorn bush not burn up?' God saw that he had turned to see, and God called to him from within the thorn bush, and He said, 'Moses, Moses!' And he said, 'Here I am'" (Exodus 3:3-4). The bush had burned for many years, but it seems that Moses was the only one to notice. "God saw that he had turned to see." As the world burns, most people keep their heads down and go on with their mundane lives. Few are willing to truly look, to confront the dangers that threaten to consume us, and to fight back. God said to Moses, "You pained yourself to look; I swear that you are worthy that I reveal Myself to you."[28]

The sages teach that "When man is led in for judgment [after leaving this world], he is asked... Did you establish times for the Bible?"[29] Simply understood, the sages are teaching us that when a person dies, God asks him: "Throughout the course of your life, did you build Bible study into your daily schedule? Was studying the Bible a priority in your life?" But Rabbi Leo Jung, one of the leading American rabbis of the early 20th century, interprets this passage differently. He explains that when a person dies, God asks him: "Did you interpret and judge the times you lived in through the perspective of the Bible and its eternal values? Or did you make the tragic mistake of doing the opposite, of interpreting the Bible through the lens of your own time, inserting your generation's popular beliefs and transitory values into God's eternal Bible?"[30]

We are permitted, indeed obligated, to interpret the Bible and apply its wisdom to our time. But we must avoid the trap of fitting the words of the Bible into our personal worldviews, for the Hebrew Bible "is here to teach us, not for us to teach it."[31] Above all else, we must not twist the Bible so that it becomes a stamp of approval for popular opinions of our time. The Bible is not what Terry Teachout calls a "theater of concurrence,"[32] in which we tell ourselves what we want to hear. If we properly study the Bible, it will challenge us and make us rethink our assumptions.

And There Was No Vision in the Land

"And the child Samuel ministered unto God before Eli. And the word of God was rare in those days; *there was no vision (chazon)*" (I Samuel 3:1). What does it mean that "there was no vision," no *"chazon,"* in Israel?

The great medieval Biblical scholar, Gersonides, explains: "'And the word of God was rare in those days': This means that prophecy was very difficult to attain, and so prophecy at the time was not opened up; there was no one capable of prophesying."[33] During the long era of the Judges, for close to 400 years, the people of Israel grew distant from God, and their leaders, though periodically heroic, were deeply flawed. For generations, the people were unworthy of prophecy - until Samuel the prophet arrived on the scene and changed everything.

After the Israelites left Egypt, Jethro advised Moses to "seek out, from among all the people, capable individuals who fear God... Set these over them as chiefs of thousands, hundreds, fifties, and tens (Exodus 21:18). When telling Moses to "seek out" these leaders, Jethro uses the Hebrew word "*techezeh,*" the active form of *chazon*. There is a difference between the Hebrew words "*re'iyah*", meaning "seeing," and "*chazon,*" meaning "vision." "*Re'iyah*" is the sight of the senses, while "*chazon*" refers to a seeing of the spirit and the soul. Jethro was telling Moses that though the masses only see with the sight of their senses, you, Moses, must see with the Divine spirit.[34]

Samuel's generation was not only lacking prophecy. It was missing "*chazon,*" a "seeing of the spirit." Immersed in their farms and businesses, God's chosen people lost sight of their unique purpose - why God had taken them out of Egypt in the first place. The people performed the sacrificial service in the Tabernacle, but the priests conducting the service were corrupt and uninspired. Though they observed many details of the commandments, the trees were obscuring the forest. The ultimate goal of the Tabernacle, to bring God's glory down to this physical earth, was forgotten. There was no *chazon*, no vision in Israel.

Our generation, like Samuel's, suffers from the same lack of *chazon*. As G.K. Chesterton wrote, "There is such a thing as a small and cramped eternity; you see it in many modern religions."[35] Religion devoid of vision and the longing for redemption is a "small and cramped eternity," a religion shorn of all its grandeur and depth. It is a stunted, shallow form of faith that our children, who long for great ideals, are likely to reject.

When God took Israel out of Egypt, He blessed them with manna that fell from the heavens. The Bible describes its taste in different ways, "like a wafer with honey" (Exodus 16:31) and like "the taste of oil cake" (Numbers 11:8). The sages explain that just as a baby tastes different flavors from the breast, since the taste of the milk changes somewhat depending on what foods his mother eats, so too with the manna; every time the people of Israel ate the manna, they found in it many different flavors, based on their preferences.[36] But what flavor would the people taste in the manna if they ate it without thinking? It seems that those who ate without reflecting on the manna and appreciating the miracle they were experiencing tasted nothing. The same is true of those who live through the time of redemption without *chazon*. Without thought, reflection and vision, we may live through awesome events and the fulfillment of prophecy and yet remain oblivious to what is happening around us.[37]

"When the Lord returns the returnees to Zion, we shall be like dreamers" (Psalm 126:2). When we fall asleep and dream, we generally do not understand the meaning of what we see in our dreams. It is difficult to grasp what we see in our subconscious, for our dreams are hazy. The same is true of our generation, the era of redemption, when the people of Israel are returning to Zion. The highs and lows, the constant turmoil - all of this is necessary to bring the redemption - but we struggle to understand it.[38] We are yearning for *chazon*, for a vision that will make sense of our dreams.

"The currents of our time demand a far greater and loftier spiritual force."[39] Our generation is no longer satisfied with a "going-through-the-motions" religious life; we are looking for a greater vision. Rabbi Hanan Porat once described his circle of idealists as "a group of friends thirsty for *chazon*." His friends were scholars, immersed in the study of the Talmud and Jewish law, but they remained thirsty for vision. "Behold, days are coming, says the Lord God, and I will send famine into the land, not a famine for bread nor a thirst for water, but to hear the word of the Lord" (Amos 8:11). The "word of the Lord" does not mean the details of the commandments, but rather *chazon*,[40] the ability to see with the Divine spirit.

With the exception of the Book of Leviticus and sections of Deuteronomy, the Hebrew Bible is not, primarily, a book of laws. Most commandments are only described in broad terms; the details of their observance are part of the oral tradition, later committed to writing by the sages in the Mishna and Talmud. The Hebrew Bible is a book of *chazon*, laying out God's vision for the people of Israel and the nations of the world. Whether we realize it or not, our generation is thirsting for the Hebrew Bible's vision, an eternal *chazon* that infuses every moment of our lives with meaning.

Ever since Israel retreated from large swaths of its biblical heartland by agreeing to the Oslo Accords, secularists have crowed "it is the end of the [messianic] dream (*chalom*) of Greater Israel." But what the secularists do not understand is that the people of Israel's bond with the land of Israel is not the fulfillment of a "*chalom*," a dream, but rather the product of a "*chazon*," the great vision of the Hebrew Bible. A *chalom* may come to an end, but a true *chazon* will, without any doubt, be fulfilled.[41] "The vision is always solid and reliable. The vision is always a fact. It is the reality that is often a fraud."[42]

"The essence of a book exists before the book or before even the details or main features of the book… The last page comes before the first… most of all, [the author] sees the color and character of the whole story prior to any possible events in it."[43] I did not know, when I began writing the articles that form the basis of this book, exactly what I intended to say - only that something *must* be said. After the horror of October 7, I understood that to live meaningfully during times such as these, I required a greater vision, a vision I did not yet possess. At a time of war, when the world as we know it is shaking, there is a need for "greater understanding, great courage, deep and penetrating thinking, and a desire for truth."[44] It was no longer enough to live as a faithful believer; I had to learn how to *think* like one. To do that, I had only one place to turn - the Hebrew Bible.

For the Sake of Zion, I Will Not Be Silent

The sages further taught that "When man is led in for judgment [after leaving this world], he is asked… Did you look for salvation?"[45] Rabbi Nissim of Geronda, a great medieval scholar, explains that God will ask every one of us: "Did you look for the fulfillment of the words of the prophets *in your days*?"

To state the obvious, we cannot look for the fulfillment of prophecies in our days if we do not know what the prophets are saying. One of Maimonides' thirteen principles of faith is "I believe with complete faith in the coming of the redemption." If we are commanded to believe in something, we are also commanded to learn the matter and understand it properly. Each of the prophets shows us a different aspect of the end times. It is only by studying them all and piecing them together that we can form a coherent understanding of the times we are living through.[46]

First and foremost, I hope to encourage readers, both Jewish and Christian, to return - or turn for the first time - to the Hebrew Bible, to see the events of our times through God's eyes. "Turn it and turn it again, for all is in it; see through it; grow old and worn in it; do not budge from it, for there is nothing that works better than it."[47]

Sadly, far too many religious leaders are blind to the great changes and events occurring in our generation, before our eyes. "Like foxes in ruins were your prophets, O Israel. You have not gone up into the breaches nor have you built a fence for the house of Israel, to stand in war on the day of the Lord" (Ezekiel 13:4-5). The role of a spiritual leader is to awaken his people from complacency and warn them of the approaching "war on the day of the Lord." But too many of our leaders stick their heads in the sand and refuse to see. As Rabbi Abraham Isaac Kook, the first Ashkenazi Chief Rabbi of British Mandatory Palestine, said: "It is hard for me to grasp how most of the great rabbis of our generation, may God protect them, want only to walk along the old path and to distance themselves from every act of vibrancy and life. It is an approach that, in my opinion, directly contradicts the will of God, and only strengthens the hands of those who reject God… Woe to us because of the 'humility' of these people, even if their intentions are good."[48] Though these men are great scholars, they do not read the Bible as a living book, and so they fail to grasp the connection between God's word and current events.

Acquiring a biblical perspective on current events is not only God's will. During times of great upheaval and uncertainty, it is also a source of great strength and comfort. It is only natural for the painful events of our time to overwhelm us and bring us to despair, but when we learn to interpret events through the metahistorical lens of the Hebrew Bible, we acquire a broader perspective that is not limited to the particular crisis overwhelming us at the moment. "Look (*habet*) from heaven and see (*re'eh*)" (Isaiah 63:15). We "see," "*re'eh*," through our physical eyes, but we must also learn to "look," "*habet*," to reflect upon events and see God's hand in history, even when it is not visible to the naked eye. Though God's hiddenness superficially remains unchanged, by "looking" we begin to realize that our generation is different, that God is shaping history in our time more actively and openly than ever before.[49] Each event takes on new meaning once we learn to interpret it as part of God's greater plan for Israel and mankind. "There are many thoughts in a man's heart, but God's plan - that shall stand" (Proverbs 19:21).

Though we cannot fully grasp God's ways, we can appreciate the broad contours of God's plan. Through the teachings of the prophets, we begin to recognize that redemption will not arrive quickly or easily, for "Can a country be born in a day or a nation be brought forth in a moment?" (Isaiah 66:8). When we recognize that our sufferings are the unavoidable "labor pains" of redemption, they take on new meaning and significance. And most important of all, we remember that we are not alone. As the prophet Haggai said in the name of God, "I am with you." We are not alone, "For the Lord will not abandon His people, nor will He forsake His heritage" (Psalm 94:14).

The Jewish people's yearning to return home to the holy land sustained generations of downtrodden Jews through two thousand years of exile. Without this yearning, there would be no State of Israel today. The same is true of our yearning for redemption. This yearning sustains both body and soul; without it, our lives become a shallow reflection of true faith. "Every eye must seek the greatness that awaits us in the future,"[50] or as the philosemite George Eliot wrote, "Every Jew should rear his family as if he hoped a Deliverer might spring from it."[51] One who believes in God and lives a righteous life in accordance with the Bible but does not yearn for redemption lives a static life bereft of greater purpose.[52]

"*Tzipita L'yeshua?*" "Did you look for the fulfillment of the words of the prophets in your days?" With this question, God will not simply ask us if we yearned for redemption and searched for signs of its coming in our generation. The Hebrew word used in this question is not "*kivita*," meaning

"Did you *hope* for redemption?" but rather "*tzipita*," meaning "Did you *watch* for redemption?" We are meant to be watchmen, as Isaiah said, "The voice of your watchmen ("*tzophayich*," from the same root as "*tzipita*") raised a voice; together they shall sing, for eye to eye they shall see when God returns to Zion" (Isaiah 52:8).

The task of a watchman is to pay close attention to events, to warn of trouble and to awaken others to act and bring salvation.[53] A watchman stands on high towers and looks out over the horizon, seeing things that those standing on the ground cannot see. So too, a watchman of God sees "eye to eye," aligning his vision with the deeper *chazon* of the prophets, the vision of God. "For Your deliverance we hope all day, and *watch* for Your deliverance."[54]

But a true watchman of God not only pays constant attention - he also *acts*. When he sees that he can do something to advance the cause of salvation, he rushes to do so. If an enemy advances, and it is possible to protect the people by retreating or defending, a watchman has an obligation to act - and to act quickly. A "watchman for salvation" has two obligations: to patiently and keenly watch for signs of salvation, and to energetically act to advance salvation when the opportunity arises.[55]

"For the sake of Zion, I will not be silent, and for the sake of Jerusalem I will not rest, until her righteousness comes out like brilliance, and her salvation burns like a torch" (Isaiah 62:1). Reading this verse, we are left to wonder; *who* will not be silent, and *who* will not rest? These are the words of God and, according to many, also the words of Israel.[56]

Yes, God will bring salvation to His people and those who stand with her. But these words are also spoken by Israel *herself*. Every one of us, as watchmen of Israel, must make this verse our mantra. "'For the sake of Zion I will not be silent': I will not be silent from arguing and proving its truth, for the salvation of Israel from their exile requires action and deed. 'For the sake of Jerusalem I will not rest': I will not sit at rest without doing anything, but will act with alacrity to rescue them."[57]

"Do not delay the end times"[58] through inaction. The great travails of our time must neither paralyze us or leave us feeling helpless. Now is the time to uncover reservoirs of strength and determination we never before realized we possess. The prophet is calling us to awaken, to *act*. Isaiah is looking each of us in the eye, demanding to know: when genocidal terrorists relentlessly attack the people of Israel, what will *you* do to strengthen and comfort God's people? Will you simply read the news, shake your head in frustration, and go on with your day? Or will you rise up and find a way to make a difference? The rebuilding of Jerusalem begins with desire, but it does not end there. "No salvation can be complete unless the one who is being saved actively works with his own hands to bring it to fruition."[59]

As the prophets make clear, the war against Israel is nothing less than a war for the future of mankind. Ishmael and Edom, Islamic jihadists and woke progressives, have joined forces, united only by their common hatred for the Bible and the people who live out its values and teachings. Though Israel is their first target, Iran and its proxies have far larger goals than the destruction of Israel and the genocide of the Jewish people. Christians and the West are next.

Through two thousand years of persecution, the people of Israel learned not to ask "what will be?" but rather "what must we do?" We will not be saved by sighing and bemoaning our fate. As the enemies of Israel take over the streets of America and Europe, it is no longer enough to passively support Israel. Every Jew and Christian who believes in the God of Abraham, Isaac and Jacob, in the God of the Bible, must become a "watchman for salvation" who is prepared to stand up and fight for God. "In the future, a voice from heaven will explode over the mountains and say: 'Who acted with God? Whomever has acted with God let him come and take his reward!'"[60]

PART II:

BIBLICAL BEGINNINGS

CHAPTER 3:

THE FOURTH KINGDOM: EDOM AND ISHMAEL UNITE

Dreams, kingdoms, oppressors and redemption - the Book of Daniel contains the secrets of Israel's long exile and nothing less than the future of humanity.

"Nebuchadnezzar dreamed dreams, and his spirit was troubled" (Daniel 2:1). The great Babylonian king, the most powerful man of his generation, was chosen by God as the conduit for a critical prophecy of exile and redemption.

"He could not sleep" - it was a dream that kept him up at night, and for good reason. Only Daniel, the exiled Jewish prince, could help the king recall and then interpret the dream. "You, o king, saw… a mighty image… and its appearance was terrible. The head of this image was of fine gold, its front and arms were of silver, its belly and thighs of brass, its legs of iron, and its feet partly of iron and partly of clay. And you watched until a stone was cut without hands, and it struck the image on its feet which were of iron and clay, and broke them. Then the iron, the clay, the brass, the silver and the gold all broke into pieces and were like the chaff of the summer threshing floors, and the wind carried them away, and no place was found for them. And the stone which had struck the image became a great mountain, and it filled the entire earth" (Daniel 2:31-35).

Daniel explained to the king that the statue's materials represent a succession of empires - four great kingdoms that will rise up but eventually fall. In the end, the eternal kingdom of God will triumph over all of these human kingdoms.

"You are the king, king of kings, to whom the God of heaven has given kingdom, power, strength and glory; and wherever mortals dwell, the beasts of the field and the birds of the sky – He has given them into your hand and has made you ruler over all of them; you are the head of gold. And after you there shall arise another kingdom, inferior to yours, and then a third kingdom, of brass, which will reign over the entire earth. And the fourth kingdom will be as strong as iron, for iron breaks to pieces and subdues all things, and like iron that shatters, so shall it break and shatter all of these. And as for your seeing the feet and the toes, partly of potters' clay and partly of iron – it shall be a divided kingdom, with some of the strength of iron in it, as you saw – iron mixed with miry clay. And like the toes of the feet which were partly iron and partly mire, part of the kingdom will be strong, and part will be broken. For as you saw iron mixed with miry clay, they shall mingle themselves with the seed of man, but they will not cleave to one another, just as iron cannot be mixed with clay. And in the days of these things, the God of heaven will raise up a kingdom which will never be destroyed, nor will this kingdom be left to another people; it shall break and consume all of these kingdoms, and it shall remain forever, just as you saw that a stone was cut out of the mountain without hands, and it broke the iron, the brass, the clay, the silver, and the gold. The great God has made it known to the king what will happen in the future, and the dream is certain, and its meaning is sure" (Daniel 2:37-45).

The head of gold symbolizes Nebuchadnezzar and the Babylonian empire, while the Kingdom of God and His people, Israel, are the stone that is cut out, representing the final and everlasting kingdom. Between these two extremes, there are three intermediary kingdoms: one is represented by the silver front and arms, the second by the belly and thighs of brass, and the third by the legs of iron and its mixture with clay. Together with the Babylonian kingdom, these four empires oppress the people of Israel until the time of redemption.

Though it is not stated explicitly in the verse, the sages have generally agreed upon the identity of the second and third kingdoms. The second kingdom, represented by two arms of silver, corresponds to the Persian and Median empires, while the third kingdom, depicted with brass, symbolizes Alexander the Great and the Greek empire that followed his reign. The great question, debated for millennia, is the identity of the fourth and final kingdom, more powerful than all the others, but also "a divided kingdom" of "iron mixed with clay."

The Fourth Kingdom

In the 3rd century, one of the sages identified the fourth kingdom as Edom, the descendants of Esau. "Why is [Edom] compared to iron and clay?... Just as iron is strong, so this evil kingdom is strong, but it is also compared to clay, because in the future God will break it, like clay."[1] Others, however, argued that Edom is included in the third kingdom with Greece, for in many ways it was a continuation of Greek culture, and that the fourth kingdom is Ishmael.[2]

Saadia Gaon, the great 10th-century philosopher and scholar, offers a third approach. For him, the key to identifying the fourth kingdom is understanding the parable of iron and clay: "You saw the feet and the toes, part potter's clay and part iron; that means it will be a divided kingdom; it will have only some of the stability of iron, inasmuch as you saw iron mixed with common clay... You saw iron mixed with common clay; that means: they shall intermingle with the offspring of men, but shall not hold together, just as iron does not mix with clay" (Daniel 2:41,43).

Saadia writes that the fourth kingdom will be divided in two, between the nation of "iron" and the nation of "clay" - between Rome (Edom),[3] and Ishmael.[4] Though Saadia does not explain further, the implication is that Edom will be physically and militarily powerful like iron, while Ishmael will be ever-present like clay, capable of overwhelming his enemies through sheer force of numbers.

Several other sources lend credence to Saadia's view. "For the conductor on the eighth, a song of David" (Psalm 12:1). The sages ask: "What is the meaning of 'the eighth'?... Some explain the eighth in regards to the four kingdoms that are eight, and Edom is the eighth. This is what is written (Daniel 2:32-33): 'Its head was of fine gold, its breast and arms of silver, its belly and thighs of bronze, its legs of iron, its feet part iron and part clay.' There are thus eight, which are really four: Babylon and Kasdim, Media and Persia, Greece and Macedon, and Ishmael and Edom."[5]

The sages also found allusions to Edom and Ishmael's joint role as the fourth kingdom in God's mysterious "Covenant of the Parts" with Abraham. "And He said to him, 'I am the Lord, Who brought you forth from Ur of the Chaldees, to give you this land to inherit it.' And he said, 'O Lord God, how will I know that I will inherit it?' And He said to him, 'Take for Me three heifers (*shor*) and three goats and three rams, and a turtle dove (*tor*) and a young bird'" (Genesis 15:7-9).

The animals listed in this verse represent nations: "In the Covenant of the Parts, God showed Abraham the four kingdoms that will rule [over Israel] and ultimately be destroyed. As it says, 'Take for Me three heifers,' this refers to the kingdom of Edom, which is like a heifer... 'And a turtle dove,' this refers to the children of Ishmael." The Hebrew words for "heifer" and "turtle dove" are "*shor*" and "*tor*," which are used interchangeably, implying that there will be a union of sorts between Edom and Ishmael. "Woe unto the land when a male *shor* and a female *tor* are joined together, for they will open and plunder all the valleys."[6]

"Now the sun was ready to set, and a deep sleep fell upon Abram, and behold, a fright, a great darkness was falling upon him" (Genesis 15:12). God showed Abraham a vision of the four kingdoms that would one day oppress his descendants, the people of Israel. The "fright" that Abraham saw was a vision of Edom and Ishmael, who together will strike fear in the hearts of Israel.[7]

Later scholars agreed that Edom and Ishmael would play key roles as Israel's tormentors at the end of time. Maimonides writes: "From the prophecies of Daniel and Isaiah and the statement of our sages it is clear that the advent of the Messiah will take place when the hands of Edom and Arabia (Ishmael) will be mighty and when their kingdoms will spread throughout the world... This fact is true beyond question or doubt. Daniel, in the latter part of his vision, alludes to the Kingdom of Ishmael, to the rise of Mohammed and then to the arrival of the Messiah. Similarly, Isaiah intimated that the coming of the Messiah will occur after the rise of Mohammed, in the verse 'A man riding on an ass, a man riding on a camel, and two men riding on horses.' (Isaiah 21:7). Now 'the man riding on an ass' is a symbolic reference to the Messiah as is evident from another verse which describes him as 'lowly and riding on an ass' (Zechariah 9:9). He will follow the 'man riding on the camel,' that is, the kingdom of Arabia. The statement 'two men riding on horses' refers to both empires, Edom and Arabia."[8]

In his Gog of Magog prophecies, Ezekiel tells of the end of days, when the nations will wage war against Jerusalem. The nations that battle Israel will fall into two groups - the Ishmaelites on one side and the princes of Edom and the kings of the north on the other.[9] The fourth kingdom will be unstable; sometimes Edom will lead, and sometimes Ishmael will be stronger.[10] These two great powers are unique; though Jewish tradition generally refers to global humanity as "the 70 nations,"[11] this category does not include Ishmael and Esau.[12]

With all due respect to the other views of the sages, I believe that the events of our time have proven Saadia's view correct. Working in tandem, Edom and Ishmael are the fourth and final kingdom to persecute the people of Israel before redemption arrives.

Who are Ishmael and Edom?

Thus far, we have spoken of "Edom" and "Ishmael," two ancient nations from the biblical era. In modern times, however, there are no nations that identify as either Edom or Ishmael, and so it is critically important to identify them by their modern names.

Before doing so, it is important to note that Edom and Ishmael must not be interpreted in a narrow or literal "physical" sense, but rather as spiritual forces at work in the world.[13] At the end of days, Ishmael and Edom will not be recognizable by their original geographic locations, but rather by their spiritual and cultural qualities, the passions and traits that make them unique.

Who, then, is Ishmael today? Before the founding of Islam, Josephus, the Roman-era Jewish historian, referred to Ishmael as the "founder of the Arabs."[14] Later on, after the establishment of Islam, Ishmael and his descendants were often equated with "Arabs" and "Islam" in Jewish literature.

In a commentary concerning Ishmael, Rabbi Shlomo Yitzchaki, one of the greatest biblical commentators, explicitly identifies Ishmael as the Arab nations: "When they led them beside the Arabs, the Israelites said to their captors, 'Please lead us beside the children of our uncle Ishmael, and they will have mercy on us.'"[15]

Ishmael is also recognized by Muslims themselves as a prophet and the ancestor of many prominent Arab tribes and nations – and most importantly, as the ancestor of Muhammad. Every year during the Hajj, the pilgrimage ritual in Mecca, pilgrims recreate Hagar's desperate quest for water to quench her infant son's thirst. In the Koran, Ishmael replaces Isaac as the chosen son of Abraham. Though it does not explicitly mention the name of the son whom Abraham was commanded to sacrifice to God, Muslims believe that this son was Isma'il (Ishmael). In Islamic tradition, when Ishmael reached an age where he could walk beside his father, Abraham received a divine command in a dream, instructing him to sacrifice his only son, as Isaac had not yet been born.[16]

Whether or not they physically descend from Ishmael, Ishmael is today identified as the Arab nations and, more broadly, as nations that have embraced Islam. The identity of Edom, however, is more complex.

Throughout the Hebrew Bible, there are many prophecies concerning the future fate of Edom, the nation that descends from Jacob's brother Esau. The problem, however, is that the physical nation of Edom no longer exists.

In biblical times, Edom was a kingdom located to the south of ancient Israel on the strategic trade route between Arabia and the Mediterranean. The Edomites were later conquered by the Nabataeans, after which many of them migrated to southern Judea, where they became known as Idumaeans. But by the time the Romans destroyed the second Temple in Jerusalem in 70 CE, the Idumeans had disappeared from history, along with almost all of the ancient nations mentioned in the Bible.

What, then, are we to make of the Book of Obadiah, which is entirely dedicated to the fate of Edom? Are Obadiah's prophecies, as well as the prophecies concerning Edom's future found in Isaiah, Ezekiel and many other prophets, still relevant today?

When the Romans ruled the land of Israel, the term "Edom" came to represent the Roman Empire, which adopted much of the Edomite belief system.[17] At the center of this connection was the reviled Herod, appointed by Rome as the king of Judea and a descendant of an Idumean (Edomite) family that had converted to Judaism. Herod had close ties to Roman officials and hoped to rise in the ranks of the Empire.

The sages despised the cruel and erratic Herod, who murdered any potential threats to his reign, including members of the heroic Hasmonean family that led Israel in revolt against the Greek Empire. The sages portrayed Herod not as a true Jew but as the epitome of Roman influence and cruelty, akin to rulers like Caligula and Nero. They despised him for his oppressive rule over Jewish lands and his brutal suppression of dissent. Herod's descendants, including Agrippa II and Berenice, were at odds with the Jewish rebellion against Rome, aligning instead with Roman interests. With Herod's lineage in mind, the rabbis naturally associated Rome with the biblical Edomites. Given Rome's dominant presence in the region and its role in the destruction of the Temple, it was only natural for the sages to draw parallels between the biblical conflict of Esau and Jacob and the contemporary struggle between Rome and the Jews.[18]

The earliest source tying Edom together with Rome is a statement attributed to the great Rabbi Akiva (50-135 CE) about an oft-cited verse in Genesis, "The voice is the voice of Jacob, yet the hands are the hands of Esau" (Genesis 27:22). "'The voice is the voice of Jacob' - the voice of Jacob cries out at what the hands, 'the hands of Esau,' did to him."[19] In another version of this teaching, the sages make Rabbi Akiva's intent explicit: "The voice is the voice of Jacob crying out because of what the hands of Esau did to him at Beitar."[20] Rabbi Akiva is referring to the devastation inflicted upon the Jewish people by the Romans during the Great Revolt (66–73 C.E.) and the Bar-Kochba uprising (132–136 C.E.), conflicts that led to the complete destruction of

Jerusalem and the city of Beitar. With this teaching, Rabbi Akiva explicitly links the Roman Empire to Esau, portraying Jews and Romans as the continuation of Jacob's ancient struggle with Esau.

As the sages sought to understand the spiritual implications of the Romans' destruction of Jerusalem, they looked back to the Book of Lamentations. The destruction of the second Temple in 70 CE corresponded eerily to the destruction of the first Temple as described by Jeremiah: "The roads of Zion are mournful because no one comes to the appointed season; all her gates are desolate, her priests moan; her maidens grieve while she herself suffers bitterly. Her adversaries have become the head, her enemies are at ease… The adversary stretched forth his hand upon all her precious things, for she saw nations enter her Sanctuary, whom You did command not to enter into Your assembly" (Lamentations 1:4,5,10). And who is guilty of committing this evil against God's people? Incredibly, Jeremiah makes no mention of Babylon or Chaldea, the nations that actually destroyed the first Temple. Instead, he points his finger at Edom: "Rejoice and be glad, O daughter of Edom, who dwells in the land of Uz; upon you also shall the cup pass, you shall become drunk and vomit. The punishment of your iniquity is complete, O daughter of Zion; He will no longer send you into exile; but your iniquity, O daughter of Edom, He shall punish - He will reveal your sins" (Lamentations 4:21-22). Though Jeremiah initially wrote the text of Lamentations in response to the hardships of his time, he crafted it with a prophetic vision that would resonate just as poignantly with the future destruction of the second Temple. Once again, Rome and Edom are intertwined.[21]

For generations, the sages considered Rome to be the modern manifestation of Edom. However, with the decline and fall of the Roman Empire, the Roman Catholic Church became the dominant power in Europe and the driving force of antisemitism in Europe. Jews who lived through the pogroms of the Crusaders or were expelled from Spain, England and France during the Middle Ages naturally began to conflate the Church with Edom.

Though many commentators associated Christianity with Edom, I believe this view does not align with the sages' original understanding of the spiritual qualities of Edom and Rome. The sages draw a compelling picture of Rome as an arrogant people who reject the God of Israel: "After Hadrian, king of Edom conquered the world, he returned to Rome and said to his officers: 'I want you to make me a god, since I have conquered the world.' They said to him: 'But you have not yet established your rule over God's city and His house.' He went, succeeded, destroyed the Temple, exiled Israel, and returned to Rome. He said to them: 'I have now destroyed His house and burned His Temple and exiled His people. Make me a god.'"[22]

This passage presents Rome, the modern Edom, as a nation that rejects the God of Israel - whose emperor yearns to make himself a god. Though the Roman Catholic Church committed great evils against the Jewish people, it does not fit this description of Edom as a God-hating, pagan empire.

"And the children struggled within her, and she said, 'If it be so, for what do I live?'" (Genesis 25:22). What was this struggle about? "Whenever Rebecca passed by the doors of the study houses of Shem and Eber [where God's word was studied], Jacob moved convulsively trying to come out, but whenever she passed by the gate of a pagan temple Esau moved convulsively trying to come out."[23] Similarly, when explaining the verse "Esau despised the birthright" (Genesis 25:34), the sages explain that "he despised the service of the Omnipresent."[24] In Jewish tradition, Esau is associated with pagan temples and the rejection of God - a description of Esau that simply does not align with the Church.

If Edom is not the Christian Church, and if Rome has long since vanished from the earth, we must once again ask the question with which we began: who is Edom in our time?

Logically, the Edomites of our time are those nations and peoples who are the cultural heirs of the pagan Roman Empire - namely, the secular Western nations who have rejected God, His Bible, and His chosen people.

In the words of Rabbi Meir Soloveitchik: "As modern Israel prospered, much of the West lost faith in itself - and in the process lost faith in faith. Many Europeans saw in a strong Jewish state a reminder of the biblical past that Europe suddenly chose to elide and eschew. In 2004, a constitution for the European Union was created whose preposterous preface described the history of Europe without a single mention of Christianity. What had once been the center of the Western world sought to forget much of what it had once believed."[25]

These Western nations are the modern standard bearers of Edom and Rome, for like the Roman emperors of old, they yearn to destroy God's house, exile His people from the biblical heartland, and make themselves into gods by submitting to their most craven desires.

Europe has abandoned its biblical heritage. What used to be the center of Christendom has turned away from Judeo-Christian values and embraced the paganism of secular woke progressivism. They have returned to the evil materialism of Esau and Rome, their spiritual forefathers. The great question is whether the United States will join them in this Edomite rebellion against God.

Haters and Enemies

Ishmael and Edom, Muslims and secular progressives - these are the enemies of Israel that together make up the fourth kingdom in our time. Though bound together by their hatred for Israel, each oppressor remains unique.

Moses distinguishes between the enemies of Israel and those who hate Israel: "And the Lord, your God, will place all these curses upon your enemies and upon those who hate you, who pursued you" (Deuteronomy 30:7).

The same distinction between enemies and haters is found in Psalm 83, where they are described as the enemies and haters of God Himself: "O God, have no silence, do not be silent and do not be still, O God. For behold, Your enemies stir, and those who hate You raise their heads" (Psalm 83:2-3).

Who are these enemies and haters of God and Israel? Rabbi Shlomo Yitzchaki explains that "Your enemies" and "those who hate you" allude to the two nations that continually persecute Israel - i.e., Edom and Ishmael.[26] Later commentators are more specific, explaining that "God's enemies" refers to Ishmael, while "those who hate God" refers to Edom, "For an enemy is worse than a hater... The children of Ishmael are worse for the people of Israel than the children of Esau... And so it is said, 'better to be under the dominion of Esau than under the dominion of Ishmael.'"[27]

The people of Edom are described as "those who hate You," for they are driven by their hatred of God and the morality and restrictions that He imposes upon humanity. Like the Roman emperors who sought to make themselves into gods, Hitler would later say 'We do not want any other god than Germany itself. It is essential to have fanatical faith and hope and love in and for Germany."[28]

Today's secular progressives, like the pagan Romans and German Nazis who preceded them, are continuing humanity's futile quest to build a tower of Babel and topple God from His throne. "Come, let us build ourselves a city and a tower with its top in the heavens" (Genesis 11:4). "They came with one scheme and said, '[God] had no right to select for Himself the upper regions. Let us ascend to the sky and wage war with Him.'"[29]

Hatred of God leads, inevitably, to hatred of Israel. Father Raymond J. de Souza writes that "An aggressively secular viewpoint that tends toward fundamentalism in keeping religion out of our common life has a challenge in dealing with the reality of the Jewish people. It is not possible to understand the origins of the Jewish people, nor their astonishingly unlikely survival in history, without reference to their religious identity... Therefore, the very idea of Israel... is an offense to [the] secular, progressive mindset... Thinking about Israel and thinking about Jews means thinking about religion and thinking about God. Some people don't like to think about that, and so have come to not like thinking about Jews."[30]

Ishmael is "God's enemy," and are even worse than the Edomite "God haters." Unlike the Edomites, the people of Ishmael call out in the name of God. But though they believe in God, they believe in a god of their own making, and use Him to justify their heinous acts. They are worse than Edom, for instead of openly and honestly rejecting God, the people of Ishmael pervert God and use Him as a justification for their evil deeds. They believe in God, but reject His Bible, and so their belief only adds fuel to their evil fire.

In its founding charter, Hamas quotes the following hadith[31]: "The hour of judgment shall not come until the Muslims fight the Jews and kill them, so that the Jews hide behind trees and stones, and each tree and stone will say: 'Oh Muslim, oh servant of Allah, there is a Jew behind me, come and kill him.'"[32]

The Islamic jihadists dedicated to Israel's destruction are driven by their twisted faith in God: "Israel will exist and will continue to exist until Islam will obliterate it, just as it obliterated others before it."[33] "Palestine is an Islamic land... Since this is the case, the liberation of Palestine is an individual duty for every Muslim wherever he may be."[34]

The chairman of Hamas's political bureau, Ismail Haniyeh, referred to Hamas' massacre of October 7, 2023 as the "advanced [battle] front of the Ummah"[35] and called for both "financial jihad" and "jihad of the teeth." Speaking to the International Union of Muslim Scholars in Doha, Haniyeh asked his audience: "Who wishes to invest in building the jihadist generation to liberate Jerusalem and to unite the blood of the Ummah with the blood of the people of Gaza, Jerusalem, and Palestine on the land of Palestine for its liberation and the liberation of Jerusalem?"[36]

Ishmael's passionate faith in Islam makes him far more dangerous than Edom, and the true enemy of God Himself.

A Terrifying Alliance

Let's return to Psalm 83: "Against Your people they plot cunningly, and they take counsel against Your protected ones. They said, "Come, let us destroy them from [being] a nation, and the name of Israel will no longer be remembered." For they have taken counsel with one accord; against You they form a pact. The tents of Edom and the Ishmaelites…" (Psalm 83:4-7)

Despite their differences, the psalmist declares that the day will come when Edom and Ishmael will join forces against Israel. This alliance has biblical precedent. Over three thousand years ago, Esau and Ishmael formed a bond through the marriage of Esau to Mahalath, the daughter of Ishmael. "So Esau went to Ishmael, and he took Mahalath, the daughter of Ishmael, the son of Abraham, the sister of Nebaioth… as a wife" (Genesis 28:9).

In his vision of the fourth kingdom, Daniel saw "iron" mixed with "common clay." Edom and Ishmael, in spite of their divergent worldviews, will join together in an unstable alliance. The sages explain that Gog of Magog's coalition against Israel will include both "circumcised" and "uncircumcised"[37] peoples, enemies of Israel who are religious (the Ishmaelites) and irreligious (the Edomites).

"For behold, darkness shall cover the earth, and a thick darkness the kingdoms, and the Lord shall shine upon you, and His glory shall appear over you" (Isaiah 60:2). The "darkness" represents the nations that have no religion at all, while the "thick darkness" represents the Ishmaelites, who believe in God and in reward and punishment, but whose religion also contains great falsehoods[38] that lead them to commit terrible evil.

Why will Ishmael and Edom unite, despite their differences? Why will they form an alliance at the end of days as they never have before?

The Zohar, the foundational book of Jewish mysticism, explains that "these nations will join together and form a covenant of peace in order to turn against Israel to destroy them."[39] Though these nations have always hated Israel, they will form this covenant against Israel in reaction to the refounding of the Israelite kingdom.[40] In other words, while Edom and Ishmael can accept the presence of Jews in the world when God's people are exiled and subservient to them, they cannot abide a strong and sovereign State of Israel. When Israel begins to rise up in strength and glory, the Edomites and Ishmaelites understand that Israel, God's people, are now a threat to their broken philosophies and twisted religions. A vibrant Israel fulfilling its role as a light unto the nations represents a fundamental challenge to their dominance and influence over humanity. And so Edom and Ishmael will set aside their differences and work to destroy the State of Israel.

"And Egypt shall become desolate, and Edom shall be a desert waste, because of the violence done to the children of Judah, because they shed innocent blood in their land" (Joel 4:19). "Egypt" refers to the Ishmaelites, for Ishmael's wife was an Egyptian. The nations of Edom and Ishmael will be "violent" and "shed innocent blood." They will remain powerful and bring evil upon Israel, who will be exiled among them, until the moment of redemption.[41]

"In the future, the nations will permit Israel to return to its land, and Israel will experience a redemption through leaving the exile. But when the redemption begins to shine in all of its glory, splendor and holiness, the nations will turn on Israel and pursue them, and then they will declare the war of Gog of Magog against them. They will fall on the hills of Israel, Israel will be completely holy before God, and the redeemer the son of David will be revealed."[42]

Despite their evil plans, the alliance of Edom and Ishmael will ultimately crumble; the iron will not hold together with the clay. It is only a matter of time. When the alliance collapses, God will set up His own kingdom, the Kingdom of the son of David,[43] which will stand forever. "You saw iron mixed with common clay; they… shall not hold together, just as iron does not mix with clay. And in the days of these kings, the God of heaven will set up a kingdom forever, it will not be destroyed, and the kingdom will not be left to another people; it will crumble and destroy all these kingdoms, and it will stand forever" (Daniel 2:43-44).

CHAPTER 4:

ISHMAEL THE WILD DONKEY

On November 24, 2023, two men were executed in the Arab town of Tulkarem in Samaria. After they were shot and killed in the street, local residents beat and stomped on their bodies. A mob of hundreds of onlookers then tried to hang their mutilated bodies from an electrical tower, as hundreds of others gawked and filmed the scene on their smartphones. When that proved too difficult, local residents tossed their bodies over the walls of a United Nations school and tied their feet to a chain link fence.[1]

The perpetrators, as you have probably guessed, were Arabs. But so were the victims - Hamza Mubarak, 31, and Azam Juabra, 29, who were accused of collaborating with Israel and providing the IDF with counter-terrorism intelligence. Unsurprisingly, this sickening story received little attention in the press. Perhaps this is because stories like this one are common among the Arabs of Judea, Samaria and Gaza, who see no contradiction between brutal violence and their Muslim faith. Footage from the incident depicted crowds shouting "traitors" at the victims and repeatedly screaming "Allahu Akbar," "God is greatest."

During one of his many visits to Israel, Captain Gary Kosak visited a small house factory of handicapped Arabs who were working at sewing machines and weaving looms. Though they were disabled, they worked hard to make wall hangings, tablecloths and other items. Some were born with their handicaps, but a beautiful young woman there was handicapped in an act of vengeance between two Arab families. Someone in her family had wronged someone from another Arab family, who then took out his rage on this young woman. Together with his accomplices, he kidnapped the young woman, held her down and cut the nerves and tendons in her legs, making her a cripple. Kosack writes, "It was an example of Arab vengeance that seems to fit the prophetic description of Ishmael's offspring. In learning more about the Arab people, I discovered that acts of blood revenge were not uncommon. These types of tragedies happened frightfully more often than one would imagine."[2]

The list of Arab atrocities committed against Jews in Israel is so long that most of the world has become numb to the horror. One example will have to suffice: the brutal slaughter of the Fogel family in the Samarian town of Itamar. On Friday night, March 11, 2011, Tamar, the eldest Fogel daughter, returned from a Sabbath youth activity to find the door closed, even though she remembered her parents had left the door open for her. Upon entering, she discovered a horror scene. Her younger brothers Yoav, 11, and Elad, 4, lay lifeless on the floor, surrounded by blood. In her parents' bedroom, Tamar found the bodies of her parents, Ehud and Ruth Fogel, alongside her three-month-old sister, stabbed in her crib. Tamar found her two remaining brothers, Roi, 8, and Shay, 2, hiding in another room.

The terrorists who slaughtered the Fogel family, teenaged cousins Amjad Awad and Hakim Awad from the neighboring Arab village of Awarta, meticulously planned their assault, targeting the Sabbath when they knew Jewish families would be at home. At their trial, Hakim - only 17 years old at the time of the massacre - said he had no regrets. As he left the court, he motioned the V sign for "victory" with his fingers.[3]

As is their custom whenever a terrorist successfully murders Jews or other infidels, the Arabs of Judea and Samaria celebrated the slaughter of the Fogel family by handing out candies in the streets to children,[4] just as they celebrated after the destruction of the twin towers on 9/11.[5] From Iran to Yemen to Lebanon, Muslims glorify jihad and the annihilation of those who do not accept their creed.

These stories are not exceptions but rather the rule. "Woe is to me for I have sojourned in Meshech; I dwelt among the tents of Kedar. Too long has my soul dwelt with those who hate peace. I am at peace, but when I speak, they come to wage war" (Psalm 120:5-7). "Kedar," explain the commentators, is one of the kingdoms of Ishmael.[6] Though they might pay lip service to peace, in their hearts they yearn for war.[7]

Ramadan, the ninth and holiest month of the Islamic calendar year, "is the month in which the Koran was revealed as a guide for humanity with clear proofs of guidance and the standard to distinguish between right and wrong."[8] In theory, it is a time when Muslims practice self-restraint, refraining from food, drink, sexual activity and immoral behavior between dawn and dusk, and also a time to focus on family, charity and kindness.

In practice, Ramadan is a month of incitement to murder Jews. Many Muslims spend the daytime hours at their mosques, praying and listening to religious lessons or sermons. These sermons are used to provoke Muslims to action against Jews. In 2023, Muslims subjected Israelis to an unprecedented wave of terror during Ramadan, committing over fifty shootings, trampling attacks, stabbing attacks, rocket barrages, and throwing dozens of Molotov cocktails. Most sickening of all, Muslim terrorists murdered my neighbors, Lucy (48), Maia (20) and Rina (15) Dee, may their blood be avenged, on the second day of Passover, as they were driving to a family get-together. On the Temple Mount, hundreds of Muslims barricaded themselves in the al-Aqsa Mosque and threw stones and fireworks at the policemen. The wave of attacks was driven by a well-oiled incendiary machine that operates in mosques, schools, and especially on social networks and through viral videos.

Making Ramadan a month of terror and war is neither new nor an aberration. Throughout their history, Muslims initiated many important battles for Islam specifically during Ramadan: the Battle of Badr (624), the Conquest of Mecca (630); the Conquest of Spain (711), the Battle of Hattin (1187); Battle of Ain Jalut (1260), the Yom Kippur War (1973), and Operation Guardian of the Walls (2021), which erupted after Hamas issued an ultimatum to the Israeli government to evacuate the Temple Mount and the Sheikh Jarrah neighborhood.

Incredibly, much of Israel's secular leadership refuses to acknowledge the explicitly religious nature of Muslim antisemitism and attacks on Jews. At the start of Ramadan in March 2024, in the midst of Hamas' holy war against Israel, Major General Aharon Haliva of the IDF's Military Intelligence Directorate warned against actions on the Temple Mount in the month of Ramadan. "Religious triggers, primarily the Temple Mount, during the month of Ramadan, may lead to a flare-up and escalation on multiple fronts or even regional, while turning the war into a religious war."[9]

Statements like these are astoundingly naive. Gazan Arabs did not attack Israel on October 7, 2023 because of economic hardship. Homes in Gaza are spacious and often furnished with luxury furniture, while the shops carry a full range of affordable items. Gaza is home to universities and luxury hotels and possesses some of the most beautiful and valuable beachfront real estate in the world.

Hamas' October 7 slaughter was committed *in the name* of Islam. Hamas called its war against Israel the "Al-Aqsa Flood," stating explicitly that it was driven by the religious goal of "liberating" the Temple Mount. Hamas terrorists murdered, kidnapped, raped and tortured in the name of Muhammad and the Koran. The duty of jihad against Israel is written in large letters on every school, house and street in Gaza, and the IDF consistently found weapons and terror tunnel shafts hidden in Gaza mosques.

It is time to accept the truth: Islam is a religion of war. From the very beginning, Islam has categorized the world into two domains: the House of Islam, *Dar al-Islam*, and the House of War, *Dar al-harb*. The "House of Islam" comprises territories governed by Muslim authorities and Islamic law, while the "House of War" refers to areas not yet under Islamic rule - where a state of perpetual jihad, or holy war, is mandated by Islamic law. Islam is not a "religion of peace," as so many in the West consistently claim. Until we recognize this basic reality, we have no hope of defeating our enemies.

Islam was born and took root in the tribal lands of Ishmael, whom Muslims consider a prophet and the forefather of Muhammed. What drives the people of Ishmael to act this way? What is the root of their hatred and predilection to murder?

Today's ongoing war between Israel and Ishmael cannot be understood in a vacuum. Though we are all children of Abraham, the people of Israel descend from Isaac, while Muslims claim Ishmael as their forefather. To understand the character and motivations of modern Ishmael, we must go back to the very beginning, to Ishmael himself.

A Wild Donkey

The seeds of Ishmael's destiny, as is often the case in the Bible, are found at the very beginning of Ishmael's story, even before his birth: "And the angel of the Lord said to [Hagar], 'Behold, you will conceive and bear a son, and you shall name him Ishmael, for the Lord has heard your affliction. And he will be a wild donkey of a man (*Pereh Adam*); his hand will be upon all, and everyone's hand upon him, and before all his brothers he will dwell'" (Genesis 16:11-12).

Though he is the firstborn son of Abraham, one of the greatest men to ever walk the earth, Ishmael is destined to be a "wild donkey of a man." It is part of his very essence.

In the Hebrew language, the adjective always follows the noun. According to the standard grammatical rules, Ishmael should have been called "*Adam Pere,*" a "man that is a wild donkey." Why does the Bible say Ishmael is a "*Pere Adam,*" a "wild donkey that is a man"? It seems that "wild donkey" is the primary word, the "noun" by which Ishmael is known, while "man" is merely an adjective.[10]

When God commanded Abraham to sacrifice Isaac, "Abraham arose early in the morning, and he saddled his donkey, and he took his two young men with him and Isaac his son." But when the fateful time came to ascend to Mount Moriah and sacrifice Isaac, "Abraham said to his young men, 'Stay here with the donkey, and I and the lad will go yonder, and we will prostrate ourselves and return to you'" (Genesis 22:3,5). The sages identify the two nameless young men as Ishmael and Eliezer.[11] As Abraham turned to climb the mountain, he turned to Ishmael and said "Stay here with the donkey" - you who are like the donkey.[12]

What is the meaning of "*Pere Adam,*" that Ishmael is a "wild donkey" of a man?

A quick survey of the classic biblical commentators fills in the picture. Ishmael will be a man who loves to hunt beasts in the wilderness. "His hand will be upon all and everyone's hand on him" - he will be a bandit, and everyone will hate and attack him. "And before all his brothers he will dwell" - for his seed will be numerous.[13]

Others write that Ishmael will be a "wild-donkey man accustomed to the wilderness, seeking food, devouring all and being devoured by all… His children will increase and have wars with all the nations."[14] He will be "unrestrained among people"[15] and "will rebel against all mankind."[16]

"*Pereh,*" the Hebrew word for "wild donkey," is similar to other Hebrew words that begin with the same two letters - "*pera,*" "to uncover," and "*perach,*" to bloom. The phrase "*Pere Adam*" describes a person who wants to be free and to shake off subjugation of any kind. Ishmael is impulsive, fiercely resisting any restrictions on his behavior. He is willing to do anything, to break any rule of decency, for he will allow nothing to stand in the way of his will.[17]

These "wild donkey" character traits were not limited to Ishmael alone, but would come to define his many descendants, for all time. Before moving to Israel, Rabbi Joseph Hayyim Sonnenfeld wondered how the Bible could compare Ishmael to a donkey. Was he not a human being created in the image of God? But after he moved to Israel and experienced the crimes of the Ishmaelites, he had the opposite question. How could a donkey be compared to Ishmael?[18]

Someone once asked Rabbi Israel Meir Kagan, who died fifteen years before modern Israel's founding in 1948, about the relationship between Jews and Arabs. He responded: "Our Bible is eternal, and when it says that Ishmael 'will be a wild donkey of a man' it means that the children of Ishmael are destined to remain wild donkeys forever. Even if the cultured nations of the world try to educate them and civilize them, they will not succeed - for they are not people of culture. Even if an Ishmaelite studies to become an attorney or a professor, he will be an attorney or a professor who remains a wild donkey of a man. His wildness will never leave him. The Bible says: 'And he will be a wild donkey of a man' - 'will be' means that he will be this way forever." Rabbi Kagan sighed and said: "Oy, who knows what this wild donkey of a man is likely to do to the people of Israel in the end of days!"[19]

Does this mean that Ishmael is destined to be evil and has no hope of repentance? Certainly not. Though Ishmael is fundamentally wild, he also possesses the ability to channel his wildness in a holy direction. By humbly accepting Isaac's leadership and recognizing the authority of the Bible, the people of Ishmael can use their great passion for holiness.

The Bible tells us that when Abraham died, Isaac and Ishmael reunited to bury their father together. "Abraham expired and died in a good old age, old and satisfied, and he was gathered to his people. His sons Isaac and Ishmael buried him in the Machpelah cave in the field of Ephron, son of Tzochar, the Hittite, which faces Mamre" (Gen. 25:8-9). The sages explain that by listing Isaac, the younger son, before Ishmael, his older brother, the Bible implies that Ishmael gave precedence to Isaac as Abraham's primary son. "From here [we may deduce] that Ishmael repented."[20] Ishmael's acceptance of the primacy of Isaac demonstrates repentance for it signifies his acknowledgment and acceptance of God's decision that Isaac, not Ishmael, would inherit Abraham's blessings exclusively.

Ishmael's reconciliation with Isaac did not last, and his descendants are once again committing acts of murder and terror in the name of God. But Ishmael's reconciliation with Isaac is a reminder that the door to repentance is always open, if only Ishmael's children can find the humility to walk through it.

Winnowing the Chaff from the Wheat

The Bible is clear: Ishmael is fated to be a "wild donkey" of a man. But *why* is the holy Abraham's firstborn son destined to be so deeply and fundamentally wild?

"Until three generations, the defilement[21] did not disappear from our Patriarchs: Abraham begat Ishmael, Isaac begat Esau, [but] Jacob begat the twelve tribes in whom there was no taint whatsoever."[22] The forefathers of Israel, for all their holiness, possessed certain characteristics that, when taken to an extreme, could lead to great evil. The sages view Ishmael and Esau, the firstborn sons of Abraham and Isaac, as the "chaff" that surrounded the "wheat," the ideal sons of Abraham and Isaac - Isaac and Jacob, respectively. Like chaff, Ishmael and Esau are seen as "inedible" produce that must be winnowed and discarded before one can enjoy the wheat itself.

Abraham's defining character trait was "*chessed*," generally translated as "kindness." His care and concern for other people, including complete strangers, was legendary. Ishmael, the firstborn son of Abraham, possessed his father's *chessed* quality to an extreme.[23] Jewish mystics explain that "many nations are defined by the trait of *chessed*, and this is from Ishmael, who is the husk and refuse of the *chessed* of Abraham."[24]

Superficially, this is difficult to understand. *Chessed*, kindness, is a laudable quality. If Ishmael possesses *chessed* in abundance, why is he compared to "chaff" that must be discarded?

Though *chessed* is generally translated as "kindness," the word is used in a radically different context in Leviticus: "And a man who takes his sister, whether his father's daughter or his mother's daughter, and he sees her nakedness, and she sees his nakedness, *it is a disgraceful act (chessed)*, and they shall be cut off before the eyes of the members of their people; he uncovered his sister's nakedness; he shall bear his sin" (Leviticus 20:17). In this verse about incest, *chessed* is not translated as "kindness" but rather as "a disgraceful act." How can this one word have such radically different meanings? What does kindness have to do with incest?

At its core, *chessed* refers to an overflowing or lack of boundaries. It is a phenomenon that is neither inherently good nor evil, but one which can manifest in many different ways.

A very positive manifestation of *chessed* is kindness, a generosity of spirit that drives good people to give more of themselves to others than that which is strictly expected or required. A person with good *chessed* is able to break free of the boundaries of his own selfishness and share with others. Abraham epitomized this kind of *chessed* in its ideal form. The sages explain that his tent was open on all four sides,[25] removing all boundaries for travelers who might need a place to sleep or eat. Even as he recovered from his circumcision, Abraham sought out guests to welcome into his home.[26]

But *chessed* can also manifest as an inappropriate overflowing of healthy and proper boundaries. Incest and other forms of forbidden relationships are precisely this: love without boundaries. This is why the Bible refers to incest as "*chessed*."

"And Sarah saw the son of Hagar the Egyptian, whom she had borne unto Abraham, making sport" (Genesis 21:9). "Making sport," explain the commentators, is code for breaking rules of normal, healthy conduct. Ishmael engaged in illicit sexual relations and sought to murder Isaac, his half-brother and rival. "His hand will be upon all, and everyone's hand upon him, and before all his brothers he will dwell" (Genesis 16:12). "His hand will be upon all," stealing that which does not belong to him. He is "a wild donkey of a man," an animal that cannot be domesticated. Ishmael is a man of extreme and negative *chessed*, a man without healthy boundaries.

A nation's character is expressed in its songs and legends,[27] through the traditions that are passed down from parents to children through generations. The most famous legend of the children of Ishmael is One Thousand and One Nights, also known as Arabian Nights. The story tells of a powerful ruler, disillusioned by his wife's betrayal, who comes to believe that all women are unfaithful. After killing his wife and her lovers, he adopts a grim practice: each night, he marries a virgin, only to have her executed the next morning to ensure she will never be able to betray him and bring him dishonor. As his disdain for women grows, the supply of virgins dwindles until only one remains - the daughter of his vizier. Unwillingly, the vizier's daughter offers herself as the next bride. On their wedding night, she begins to weave captivating tales, each one left unfinished until the following night, when the king spares her life in anticipation of hearing the conclusion. Night after night, she staves off her execution with her enthralling tales, eventually totaling one thousand and one nights.

One Thousand and One Nights is extraordinarily revealing, highlighting the negative *chessed* of Ishmael. The unfaithfulness of the king's wife reflects his love without proper boundaries, while the king's cruel treatment of unknown numbers of virgins expresses Ishmael's tendency to take that which does not belong to him, for "His hand will be upon all."

Ishmael's flaws exist together with the strengths he inherited from Abraham. Like Abraham, Ishmael and his descendants are monotheists who reject idolatry with great clarity. And like Abraham, they are renowned for their hospitality. Given these strengths, why does Ishmael's *chessed* manifest in such dangerous and evil ways, unlike the holy *chessed* of his father?

The answer lies in the other half of Ishmael's DNA: his mother, Hagar the Egyptian. "The descendants of Ishmael carry all of Ishmael's nature: warm sensuality, Hagar's desire for freedom, and the spirit of Abraham. Therefore, the Ishmaelites express their faith in the one God with great clarity, and this was developed greatly by Arab and Jewish philosophers. However, they do not bind themselves to the commandments and the ways of the God of righteousness and justice. For this they would have needed the motherhood of Sarah, who conquered all of the desires and temptations and learned to control them – and this was the foundation of Judaism."[28]

Though Islamic theology calls on its adherents to serve God, they lack subservience to the Divine will as expressed in the Bible. They possess the faith of "wild donkeys," but it is *they* who decide what is God's will. Without Sarah as a balancing force of righteousness, limits and controls, Ishmael took his father's trait of *chessed* to dangerous extremes.

The names "Israel" and "Ishmael" both contain the word "*El*," one of the names of God. But there is a critical difference between them. The name "Israel" is read as "*Yashar-El*," meaning "straight with God." Ishmael, however, means "*Yishma-El*," "God will hear my requests and answer me." Whereas Israel is "straight" with God and follows God's will, Ishmael expects God to fulfill his *own* will.

In other words, the people of Ishmael do not bend their will to God, but rather bend God's will to theirs. They justify their actions by attributing them to God's will, using this belief to sanction whatever they choose to do. This is how Hamas terrorists could scream out their faith in God while raping, torturing and massacring women and children on October 7. This form of faith, faith without the moral regulations of the Bible, only increases the evil of Ishmael, for it provides a divine stamp of approval to their heinous crimes.

The Kabbalists argue that Ishmael is particularly dangerous because his circumcision was incomplete. Unlike pagans, Ishmael was circumcised (Genesis 17:25), but only partially. The commandment of circumcision has two elements: *milah*, removing the foreskin, and *periyah*, peeling back a thin membrane to reveal the corona. Ishmael only fulfilled the first part of the circumcision, symbolizing his imperfect relationship with God.[29] "Come and see: for four hundred years, the angel of the children of Ishmael stood and begged before God. He said to God, 'whoever is circumcised has a portion in Your name.' God said to him, 'it is so.' He said to God, 'Behold Ishmael who is circumcised. Why does he not have a portion in You like Isaac?' God said to him, 'It is not so, the one was circumcised properly and according to the full requirements, while the other was not so. And in the future, the children of Ishmael are destined to rule over the Holy Land for a long time when it is empty from anything, like their circumcision which is empty and imperfect.

And they will prevent the children of Israel from returning to their place until the reward for the merit of the children of Ishmael reaches completion.'"[30]

The commandment of circumcision symbolizes man's need to restrain his urges and desire for gratification. The foreskin represents unchecked lust, which is detrimental to our spiritual well-being, while its removal represents the proper and healthy channeling of physical desire within appropriate boundaries.[31] As British Chief Rabbi Jonathan Sacks wrote, "Circumcision turns biology into spirituality. The instinctive male urge to reproduce becomes instead a covenantal act of partnership and mutual affirmation."[32]

Ishmael is not Abraham's chosen son, for he is not capable of carrying on Abraham's legacy. "But My covenant I will establish with Isaac, whom Sarah will bear to you at this time next year" (Genesis 17:21). Ishmael possesses faith, symbolized by his circumcision, but God did not choose to establish a covenant with him for his circumcision was imperfect. He accepted faith in God, but would not submit to God's will.

Ishmael and Israel

"Why is his name called Ishmael ("God will hear")? For in the future, God will hear the painful cries of His nation [the people of Israel] in the land, who will cry because of what the descendants of Ishmael will do to them at the end of days. Therefore, his name was called Ishmael, as it says 'May God hear and answer them [Israel]' (Psalm 55:20)."[33]

Ishmael is destined to inflict terrible pain and suffering upon the people of Israel. Though other nations that exile and oppress Israel are compared to animals in the Book of Daniel, Ishmael is called a "wild donkey of a *man*," part animal and part human, for he was partially circumcised. "Therefore his oppression is worse than that of the other four oppressors,"[34] and "There is no exile more painful for the people of Israel than the exile of Ishmael."[35]

Maimonides personally experienced the painful oppression of the Ishmaelites. In 1148, the Almohads - a North African Berber Muslim empire founded in the 12th century - conquered Córdoba, the city of his birth, and the Jewish community was forced to choose between conversion to Islam, death or exile. Maimonides' family chose exile, and spent the next decade on the run in southern Spain and North Africa. Given his personal experiences, his assessment of the Ishmaelites is not surprising: "Remember, my co-religionists, that on account of the vast number of our sins, God has hurled us in the midst of this people, the Ishmaelite Arabs, who have persecuted us severely, and passed baneful and discriminatory legislation against us… Never did a nation molest, degrade, debase and hate us as much as they… We do not escape this continued maltreatment which well nigh crushes us. No matter how much we suffer and elect to remain at peace with them, they stir up strife and sedition, as David predicted, 'I am all peace, but when I speak, they are for war.' (Psalm 120:7)."[36]

Though Ishmael's chronic refusal to recognize boundaries leads him to conflict with many nations, Ishmael possesses a unique hatred for the people of Israel - a hatred that goes back to the very birth of Isaac. Ishmael was Abraham's firstborn, and while his mother was only Sarah's handmaid, he considered himself to be Abraham's rightful heir. It was only natural for him to resent Isaac, whom God chose instead of him. As the sages teach, "When Isaac was born, everyone was happy. Said Ishmael: "You are fools! I am the firstborn, and I will take a double portion [which is the firstborn's right]!"[37]

Unfortunately for Ishmael, Isaac received the rights of the firstborn in his stead. Most importantly, that meant that the land of Israel would belong to Isaac's descendants, as God later made explicit in His promise to Isaac: "Sojourn in this land, and I will be with you, and I will bless you, for to you and to your seed will I give all these lands, and I will establish the oath that I swore to Abraham, your father" (Genesis 26:3).

As of 2024, there are 50 Muslim-majority nations in the world, including 22 Arab countries. Yet hundreds of millions of Muslims demand that tiny Israel (approximately the size of New Jersey), the world's only Jewish state, be transformed into a Muslim caliphate. "From the River to the Sea, Palestine will be Free!" If they succeed in their plans to erase Israel from the map and transform it into "Palestine," where will the 7 million Jews of Israel go? The children of Ishmael are not particularly concerned with that issue. Given the widespread approval of the atrocities of October 7 in the Muslim world, it is fair to assume that a second Holocaust is not out of the question if they have their way.

How should Israel respond to Ishmael's undying hatred? Just as the roots of Islam's astonishing and undying Jew hatred reach all the way back to Ishmael, the proper response to this evil is also found in the Bible itself.

"And Sarah saw the son of Hagar the Egyptian, whom she had borne unto Abraham, making sport. Wherefore she said unto Abraham: 'Cast out this bondwoman and her son; for the son of this bondwoman shall not be heir with my son, even with Isaac.' But the matter was very evil in the eyes of Abraham, concerning his son. And God said to Abraham, 'Be not displeased concerning the lad and concerning your handmaid; whatever Sarah tells you, hearken to her voice, for in Isaac will be called your seed'" (Genesis 21:9-12).

When Sarah saw Ishmael "making sport" - a euphemism for his plans to murder Isaac - she understood that there was no choice but to banish Ishmael from her home. It's common sense; what else can you do when someone in your own home is trying to murder you?

Nevertheless, the prospect of banishing his firstborn son Ishmael was not merely distasteful to Abraham; it was "very evil" in his eyes. Abraham was a man of awesome kindness and love. Despite the threat that Ishmael presented to Isaac – the commentators write that Ishmael "would take his bow and shoot arrows at him"[38] - banishing Ishmael went against every fiber of Abraham's being.

God made clear that in this argument, Sarah was right. When Ishmael threatened Isaac, the proper response was not lovingkindness, but banishment. Isaac was Abraham's true heir. He was Abraham's future, and so Abraham and Sarah were obligated to do whatever was necessary to protect Isaac. Ishmael had to be expelled from Abraham's home, however unpleasant it would be.

The lesson for our time is unambiguous and must be stated clearly and without apology. For over 150 years, the descendants of Ishmael have repeatedly refused to live in peace with the people of Israel, the descendants of Isaac. They have murdered one precious and irreplaceable Jew after another. The vast majority of the Arabs of Gaza, Judea and Samaria have made their intentions absolutely clear: they support Hamas and other terrorist groups that seek to murder Jews and remove them from the land of Israel.

Understandably, "Sarah Jews" – and I count myself as one of them – have had enough. We cannot live safely and happily in our land together with the children of Ishmael. These people are our enemies – and they must go.

Nevertheless, the more liberal "Abraham Jews" among us find the prospect of banishing the children of Ishmael to be deeply distasteful. These are good people, people of love and kindness, and I completely understand why the prospect of expelling the children of Ishmael from Gaza, Judea and Samaria is "very evil" in their eyes. However this happens, it will be distasteful and unpleasant.

And yet, as God so clearly told Abraham, "whatever Sarah tells you, hearken to her voice." With these words, God is telling our generation: "My dear 'Abraham Jews': I understand that you are filled with love and kindness, and that you desperately want to live in peace together with the children of Ishmael. I love you for your idealism! But precisely because I love you, I need you to do this for Me. Listen to the 'Sarah Jews,' the Jews of Israel who have lived for decades with the constant threat of Arab terror. They have buried their sons and daughters, their husbands and wives, because the 'Abraham Jews' refuse to see the truth: that the children of Ishmael are not interested in peace. I beg of you, 'Abraham Jews' – listen to the 'Sarah Jews', and banish Ishmael from My land!"

The people of Israel will never live in safety and security until Israel banishes the millions of Ishmaelites who either murder Jews or aid and support the terrorists who do so.[39] "But if you do not drive out the inhabitants of the Land from before you, then those whom you leave over will be as spikes in your eyes and thorns in your sides, and they will harass you in the land in which you settle" (Numbers 33:55). The wild donkey must be banished from the land.

"[Ishmael] will beget twelve princes (*nesi'im*), and I will make him into a great nation" (Genesis 17:20). The sages point out that the word "princes," "*nesi'im*," used in this verse is missing a letter, alluding to a verse in Proverbs, in which the word "*nesi'im*" is used with a different meaning. "Clouds (*nesi'im*) and wind, but no rain" (Proverbs 25:14). Like clouds which disappear without a trace, so will the princes of Ishmael.[40]

"And they [Ishmael's descendants] dwelt from Havilah to Shur, which borders on Egypt, going towards Asshur; against all his brothers he dwelt [*nafal*, literally "fell"]. And these are the generations of Isaac the son of Abraham; Abraham begat Isaac" (Genesis 25:18-19). Rabbi Jacob ben Asher explains: "Immediately following the verse 'against all his brothers he fell' is written 'And these are the generations of Isaac.' This teaches us that when Ishmael falls at the end of days, then will sprout forth the son of David, who is a descendant of Isaac."[41]

May we soon see that day!

CHAPTER 5:

ESAU: THE DECEPTIVE PIG

From 2015-17, Germany welcomed over 1.4 million refugees from Syria, Afghanistan and other Muslim countries. Germany's chancellor Angela Merkel famously declared "we can handle this," and that there were no limits to the number of refugees Germany could accept.[1] Incredibly, the nation that only 70 years earlier slaughtered 6 million Jews and millions of other innocents had become a model of love and acceptance. Or at least it *seemed* that way.

To better understand what drove Germany to fling open its doors to refugees, Tuvia Tenenbom toured Germany while presenting himself as half-Jordanian. He gained entry to squalid refugee camps and mingled with Muslim refugees and local Germans.

While in Munich, Tenenbom asked two German university students why Germany was accepting more refugees than any other country. The answer? "History." If the Germans didn't accept all the refugees, they would be called "Nazis" by other countries. In their view, the Germans were better than all other countries when it came to the refugee situation.

Tenenbom challenged them: "Your statements are contradictory. If Germany's refugee policy is a result of a fear of being called "Nazis," then Germany is not 'better' than other countries, just more fearful than others." Instead of replying to the question, one of the students told Tenenbom "I think you are of Jewish origin." "Why?" asked Tuvia. "Because you are critical of me and my country."

The other student then chimed in and said that Israel is an "aggressive" and "inhumane" state. Why? The student explained that about two years ago, a Palestinian killed an Israeli and Israel responded with a military action that killed about 36 Palestinians. They didn't know anything more about the story. In short, as Tenenbom writes, "the Israelis, meaning the Jews, are inhumane, and the Germans are angels."[2]

In Hannover, Tenenbom met three young Swedes, who argued that Sweden is even more humane than Germany, for in proportion to their population, the Swedes took in more refugees than any other country. They said that Sweden cares more about human rights than any other nation, and that its people despise racists.

Tenenbom asked them: "The Swedish people are quite obsessed with the Arab-Israeli conflict. Why is that?" "Israel is a Nazi state," one of them answered, and the others agreed. "The Jews should never have been allowed to live in what is today 'Israel.' They should have been directed to settle somewhere else." They went on to describe the unique evil of the Jews: "When a Palestinian kills a Jew, the Jews retaliate and kill one hundred Palestinians."[3]

Throughout Germany, Tenenbom heard the same sentiment. "Germany wants to do good, wants to feel like they are doing good, and wants the world to see them as good."[4] Yet, many of those who professed to love the refugees were certifiable antisemites who despised Jews and the Jewish State.

Hatred of Israel is par for the course for most Western nations. UNRWA, the UN Relief and Works Agency, exclusively serves Arab "refugees" from Israel and their descendants - i.e., Arabs who have never resided in the territories they are deemed refugees from. IDF intelligence has shown that about 450 terror operatives in Gaza, mostly Hamas members, were also employed by UNRWA - an ostensibly neutral organization.[5] Hamas military equipment was found hidden in UNRWA schools during the IDF's ground operation in Gaza. Meanwhile, UNRWA staff expressed support for Hamas's October 7 massacre, hailing the terrorists as "heroes," sharing images of dead or captured Israelis, and advocating for the execution of Israeli hostages.[6]

Why do the people of progressive Western democracies like Germany and Sweden hate Jews? Why does the European Union repeatedly condemn Israel while ignoring the evils perpetrated by autocracies like China and Iran?

To understand the West's obsession with Jews and Israel, we must better understand the spiritual forefather of today's secular, progressive West: Esau, the brother of Jacob.

His Father's Son

In Jewish tradition, Esau is almost universally considered an evil man. In sharp contrast to Jacob, the father of the people of Israel, Esau is condemned as a murderer and rapist and compared to a pig. Though his sins are not spelled out in the Bible, Esau was clearly a bloodthirsty man, evidenced by his plan to murder his brother. "Let the days of mourning for my father draw near, I will then kill my brother Jacob" (Genesis 27:41).

Yet somehow, Esau was his father Isaac's favorite child. "Isaac loved Esau because [his] game was in his mouth, but Rebecca loved Jacob" (Genesis 25:28). Esau clearly respected and loved his father; even when he was consumed with hatred for Jacob, he controlled himself while his father was still alive so as not to cause him pain. The commentators, so critical of Esau, nevertheless acknowledge that he excelled at honoring his father.[7]

What drew Isaac to his eldest son, the "ruddy (red)" boy covered in hair, the hunter and man of the field? And how could the righteous Isaac produce a son as evil as Esau?

The sages suggest that Isaac's relationship with Esau is rooted in the most dramatic - and traumatic - moment of his life: when Abraham bound Isaac at the altar on Mount Moriah. "'Isaac's eyes became dimmed from seeing' (Genesis 27:1). [Isaac went blind] from the impact of that vision. For when Abraham bound his son on the altar, the ministering angels cried… And tears dropped from their eyes into his eyes, and were imprinted into his eyes. And when he became old, his eyes became dimmed from seeing."[8]

In other words, Isaac's experience at the altar, where Abraham almost sacrificed him to God, shaped the course of his life and caused him to lose his vision as he grew old. The binding of Isaac was an awesome moment that demonstrated both Abraham and Isaac's complete dedication to God, but the experience was not without cost. Though Isaac lived a successful life and was wealthy and respected by all who knew him, the memory of the binding stayed with him. Shackled and prepared to die, he stared up at the heavens and confronted death.

"In old age, the vision [of the binding] explodes in fatal bloom; his awareness of death fills every moment of life."[9] "Behold now, I have grown old; I do not know the day of my death... Let my soul bless you before I die" (Genesis 27:2,4). Isaac was intensely aware of his mortality, and as the years went by he became detached from the comings and goings of this physical world. His blindness was symptomatic of his separation from the world of sight, from the material things that consume us in this life.

Used properly, an awareness of death and mortality can encourage us to live righteously. "The righteous ones would imagine, just before they got up to pray, that they were lying in their graves, experiencing much suffering, until someone came by and said, 'Rise, stand up and pray.' You can picture how imagining that scenario in a vivid way would add tremendous vigor and intensity to prayer."[10] Isaac lived with this thought his entire life and reached awesome levels of holiness. But a constant awareness of death can also lead to depression, meaninglessness and nihilism - as it did for Esau.

Immediately after recounting the birth of Esau and Jacob, the Bible relates the turning point in Esau's life. "Now Jacob cooked a stew, and Esau came from the field, and he was exhausted" (Genesis 25:29). As it often does, the Bible begins in the middle of the story, leaving us to wonder about the background to this incident. Why did Jacob cook a stew, and why was Esau exhausted?

The sages explain that Jacob cooked a stew in response to an event recorded earlier in the same chapter: "And Abraham expired and died in a good old age, old and satisfied, and he was gathered to his people" (Genesis 25:8). Mourners traditionally eat lentils,[11] so Jacob cooked a stew of lentils for his father Isaac who was mourning over Abraham.

Though Jacob certainly mourned his grandfather, Abraham's death was deeply traumatic for Esau. "Esau asked Jacob: 'What is the stew for?' Jacob answered: '[Abraham] has died.' Esau said: 'That old man has been struck down by fate!?' He answered: 'Yes.' Esau then said, 'If so, there is no reward and no resurrection of the dead.' The Holy Spirit cried out, 'Do not cry for the dead and do not lament for them' - this refers to Abraham; 'Weep rather for him who is going' (Jeremiah 22:10) - this refers to Esau."[12]

For Esau, Abraham's death was not simply a painful familial loss of a beloved grandfather who died at a ripe old age. It was proof that life is fundamentally random and unfair. If even the great and holy Abraham, who deserved to live forever, could die, it meant that "there is no judgment and there is no judge."[13] The irony is that Abraham's death led Esau to reject the very principle that defined Abraham's life - the belief in one God Who is both just and merciful and Whose existence lends meaning to our lives. Like his father, Esau became obsessed with death. But unlike his father, his constant consciousness of death convinced him that life is unintelligible and ultimately meaningless.

"And Esau said to Jacob, 'Pour into [me] some of this red, red [pottage], for I am exhausted'; he was therefore named Edom" (Genesis 25:30). Here again we read of Esau's exhaustion. Why does Esau demand the stew? "For I am tired," "*ki ayef anochi.*" Read literally, Esau is saying that his "*anochi,*" his sense of "I am," is exhausted.[14] Esau was *spiritually* weary, for his life was empty of purpose. "Out, out, brief candle! Life's but a walking shadow, a poor player, That struts and frets his hour upon the stage, And then is heard no more; it is a tale, Told by an idiot, full of sound and fury, Signifying nothing."[15]

"And Jacob said, 'Sell me as of this day your birthright.' Esau replied, 'Behold, I am going to die; so why do I need this birthright?'" In Hebrew, the phrase is "*Anochi holech la'mut,*" "I am *going towards* death." Obsessed with his ever approaching death, the birthright - and all the privileges and responsibilities that come with it - no longer mattered to Esau.[16] When Jacob understood this, he realized that Esau was no longer capable of possessing the birthright. A spiritually exhausted leader must step down and be replaced.

"[Esau] committed five sins on that day. He dishonored a betrothed maiden, he committed a murder, he denied God, he denied the resurrection of the dead, and he spurned the birthright."[17] Once he determined that life is meaningless, it was only natural for Esau to submit to his worst inclinations and remove all moral restraints from his life. He became a "vacant" man, who spent his days hunting animals with his bow and arrow,[18] like a wealthy and aimless British nobleman who only feels truly alive while hunting game.

In severing his relationship with God, Esau also denied the existence of a deeper, spiritual realm, essentially committing himself to a life dedicated to materialism and the pursuit of pleasure. "And Esau said to Jacob, 'Pour into [me] some of this red, red (*edom*) stew, for I am faint'; he was therefore named Edom" (Genesis 25:30). The word *edom*, red, shares the same root as *adama*, earth. "He was a man of the field, meaning a man of the earth (*adamah*), and that is why his name was called *Edom*, for it is derived from [the Hebrew word] *adama*, the earth."[19]

Esau's new identity, latent in him from the time of birth,[20] would now be *Edom* - red earthiness, physical strength and boundless desire. "The eyes of man (*adam*) will not be sated" (Proverbs 27:20). Though this is true of all mankind, the sages interpreted this verse as a reference to Esau and *Edom*, which shares the same root as *adam*, the Hebrew word for "man."[21] "Pour into me some of this red, red (*edom*) stew." Esau became a man of overwhelming appetite, an appetite that would never be satisfied. "That wicked one opened his mouth wide like a camel. He said to [Jacob]: 'I will open my mouth and you continuously pour.'"[22]

Esau's materialism and desire would later characterize his spiritual descendants, the upper classes of the Roman Empire. Roman elites frequently engaged in extravagant, extensive banquets that flaunted their riches and social standing in ways that far surpassed modern notions of luxurious dining. For the Romans, "eating was the supreme act of civilization and celebration of life."[23] Epicureanism, a philosophy in line with that of Esau, flourished in the Roman Empire. Like Esau, the Epicureans believed that death brought complete extinction, a belief which shaped their way of life. Epicurus' rejection of Divine providence and denial of the immortality of the soul led him to the same materialistic hedonism that drove Esau.

"Turnus Rufus, [the Roman governor of Judea], once asked Rabbi Akiva a question: 'Why does God hate us such that He said, 'I hated Esau' (Malachi 1:3)?' Rabbi Akiva replied, 'I will answer you tomorrow.' The next day Turnus Rufus asked him, 'What did you dream last night and what did you see?' Rabbi Akiva responded, 'In my dream there were two dogs. One was named Rufus and the other, Rufina.' Turnus Rufus immediately grew angry and said, 'You called your dogs by my name and my wife's name. You have incurred execution.' Rabbi Akiva replied, 'What difference is there between you and them? You eat and drink, and they eat and drink. You produce offspring, and they produce offspring. You die, and they die. Because I gave them your names, you are angry?'"[24]

God created man as a being with a soul that transcends the animal kingdom. But when man denies God and the spiritual uniqueness of man, his whole life is nothing but an approximation of the lives of animals, erasing any meaningful difference between the two. Without faith in God, without a higher purpose to life, people become highly sophisticated "dogs" dedicated solely to the pursuit of financial security and pleasure. This was the emptiness at the heart of Roman society, and it is the very same emptiness that lies at the heart of today's spiritually bankrupt progressive secularism. Today's atheists are the secular successors to the pagans of the Roman Empire.

The blessing that Esau received from Isaac confirmed that Esau's materialism would bring him greater prosperity than other nations. "Behold, your dwelling place shall be the fat places of the earth and of the dew of the heaven from above" (Genesis 27:39). The Roman Empire and the modern Western nations are fulfillments of this blessing - but also of its accompanying curse.

Physical desire can never be satisfied. Esau's materialism is a recipe for anxiety, depression and misery. If it wasn't already clear to the naked eye, research studies[25] have shown that as people become more materialistic, their emotional health diminishes. The pursuit of material possessions leads inevitably to competition and comparisons with others. No matter how rich you become, there is always someone richer.

But there is a deeper reason for Esau's unhappiness. With no higher purpose to his life, Esau was essentially "complete." He had nothing lasting to strive for, no reason to work on himself, to grow or change. "Esau" derives from the Hebrew word "*asuy*," meaning "complete." Unlike his twin brother Jacob, Esau was born with adult features; "he was completely like a coat of hair" (Genesis 25:25). He was called Esau because he was born fully developed with hair, like one who is many years old.[26] From the very start, he was complete, as if he were already a finished product.

Though it made him physically powerful even as a child, Esau's completeness was a recipe for misery. Without meaningful goals, without a desire to improve oneself, life loses its vitality and joy. Each day brings us closer to death. "Religion and its carrier wave, traditional culture, offer mortal individuals the hope that some trace of their personhood will survive their physical demise. Whether one expects an eternal reward singing psalms in heaven or hopes to live on in the hearts of one's countrymen, the prospect of immortality is what makes mortality tolerable."[27] By rejecting belief in God and immortality, Esau condemned himself to a life of sadness and a terrifying fear of death.

Describing the tragic story of his talented father who descended into madness, the writer Edmund Wilson explained that what "laid him open to neurotic depressions was his lack of objectives in life. He had given up political ambitions, he had had every possible success at law… More and more… he would retire to a sanitarium or to a plantation in North Carolina or shut himself up at home in a room with a felt-covered door."[28] This is the misery of Esau, and the misery at the heart of secular progressivism.

Just as Ishmael is the "chaff" that was winnowed from Abraham, Esau is the "chaff" of Isaac that had to be discarded. Isaac's constant awareness of his own mortality drove him to holiness, but it contained the ever-present danger of despair, materialism and nihilism, which would come to define his favorite son Esau. Isaac loved Esau because he saw so much of himself in his elder son. But it was only after Isaac blessed Jacob instead of Esau that Isaac finally understood that Jacob, not Esau, would be his spiritual heir. Only then did he realize what Esau had become. "And Isaac shuddered a great shudder" (Genesis 27:33). At that moment, the darkness of Esau became apparent, and "he shuddered because he saw *Gehinnom* (hell) open up beneath him."[29]

From Falsehood to Victimhood

Deep down, Esau was aware of the emptiness of his life. Of course, he could not openly admit to the world that he believed in nothing but pleasure-seeking, raw power and worshiping himself and his own desires. So Esau convinced himself that *he* was the victim, that *he* was wronged by his brother Jacob. "Is it for this reason that he was named Jacob? For he has deceived me twice; he took my birthright, and behold, now he has taken my blessing" (Genesis 27:36). In a pattern that continues among Esau's descendants to this day, Esau obscures his own evil and guilt by projecting it onto Jacob.

From the very beginning, Esau worked to create a self-image of righteousness, even as he descended into nihilism. "Esau was a man who understood hunting" (Genesis 25:27). The sages explain that Esau was a man who knew how to hunt his father, by entrapping and deceiving him with his words. He would ask Isaac, "Father, how should salt and straw be tithed?" - though he well knew that there is no obligation to tithe salt or straw. Because of questions like these, Isaac believed Esau was punctilious in following God's will. By contrast, "Jacob was an innocent man," a person who is not astute at deceiving others.[30] "And Isaac loved Esau because [his] game was in his mouth" (Genesis 25:28). Isaac loved Esau because Esau used his mouth to fool his father.[31]

"And they named him Esau. And afterwards, his brother emerged... and he named him Jacob... And Isaac loved Esau because [his] game was in his mouth, but Rebecca loves Jacob" (Genesis 25:25-26, 28).

They named him Esau, but *he* named him Jacob. Isaac *loved* Esau, in the past tense, while Rebecca *loves* Jacob, in the present tense. This is the difference between a man of truth and a man of falsehood. The man of falsehood is always more famous and popular, while the man of truth is generally underappreciated. Esau was named by many people, for many sought him out and honored him. But in the end, the people saw through him and turned away from him; his love became a matter of the past. But Jacob, the man of truth, is named only by "one" - by God, the One Who sees the heart and from whom nothing is hidden. When he is finally recognized for his truth and sincerity, the people's love for him will continue on and never disappear.[32] As the sages write, "Truth stands, but falsehood will fall."[33]

Years later, after Jacob sent gifts to Esau, the two brothers shared an emotional moment. "And Esau ran toward him and embraced him, and he fell on his neck and kissed him, and they wept." Yet even here, the sages believe that Esau's kiss was not the moment of true reconciliation that it appeared to be. Traditionally, the Hebrew word "*vayishakehu*," "and he kissed him," is written in Torah scrolls with three mysterious dots above the word. The sages view this as an indication that Esau did not kiss Jacob wholeheartedly,[34] that it was a kiss that concealed hatred.[35]

Esau's penchant for phony virtue and dishonesty returns to the biblical scene during the time of King Saul and King David, through the fascinating character Doeg the Edomite. When David first escaped the assassins sent by Saul to murder him in his home, he ran to Ahimelech the high priest in the town of Nob, which served as Israel's religious center after the destruction of Shiloh and the Tabernacle. Pretending to be on a secret mission on Saul's behalf, David asked Ahimelech for bread and a sword. The high priest immediately sensed that something was amiss, as it was highly unusual for the king's son-in-law and top general to arrive alone. Reluctantly, he gave David some bread, told him where Goliath's sword was kept, and sent him on his way.

Watching this interaction unfold was a man of mysterious origins. "And there was a man of Saul's servants on that day, detained before the Lord: and his name was Doeg the Edomite, the chief of Saul's shepherds" (I Samuel 21:8). Simply understood, Doeg was a descendant of Esau, a convert who rose to become one of Saul's most trusted servants. It's also possible that Doeg was an Israelite who had lived in Edom and came to be identified with its people.[36]

Either way, Doeg is a fascinating character who is described, in one verse, as an "Edomite" - a descendant of the wicked Esau - and also as one who was "detained before the Lord." What, exactly, does it mean to be "detained" before God? The commentators offer different explanations, which together create a portrait of a seemingly saintly man. After traveling to Nob with others on a pilgrimage to offer sacrifices to God, Doeg remained there after the others left to continue praying,[37] to study the Bible[38] or simply to commune with God.[39] Some even argue that his title, "the chief of Saul's shepherds," is an allusion to a far loftier role - that Doeg was the chief of Saul's religious court![40] One way or another, Doeg presented himself as a holy man, dedicated to the service of God.

Doeg's righteous image makes his ensuing evil even more disturbing. "Then Doeg the Edomite, who was appointed over Saul's servants, answered and said, 'I saw the son of Jesse come to Nob, to Ahimelech the son of Ahitub. And he inquired of the Lord on his behalf, and gave him provisions, and gave him the sword of Goliath the Philistine" (I Samuel 29:9-10). Doeg witnessed Ahimelech's interaction with David and saw firsthand that the high priest was innocent of any crime and entirely unaware that David was running from Saul. If Ahimelech were truly conspiring against Saul, why would he help David in public, in front of the prying eyes of Saul's servant Doeg? Yet Doeg twisted the story to portray Ahimelech in the worst possible light. Unlike Doeg claimed,

David did not specifically seek out Ahimelech as a co-conspirator but rather came to the house of God seeking food, for he was starving. And though Doeg implied that Ahimelech gave Goliath's sword to David to help David rebel against Saul, we know the truth is otherwise - Ahimelech only gave Goliath's sword to David because David asked for a sword and no other was available.

Doeg's clever twisting of the truth would have dire consequences for Ahimelech and the priests of Nob. "And the king said to the footmen who were standing beside him, 'Turn and put the priests of the Lord to death, for their hand is also with David, and because they knew that he was fleeing, and they did not inform me'" (I Samuel 29:17). The other servants present refused to slaughter God's priests, and so Saul commanded Doeg himself to complete his evil deed. "And Doeg turned, and he fell upon the priests, and slew on that day eighty-five men, wearers of the linen ephod. And Nob, the city of the priests, he smote with the sharp edge of the sword, both man and woman, infant and suckling, and ox and ass, and lamb, with the sharp edge of the sword" (I Samuel 29:18-19).

Saul would later die in battle for his sins,[41] the most unforgivable of which was the slaughter of Nob[42] - a stain brought about by Doeg. More than anyone else, it was Doeg, the duplicitous Edomite Bible scholar, who brought about the downfall of Saul and his kingdom.

"But to the wicked God says: Who are you to declare My statutes, and that you have taken My covenant in your mouth?" (Psalm 50:16). God says to the wicked Doeg: "Why do you bother to study my laws? When you get to the sections about murderers and slanderers, how do you interpret them?"[43] God is particularly disgusted by a wise man who is wicked, who studies His Bible yet does not keep its laws.[44]

"His speech is smooth as butter, yet war is in his heart; his words are more soothing than oil, yet they are drawn swords" (Psalm 55:21). Doeg's learning was only insincere lip service,[45] a dangerous facade that fooled everyone but David himself. When evil dresses up as good, it is more dangerous than evil openly declared. This is the great strength of Esau, who hid his evil intentions and portrayed himself as a kosher and righteous man.[46] "Who is this coming from Edom… this one who was stately in His apparel, girded with the greatness of His strength?" (Isaiah 63:1). The people of Edom are "stately in their apparel" - they come wearing "clean clothing" and speaking smooth words of righteousness as if they speak for God Himself. But their righteous facade conceals a dark and dangerous anger. If their demands are not met, they will strike with vengeful fury.[47]

The sages frequently compare Esau to a pig, for the pig superficially appears to be a kosher animal. It possesses split hooves, one of the requirements for an animal to be kosher, but it does not chew its cud. Unlike other non-kosher animals that do not have split hooves and are easily identifiable as forbidden to Jews, like the camel, hyrax and hare, "the pig, when it lies down, stretches out its hooves, as if to say, 'See, I am a clean (kosher) animal.' So do these, the chiefs of Esau, rob and plunder and then pretend to be honorable."[48] This trait has continued throughout all the generations. Though the people of Edom portray themselves as men of proper character, they ultimately reveal themselves to be full of poison.[49]

In Daniel's second prophecy concerning the four kingdoms that will oppress Israel, he describes the fourth kingdom as a "beast, awesome and dreadful and exceedingly strong" with "huge iron teeth." "It ate and crushed, and trampled the rest with its feet" (Daniel 7:7). But though this beast is more terrible than the three beasts that preceded it, it has "eyes like human eyes," and a "mouth speaking arrogantly" (Daniel 7:8). The fourth beast, the pig of Edom, will pretend to be "human" and obscure its beastly evil with fancy words and lofty slogans.[50] In the name of "human rights" and "anticolonialism," the Edomites support the mass murder of Israelis, as so many academics did after October 7, claiming "Hamas has challenged the monopoly of violence" and "shifted the balance of power" while accusing Israel, the victim, of committing genocide.[51]

Phyllis McGinley, a Pulitzer Prize winning poet despised by the left for her celebration of the stay-at-home mom, well understood the modern manifestation of Edom. Before her death in 1978, she witnessed the rise of the modern social warrior who used words like "tolerance" and "liberty" as a hypocritical veneer to mask their own anger and intolerance.

> *The other day I chanced to meet*
> *An angry man upon the street —*
> *A man of wrath, a man of war,*
> *A man who truculently bore*
> *Over his shoulder, like a lance,*
> *A banner labeled "Tolerance."*
>
> *And when I asked him why he strode*
> *Thus scowling down the human road,*
> *Scowling, he answered, "I am he*
> *Who champions total liberty —*
> *Intolerance being, ma'am, a state*
> *No tolerant man can tolerate.*
>
> *"When I meet rogues," he cried, "who choose*
> *To cherish oppositional views,*
> *Lady, like this, and in this manner,*

> *I lay about me with my banner*
> *Till they cry mercy, ma'am." His blows*
> *Rained proudly on prospective foes.*
>
> *Fearful, I turned and left him there*
> *Still muttering, as he thrashed the air,*
> *"Let the Intolerant beware!"*[52]

Can there be any better description for self-righteous pro-Hamas rioters screaming "ceasefire" while assaulting American police officers?[53] For penetrating verse like this, McGinley earned the disdain of the allegedly open-minded leftists who have worked hard to ensure that she and her brilliant poetry are forgotten.[54]

The very same dynamic is at play among today's Edomites at the United Nations. "From Israel there descended prophets; from Esau there descended diplomats."[55] Dressed in designer suits and wearing their fabricated moral superiority on their sleeves, UN bureaucrats take great pleasure in excoriating Israel for imaginary war crimes while hobnobbing with representatives from dictatorships in Iran, China and Russia. On October 9, as Israel was only beginning to identify the mutilated bodies of over 1,200 victims of Hamas brutality and weeks before the war in Gaza began, United Nations Secretary-General António Guterres said "I am deeply distressed by today's announcement that Israel will initiate a complete siege of the Gaza Strip, with nothing allowed in – no electricity, food, or fuel. The humanitarian situation in Gaza was extremely dire before these hostilities; now it will only deteriorate exponentially."[56] Guterres would later smear Israel and claim that "Israel's military operations have spread mass destruction and killed civilians on a scale unprecedented during my time as secretary-general."

The truth, of course, is the opposite. As John Spencer, chair of urban warfare studies at the Modern War Institute at West Point has explained, "Israel has taken more measures to avoid needless civilian harm than virtually any other nation that's fought an urban war." In modern history, no military force has had to fight over 30,000 urban terrorists spread across seven cities, utilizing human shields and concealing themselves within extensive underground networks spanning hundreds of miles deliberately constructed beneath civilian areas, all while holding hundreds of hostages. Yet despite the unparalleled challenges Israel faces in its war against Hamas, it has implemented more measures to prevent civilian casualties than any other military force in history.[57]

As Gutteres and the United Nations repeatedly attacked Israel for defending itself, they also found the time to appoint Iran - the nation of state-sponsored torture and executions - as the chair of the UN Human Rights Commission.

Guterres could also be found at China's Belt and Road Initiative Forum, praising China's infrastructure investments around the world. Somehow, Guterres neglected to mention China's ongoing human rights abuses against Uyghurs in Xinjiang, including enforced sterilizations and forced labor.

Esau, it seems, is alive and kicking today.

From Esau to Amalek

Over time, Esau's toxic mix of materialism, nihilism, and hatred of Jacob developed into the monstrous evil known as Amalek. "And Timna was a concubine to Eliphaz, son of Esau, and she bore to Eliphaz, Amalek" (Genesis 36:12). Timna, as we read a few verses later, was the sister of Lotan and the daughter of Seir the Horite.[58] With these seemingly innocent verses, the Bible introduces the grandson of Esau, a man who will become the epitome of evil in the Jewish tradition.

The very conception of Amalek is a reflection of Esau's rejection of God and morality. The Book of Chronicles hints at a shady backstory: "The children of Eliphaz: Teman, and Omar, Zephi, and Gaatam, Kenaz, and Timna, and Amalek" (I Chronicles 1:36). Is Timna Eliphaz's concubine, or his daughter? Is Timna Amalek's mother, or his sister? It appears that she was *all* of these things. "This teaches us that Eliphaz was intimate with the wife of Seir, and Timna emerged from [the adulterous relationship] between them. And when Timna grew up, she became Eliphaz's concubine."[59] Timna and Amalek are the bastard children of adulterous and incestuous relationships - the inevitable result of Esau's evil choices.

During the ensuing centuries, as Jacob's family grew into a nation in Egypt, Amalek's descendants became a cruel and predatory tribe that plundered, looted and left destruction in its wake. Shortly after the miracle at the sea, the people of Israel became another of its victims.

"You shall remember what Amalek did to you on the way, when you went out of Egypt, how he happened upon you on the way and cut off all the weakest people at your rear, when you were faint and weary" (Deuteronomy 25:17-18). Amalek specialized in war crimes, kidnapping helpless women and children "from the rear," and selling them into slavery. For the Israelites, who were only beginning to recover from the trauma of slavery, Amalek's surprise attack - without any provocation - was particularly devastating.

"And he did not fear God" (Deuteronomy 25:18). Amalek's disdain for God, an extreme expression of his grandfather's rebellion, led his descendants to commit unspeakable evil. Amalek "cut off (*vayzanev*) all the weakest people at your rear." *Vayzanev*, Hebrew for "cut off," is derived from the word *zanav*, meaning "tail." The sages explain that the Amalekites "cut off the tail" - that they cut off the members of the male Jews, where they had been circumcised, and cast them up provocatively towards Heaven, exclaiming to God: "See! What good has Your commandment of circumcision done for them?"[60]

About 400 years later, when David and his militia returned to the town of Ziklag, they discovered that a large raiding party of Amalekites had burned their village to the ground and taken their wives and children as captives. The Amalekites waited for David and his soldiers to leave, ready to pounce on the weak and helpless. Later, as David and his men pursued the Amalekites, they found a sick and starving Egyptian slave whom the Amalekites, in their utter cruelty, abandoned in the desert. The Egyptian led David's army to the Amalekite camp, where "they were scattered over the entire landscape, eating and drinking and dancing, because of all the great spoil which they had taken" (I Samuel 30:16). As their innocent captives wept in pain and terror, the men of Amalek callously ate, drank and danced. Nothing could arouse mercy or pity among this nation.

Like their forefather Esau, the Amalekites possessed a unique hatred for the Jewish people. Even after Haman the Agagite - a descendant of Agag, the king of Amalek - became Ahaseurus' vizier and reached the pinnacle of political and financial success, Mordecai the Jew's refusal to bow to him would not let him rest. "Haman went out on that day, happy and with a cheerful heart, but when Haman saw Mordecai in the king's gate, and he neither rose nor stirred because of him, Haman was filled with wrath against Mordecai" (Esther 5:9). He was invited to an exclusive feast with the King and Queen, but when he came home he complained to his wife: "All this [success] is worth nothing to me, every time I see Mordecai the Jew sitting in the king's gate" (Esther 5:13). One Jew refused to bow to him, and all of his success was worthless? It seems that the very presence of a proud Jew, confident in his faith in God and the Bible, was enough to remind Haman of the emptiness of his own way of life.

"Therefore, it will be, when the Lord your God grants you respite from all your enemies around you in the land which the Lord, your God, gives to you as an inheritance to possess, that you shall obliterate the memory of Amalek from beneath the heavens. You shall not forget!" (Deuteronomy 25:19). The inevitable result of Esau's pagan materialism, Amalek is an evil that must be removed from the world.

The Kabbalists explain that our world is made up of a mix of good and evil. In every positive thing, there may lurk a trace of negativity, and within every negative occurrence, a small glimmer of goodness can be found. However, there exists one exception to this rule: Amalek. The DNA of this nation is steeped in pure, distilled evil, driven by a relentless urge for destruction and devastation.[61]

Amalek represents the evil of Esau, distilled into its purest and most terrible form. Though the Bible teaches us to be merciful and compassionate, our approach to Amalek is an exception to this general rule. A malignant growth within humanity, Amalek's evil is so dangerous to Israel and humanity that "emergency surgery" is necessary to remove this "malignant lesion" from the world. "Obliterate the memory of Amalek from beneath the heavens." Other descendants of Esau may repent of their evil and change their ways, but Amalek must be actively destroyed. It is the only way to save the world and achieve the vision of peace envisioned by the God of Israel.

An Iron Clad Rule of Hate

Over 1,700 years ago, the sages summed up a simple but powerful truth: "It is a well-known rule that Esau hates Jacob."[62]

Why do Esau and his descendants, from the Roman Empire until today, possess an undying hatred for God's people? Why are woke progressives attending Ivy League universities obsessed with Israel? Why are they consumed by the supposed evils of the world's only Jewish state (a democracy!), but can't be bothered with the atrocities perpetrated by dictatorships in China, Russia and Iran?

The answer is rooted in Esau's rejection of the birthright and the blessing of the firstborn that Isaac gave to Jacob in Esau's stead. "And Esau hated Jacob because of the blessing that his father had blessed him" (Genesis 27:41). Though Esau freely chose to reject God, he will never forgive Jacob for the consequences of his own decision.

But Esau's resentment of Jacob goes even deeper than the "stolen" blessings. The people of Israel and their stubborn refusal to assimilate and disappear from the world stage expose the nihilistic lie at the heart of Esau's philosophy. Jacob's very existence is a constant reminder to Esau that God is *real* - and that God makes demands of mankind that must not be ignored. Merely by existing, the Jew is a constant bone in Esau's throat.

Adolph Hitler, the ultimate Edomite, infamously wrote that "conscience is a Jewish invention. It is a mutilation, like circumcision."[63] Through the Bible, it was the Jew who taught humanity that people are created in God's image, that we are greater than the animals and have the capacity to decide our future for ourselves.[64] Hitler's Nazi Germany, like the Roman Empire before it, separated law from morality; in these Edomite systems, raw power was decisive. Nothing infuriates the children of Esau more than the Bible's system of moral values and its laws that protect the basic rights of all people, defend the weak and temper the excesses of the powerful.

The miraculous return of the Jews to the land of Israel did not impress the children of Esau. Edomites do not like miracles, for miracles bear witness to the supernatural. They awaken the Edomites from their dreams of endless power and thousand-year Reichs, reminding them of what they do not wish to be reminded of - that there is a God in this world. Whether they sit on thrones or occupy academic chairs ruled by the unyielding ideology of historical necessity, Edomites do not acknowledge miracles. Miracles reveal the shallowness of their worldviews, that there is more in heaven and earth than is dreamt of in their philosophies.[65]

"Deliver me, please, from the hand of my brother, from the hand of Esau, for I fear him, lest he come and smite me, mother and children alike" (Genesis 32:12). Jacob's cry to God was for himself, his wives and children, but also for future generations. "Deliver my future descendants from the hand of his descendants, who come with the power of Esau."[66]

From the very beginning, Esau and Jacob were destined to battle one another for supremacy. "Two nations are in your womb, and two kingdoms will separate from your innards, and one kingdom will become mightier than the other..." (Genesis 25:23). Either God is real or He is false; there can be no compromise. "One of the faiths is justified, one of the horses does win."[67] The Jew and Edomite cannot coexist; when one rises, the other must fall. As the sages said, "Caesarea, the daughter of Edom[68]... and Jerusalem are rivals. If one says to you that both are destroyed, do not believe him; if he says that both are flourishing, do not believe him; if he says that Caesarea is waste and Jerusalem is flourishing, or that Jerusalem is waste and Caesarea is flourishing, you may believe him, as it says, 'I shall be filled, she is laid waste' (Ezekiel 26:2). If this one is filled, that one is laid waste, and if that one is filled, this one is laid waste."[69]

"The elder will serve the younger" (Genesis 25:23). During Israel's two thousand years of exile, Edomite kings arrogantly believed that "the virgin of Israel has fallen and will never again rise" (Amos 5:2). But Israel has risen from the ashes. The people of Israel live! And so the day must soon come when Esau's hypocrisy and deception will be revealed for the entire world to see, when the truth of the children of Jacob will permanently rule over the falsehood of the children of Esau. "'Was not Esau a brother to Jacob?' says the Lord. 'And I loved Jacob'" (Malachi 1:2).

"And saviors shall ascend Mt. Zion to judge the mountain of Esau, and the kingdom shall be the Lord's" (Obadiah 1:21).

CHAPTER 6:

FROM JACOB TO ISRAEL: THE SECRET POWER OF THE MOON

In November 2023, only a few weeks after Hamas terrorists slaughtered 1,200 Jews on October 7, a young Jewish freshman at NYU interviewed me for her college newspaper. Emily was the valedictorian of her high school class and came to NYU with big plans for her future career. But a few weeks after the semester began, Hamas invaded Israel - and everything changed. NYU is one of the most antisemitic universities in America, where pro-Hamas students hold protests every day, screaming "From the River to the Sea, Palestine will be free" and "Death to the Jews!" Unsurprisingly, NYU did nothing to curtail the riots or reassure its Jewish students, and so Emily and her Jewish friends launched their own new newspaper to fight back. Incredibly, as we spoke on Zoom, I could hear antisemites protesting and screaming outside of the building.

I soon discovered how little Emily knew about Israel, the Bible and what it means to be Jewish. And so I told her about the greatness of our people - how young soldiers her age saved thousands of lives on October 7, sacrificing themselves to defend Israel's southern communities. I told her about the thousands of young Israelis traveling all over the world who raced back to Israel to reenlist after October 7. I explained that Israel is a nation of lions, "a people that rises like a lioness and raises itself like a lion" (Numbers 23:24).

Emily's eyes opened wide; nobody had ever told her that Jews are lions. But then she asked me an important question. "But if we are lions, why are we so afraid?" Emily struggled to understand why most Jewish students at NYU were afraid to push back against the pro-Hamas rioters. "Why are Jewish students hiding in their dorm rooms, like scaredy cats?"

Emily's question was more profound than she realized. Are Jews frightened cats or fearless lions? To understand the true character of the Jews, we must go back to the beginning of Jewish history - to Jacob, the father of the people of Israel.

Jacob or Israel?

Abraham, Isaac or Jacob - who is the greatest of the forefathers of Israel?

According to Rabbi Zvi Yehuda Kook, "the holiness and unique greatness of the forefathers are revealed through their accomplishments," what they left behind after they died. "By this measure, Jacob, the last of the forefathers, is the greatest. Abraham and Isaac were unique in their greatness, but Jacob is our father... He added the missing piece that was necessary to create the nation of Israel."[1] "Jacob is the chosen one of our forefathers, as is written, 'For God chose Jacob for Himself, Israel for His treasure' (Psalm 135:4)."[2]

All of Jacob's children would be included in the people of Israel. Unlike Abraham and Isaac, who fathered Ishmael and Esau - children unworthy of being part of God's chosen nation - "Jacob's bed was whole."[3] The sages say that "Jacob our forefather never died,"[4] for his legacy continued through all of his children, the children of Israel.

Though Jacob's children struggled to get along, they are undeniably his greatest legacy. Still, if we're honest, Jacob's life doesn't stack up to the lives of other great biblical personalities. Abraham was the great revolutionary, the first man to bring knowledge of God to humanity. We stand in awe of Isaac's extraordinary spiritual strength and willingness to be offered up as a sacrifice to God. Joseph sustained his family and all of Egypt through years of famine, even after his brothers sold him into slavery. Moses took the people of Israel out of Egypt and gave us the Bible, while Joshua led us to victory in the promised land. David, God's beloved king, united the nation and authored Psalms, while Solomon built the Temple and brought the nation to the heights of glory.

Compared to the accomplishments of the heroes who came before and after him, Jacob's life seems underwhelming. Why is Jacob the greatest of the forefathers? Why was he chosen to be the father of Israel?

In the Bible, God changes the names of several important characters. Abram became Abraham, Sarai became Sarah, and Hoshea became Joshua. But the changing of Jacob's name to Israel is unique. Whereas the other name changes were permanent, Jacob was henceforth known by *both* of his names, with God Himself restoring Jacob's original name[5]: "And God said to Israel in visions of the night, and He said, 'Jacob, Jacob!'" (Genesis 46:2). The Bible continues using both names even after Jacob's death. "Now these are the names of the sons of Israel, who came into Egypt with Jacob; every man came with his household" (Exodus 1:1). Though God Himself tells Jacob "Your name shall no longer be called Jacob, but Israel shall be your name" (Genesis 35:10), God did not intend to completely uproot the name "Jacob," but rather to make "Israel" primary and "Jacob" secondary.[6]

Why did God change Jacob's name, but not completely? Why must Jacob and his descendants live, for all generations, with a dual identity?

From Flight to Fight

From the very beginning, Jacob's life was defined by conflict. "And after that came forth his brother, and his hand had held onto Esau's heel; and his name was called Jacob" (Genesis 25:26). The sages go so far as to say that Jacob was formed before Esau in utero. But Jacob, though formed first, emerged last from the womb, holding onto Esau's heel in an unsuccessful bid to be the firstborn.[7]

Jacob's name, deriving from "*ekev*," "heel," presciently alluded to the way Jacob would respond to future conflicts. "Jacob was an innocent man, dwelling in tents" (Genesis 25:27) - and like most innocent people, he would be stepped on by those unbothered by notions of fairness or morality. Along the same lines, Esau is described as "hairy," and so we can assume that Jacob, in contrast, was "smooth." Whereas hair conceals, a "smooth" person is pure, with nothing to hide from others.

Though Jacob's purity was admirable, it also implied a simple naiveté and vulnerability. Esau, the "cunning hunter and man of the field" (Genesis 25:27), succeeded in capturing the favor of their father Isaac, a dangerous situation that Jacob passively accepted. Even when Esau was about to receive the blessing of the firstborn from Isaac - a terrible mistake that would have brought eternal suffering to Jacob's descendants - Jacob only acted because Rebecca commanded him to do so and told him exactly what to do. Left to his own initiative, he would have allowed Esau to take the blessings. Against his will, Rebecca forced Jacob to behave like his brother Esau, to combine "Jacob's voice with Esau's hands" (Genesis 27:22), beginning a process of transformation that would ultimately change his destiny.

Even after taking the blessings from Esau, Jacob was not ready to change his modus operandi. When facing situations of conflict, his first instinct was to run. He was a man of flight, not a man of fight.

Understanding her son's nature, Rebecca advised Jacob to flee. "She said to him, 'Behold, your brother Esau is consoling himself by planning to kill you. And now, my son, hearken to my voice, and arise, flee to my brother Laban, to Haran'" (Genesis 27:42-43). Instead of confronting Esau, Jacob fled to the house of Laban in Padan Aram - where he once again faced a foe determined to take advantage of him. In love with Rachel, Jacob agreed to work for seven years to earn her hand in marriage, but on their wedding night, the conniving Laban secretly replaced Rachel with Leah. Awaking in the morning to discover that he had been tricked, Jacob initially protested the injustice done to him: "What is this that you have done to me? Did I not work with you for Rachel? Why have you deceived me?" (Genesis 29:25). But when Laban claimed that the older daughter must be married off before the younger and demanded that Jacob work another seven years for Rachel, "Jacob did so" (Genesis 29:28), passively agreeing to Laban's demands.

Years later, after God told Jacob to leave Laban's house and return to the land of his birth, Jacob left in the only way he knew how - by fleeing. "And Jacob concealed from Laban the Aramean by not telling him that he was fleeing. So he and all that were his fled" (Genesis 31:20-21).

Time after time, Jacob passively allowed deceitful people to take advantage of him while fleeing all potential conflicts. But upon returning to the holy land and facing an unavoidable conflict with Esau and his army of 400 men, Jacob had nowhere to run. The night before they met, Jacob underwent a transformation that would forever alter his destiny. "Jacob was left alone, and a man wrestled with him until the break of dawn. When he saw that he could not prevail against him, he touched the socket of his hip, and the socket of Jacob's hip became dislocated as he wrestled with him. And the angel said, 'Let me go, for dawn is breaking,' but Jacob said, 'I will not let you go unless you have blessed me.' So he said to him, 'What is your name?' and he said, 'Jacob.' And he said, 'Your name shall no longer be called Jacob, but Israel, because you have struggled with God and with men, and you have prevailed'" (Genesis 32:25-29).

Confronted by a mysterious angel,[8] Jacob, for the first time in his life, did not flee. He fought his attacker through the night, even as the angel dislocated his hip - an injury so significant that God would forbid Jacob's descendants for all generations from eating the hip sinew of an animal. As morning broke, the two combatants wrestled to a stalemate, with no clear winner.

Though Jacob did not completely defeat the angel, he refused to let him leave until receiving his blessing. Yet strangely, in blessing Jacob, the angel admitted that Jacob did, indeed, defeat him: "Your name shall no longer be called Jacob, but Israel, because you have struggled with God and with men, and *you have prevailed.*" The exchange leaves us wondering - did Jacob defeat the angel or not?

The key to understanding this strange conversation are the words "you have struggled." The very fact that Jacob struggled with the angel and did not flee was *itself* the victory. This is the meaning of his new name, Israel. From this point on, Jacob would no longer passively allow others to take advantage of him, but would stand up to evil and *fight*. It was a change that would shape the course of human history, for by becoming Israel, Jacob gave his future descendants the ability to not only survive but to thrive and fulfill their role as God's chosen nation.

Though the angel told Jacob that his name would be changed to Israel, God did not actually change Jacob's name until a few chapters later. There was a delay; in between Jacob's struggle with the angel and his formal name change there occurred the traumatic story of Dina and Shechem.

When Jacob's beautiful daughter Dina went out to meet the local girls of Shechem, she was spotted by the city's prince, Shechem, for whom the city was named. Shechem abducted Dina, raped her and refused to let her go. When word of the scandal reached Jacob, he remained silent, and waited for his sons to return from the fields. His sons received the news with less composure. "And the men were grieved, and they burned fiercely, because he had committed a scandalous act in Israel, to lie with a daughter of Jacob, and such ought not to be done" (Genesis 34:7). The contrast between Jacob and his sons is jarring; "Jacob remained silent" while his sons "burned fiercely." Jacob appeared willing to negotiate with Shechem's father while his sons plotted their revenge. "Jacob's sons answered Shechem and his father Hamor with cunning," demanding that all of the men of Shechem be circumcised as a condition for intermarrying with Jacob's family.

The men of the city took the bait and circumcised themselves, playing directly into the hands of Jacob's sons. "Now it came to pass on the third day, when they were in pain, that Jacob's two sons, Simeon and Levi, Dina's brothers, each took his sword, and they came upon the city with confidence, and they slew every male. And Hamor and his son Shechem they slew with the edge of the sword, and they took Dina out of Shechem's house and left" (Genesis 34:25-26). Afraid that the other local tribes would gather together and attack his family, Jacob rebuked Simeon and Levi. But it was his sons who had the last word, asking Jacob: "Shall our sister be made into a prostitute?" (Genesis 34:31).

Growth is not linear. Despite his heroic struggle against the angel, it seems Jacob slipped back into his classic approach to conflict - flee from danger and do not respond to aggression, or it will only make things worse. It's an approach we see all too often from American university presidents who are afraid to push back against radicals on college campuses.

But Jacob's sons knew better. Though God had not yet changed Jacob's name, his sons angrily said that Shechem "had committed a scandalous act in *Israel*" (Genesis 34:7). They understood that a nation's status in the eyes of the world is determined by whether its people allow themselves to be pushed around. They recognized that the future existence of Israel depended upon how they would respond to Shechem's aggression. Like Winston Churchill, they understood that "when a nation that needs to choose between shame and war chooses shame, in the end it will get both."

"Shall our sister be made into a prostitute?" Yes, it is often unpleasant to be Israel, to struggle and fight back against evil. It's easier to be "an innocent man, dwelling in tents," and avoid the battles of this world. But in the end, Simeon and Levi were right. Their ferocious attack on the city terrified the other tribes of the land, intimidating potential enemies. A nation of gentle tent-dwellers is a nation that will not survive in the jungle of the Middle East. Only a people possessing courage, bravery and the fortitude to stand up to its enemies can flourish over time.

Dina's tragedy and Simeon and Levi's response taught Jacob the essential lesson he needed to become Israel. He now understood that his family could only become a free nation in its land and fulfill its Divine mission as God's chosen people by standing up to the other inhabitants of the land - and destroying them if necessary.[9] Unfortunately, this is a lesson Jacob's descendants would have to relearn, time and again, in future generations.

Jacob's evolution does not come quickly or easily. The "socket of Jacob's hip became dislocated as he wrestled with him." Becoming Israel, a man who struggles and overcomes, is a painful process that demands action. "Jacob was a Beethoven, not a Mozart. His life was a series of struggles. Nothing came easily to him. He, alone of the patriarchs, was a man who chose to be chosen… It was he who bought the birthright and took the blessing, he who chose to carry Abraham's destiny into the future."[10]

There is a cost to standing up for yourself, a cost the people of Israel are commanded to remember for all time: "Therefore, the children of Israel may not eat the displaced tendon, which is on the socket of the hip, until this day, for he touched the socket of Jacob's hip, in the hip sinew" (Genesis 32:33). Like Jacob, it is the destiny of the children of Israel to struggle and, all too often, to suffer. "Rare and brief have been our interludes of peace."[11]

It is a difficult path, but when Jacob's descendants embrace their identity as Israel, they attain a glory unlike that of any other nation. "You are My servant, Israel, about whom I will boast" (Isaiah 49:3).

When former hostage Rimon Kirsht was released by Hamas through an agreement with Israel in November 2023, the scene was caught on video. Dressed in pink pajamas, she stepped out of the Hamas van and defiantly glared at one of the terrorists. Kirsht then draped her arm around fellow hostage Merav Tal and strode confidently, chin held high, toward the International Committee of the Red Cross vans, while hundreds of Gazans screamed and whistled at her in the night. With one stare, Rimon Kirsht reminded the world - and the Jewish people themselves - about what it means to be a daughter of Israel.[12]

Though the Bible is silent regarding Dina's emotional state when her brothers freed her, my heart tells me that when Simeon and Levi rescued her from the house of Shechem, she first glared at the dead bodies of her captors and then held her head high as she emerged to freedom. For Dina, like her brothers, was not only a daughter of Jacob; she was a proud woman of *Israel*.

Why is Jacob the greatest of the forefathers? Abraham and Isaac were awesome and holy men who became the best possible version of themselves. "Abram," "the father of Aram," became "Abraham," "the father of many nations" (Genesis 17:5). But Jacob accomplished something even greater. He transformed his fundamental nature, forcing himself - for the sake of God - to overcome his passivity and become a man who battled and struggled to fix a broken world. Unlike Esau, whose name derives from "*asuy*," "complete," Jacob was a man who perpetually struggled and grew. For "you have struggled with God and with men, and you have prevailed."

Reverting to Jacob?

In the January Uprising of 1863, Polish nationalists rebelled against the Russian Empire with the goal of ending Russian occupation and regaining independence. Hasidic leader Rabbi Isaac Meir Alter, a man who passionately yearned for the Jewish people to return to the holy land, followed the events with keen interest. On Friday evening, the day after the start of the rebellion, Rabbi Alter was about to recite the Sabbath eve prayer when he paused and spoke to his congregation. "I am worried that there is, God forbid, a complaint in heaven against the Jewish people. We see that the Polish nation is willing to sacrifice terribly to fight for its freedom and to free its land from foreign conquerors. And we? What are we doing?"[13]

Rabbi Alter's challenge was directed not only to his own generation, but to Jews of all generations of the diaspora. Why did a people who prayed three times each day to return to Jerusalem do so little to actualize those dreams?

A German "man of rank" once suggested to Moses Mendelssohn, the great 18th-century German-Jewish philosopher, that the Jewish people work towards the establishment of a Jewish state in the holy land. Mendelssohn praised the man's courage and lauded his "bold idea," but then rejected it. "The greatest obstacle in the way of this proposal is the character of my people. It is not ready to attempt anything so great. The pressure under which we have lived for centuries has removed all vigor from our spirit... the natural impulse for freedom has ceased its activity within us. It has been changed into a monkish piety, manifested in prayer and suffering, not in activity."[14]

The Jewish people are the proud "children of Israel" - but they are also the meek "children of Jacob." Unlike Abraham, whose name was permanently changed from "Abram," Jacob was called by his original name even after God changed his name to Israel. He was a man of dual identity, and so would be the fate of his descendants.

Generations later, when Jacob's children were forced out of their homeland and into exile, they reverted to the passivity and fear that defined the first half of Jacob's life. "I will bring fear in their hearts in the lands of their enemies, and the sound of a rustling leaf will pursue them; they will flee as one flees the sword, and they will fall, but there will be no pursuer" (Leviticus 26:36). Exile is synonymous with *fear* – a debilitating spiritual condition. The "exile Jew" has fear in his heart; at every moment he thinks that someone is chasing him.[15] Even worse than the persecutions of exile, this deep-seated fear is the most terrible curse of the Jewish exile, for it warps the spirit of God's people.

"It is impossible for the Divine spirit and the light of God to rest upon the people of Israel unless they first remove from within their souls the terrible fear which has clung to them like an infected wound from their years of exile and persecution at the hands of lowly and evil enemies."[16] In exile, the people of Israel's vision is impaired, for they desperately hope to find favor in the eyes of the dominant majority. "In exile, Jews constantly think: 'What will the gentiles say?' instead of 'What will the Jews say?'"[17] In exile, Jews are like Jacob, "holding onto the ankle" of Esau instead of fully embracing their unique greatness.

When Jacob received the name "Israel," he did not merely receive a new name to replace Jacob. The name "Israel" symbolized Jacob's elevation from an individual to the father of a great *nation*. "'Your name shall no longer be called Jacob, but Israel shall be your name.'... And God said to him, 'I am the Almighty God; be fruitful and multiply; a nation and a multitude of nations shall come into existence from you, and kings shall come forth from your loins'" (Genesis 35:10-11). This prophecy would come true during the heady days of David and Solomon's kingdom, when the united Israelite kingdom was truly a light unto the nations. But when the kingdom was shattered and the people were sent into exile, the vision of nationhood, of *Israel*, came to seem like an impossible dream.

Living in exile, scattered across the world, most Jews naturally forget that they are part of a nation, "Israel," and revert to being "Jacob," mere individuals. They concern themselves with their local communities and fail to realize that they are part of the nation of Israel, the most glorious nation on earth. Their tunnel-vision focus on their own communities and indifference to the suffering of their fellow Jews in Israel and other parts of the world is, in Rabbi Isaac Nissenbaum's words, "the greatest sin of all," a sin that can only be atoned through action on behalf of the nation.[18]

Tragically, this "exile mindset" plagues the rabbis of diaspora Jewry even more than the average Jew.[19]

"The weakness among many men of the spirit comes because of their lack of connection to the greater soul of Israel. It is impossible for an Israelite to live a full life... without being attached to the broader nation. The air of exile causes them to forget that true life can only be drawn from the root of the nation's soul."[20] This loss of national consciousness is why Moses Mendelssohn described the Jews of exile as "lacking all vigor from our spirit."

When pro-Hamas Columbia University students pitched tents on the university's south lawn, they began a two week-long intimidation campaign targeting Jewish students. Incredibly, though over two million Jews live in New York and New Jersey, the Jewish community failed to organize even one rally of any size at Columbia in support of the Jewish students. Instead, one of the rabbis servicing the Columbia student body told Jewish students to leave the campus "as soon as possible," because "the NYPD cannot guarantee Jewish students' safety in the face of extreme antisemitism and anarchy."[21] Instead of rallying the Jewish students and the surrounding Jewish communities to stand up to the pro-Hamas students on campus, Jewish leaders followed the path of Jacob and fled the scene. Detached from the "soul of Israel," they lack the pride and courage necessary to confront evil.

"And his hand had held onto Esau's heel; and his name was called Jacob." In exile, many Jews feel privileged simply to hold onto Esau's heel - even as Esau despises the Jews among him and kicks him in the face. But even this kick many Jews accept with love and humility, for they will accept any humiliation in the hopes of one day being accepted as Esau's brother and friend. How else can we explain American Jews who continue to vote for and publicly support the very left-wing politicians who despise them most? But this humiliating desire for acceptance does not work; instead, it causes the Edomites to despise the children of Jacob even more. "Judah went into exile... and found no rest" (Lamentations 1:3).

"Come, let us destroy them from being a nation, and the name of Israel will no longer be remembered" (Psalm 83:5). Israel's enemies can usually accept "Jacob Jews" who are willing to live in exile as a lowly and weak minority. But they cannot abide "Israel Jews" who are part of a proud and glorious nation, the nation of Israel. This, too, is the curse of exile.

Nevertheless, God does not abandon Israel, even when she is forced into exile and reverts to being Jacob. "May the Lord answer you on a day of distress; may the name of the God of Jacob fortify you" (Psalm 20:2). Though God's people sometimes doubt God's love, God reassures them that He loves them at their lowest moments. "I loved you, said the Lord, and you said, "How have You loved us?"... And I loved Jacob" (Malachi 1:2).

But if Israel can revert to Jacob, so too can Jacob once again become Israel. The secret of this renewal is found in the cradle of Jewish nationhood - the Exodus.

The Secret of the Lunar Calendar

In the early 1990s, my father worked for the New York branch of a Swiss bank. This was before the news broke that the bank had been complicit in hiding billions of dollars in assets of Jews slaughtered in the Holocaust. Many of my father's Swiss colleagues did little to hide their disdain for Jews and the State of Israel. One pompous senior manager made a point of telling him that because of its precarious security situation, "Israel would be gone within 25 years - guaranteed."

25 years later, my father - not one to forget a smug antisemite - made sure to track down his former Swiss colleague, at that point retired in Zurich, and sent him a registered letter from the thriving State of Israel. He wrote, "My reason for contacting you now, after all these years, was to deliver a brief message to you... You may or may not recall that you confidently stated that 'in 25 years the State of Israel will no longer exist.'... Today, I live in Israel with my wife, children and grandchildren. We live in a beautiful and thriving country that contributes to, and is the envy of, much of the world, including static and irrelevant Switzerland. From my viewpoint, it doesn't look like Israel is going to disappear any time soon. By the way – how are things working out for you and the Muslim immigrants over there? Any predictions on the future of *your* country and the rest of Europe?"

Nikolai Berdyaev, an early 20th-century Russian Marxist, left the movement following the Russian Revolution and its aftermath. He became an independent-minded Christian and was forced into exile, ultimately settling in Paris. In his work *The Meaning of History*, he explains why he abandoned the Marxist philosophy of history.

"I remember how the materialist interpretation of history, when I attempted in my youth to verify it by applying it to the destinies of peoples, broke down in the case of the Jews, whose destiny seemed absolutely inexplicable from the materialistic standpoint... Its survival is a mysterious and wonderful phenomenon demonstrating that the life of this people is governed by a special predetermination, transcending the processes of adaptation expounded by the materialistic interpretation of history. The survival of the Jews, their resistance to destruction, their endurance under absolutely peculiar conditions and the fateful role played by them in history: all these point to the particular and mysterious foundations of their destiny."

In other words, the people of Israel do not follow the standard trajectory of nations. "Normal" nations rise to prominence, reach their zenith and then decline. But the survival and strange success of the Jewish people - consisting today of a mere 15 million people worldwide - shatters the standard model. No nation has experienced more persecution, yet no nation has proven more resistant to destruction. After every national trauma - and there have been many - the Jews rise again. Most astoundingly, the Jewish people have survived and often thrived not by building remote communities far from the center of human civilization, but while living in the crosshairs of their enemies.

Many historians and theologians have tried to explain the phenomenon of Jewish survival. St. Augustine's doctrine of Jewish witness maintains that while Christianity has surpassed Judaism as the sole true faith, it is God's will for Jews to endure until the end times, for they serve a crucial role in safeguarding and validating the Hebrew Bible, which, according to Christian doctrine, prophesied the arrival of Jesus. The doctrine was Augustine's way of resolving the tensions Catholic tradition brought upon itself in retaining the Hebrew Bible while renouncing Judaism itself. In Augustine's view, the destruction of the Temple in 70 CE and the failure of the Bar Kochba rebellion in 135 CE had eternal consequences: the Jews would never go home again. Because of their rejection of Jesus, Augustine believed the Jews were condemned to perpetual exile and powerlessness as an eschatological fact.[22]

More recently, many Christians believed that Jewish history would soon come to an end. Rabbi Joseph Soloveitchik writes that "during the Hitler era, thousands of missionaries and plain theologians, including the great Karl Barth, would regularly claim that… the Jewish people was being obliterated because it had not accepted the Nazarene. Lectures to this effect could be heard on America's great university campuses." But the establishment of the State of Israel in 1948 changed everything. "Do you know who, with a single declaration, negated all of their theological claims and arguments? The people assembled at that late Friday afternoon gathering at which Ben-Gurion presided and which declared Israel's independence. You know who else? The Jewish army, the girls and boys with their rifles and self-sacrifice. 'Today I have rolled away from you the disgrace of Egypt' (Joshua 5:9)."[23]

All at once, the founding of the State of Israel shattered Augustine's claim that the Jews would never again rise as a political power, as well as claims that Jewish existence was finally coming to an end. Israel's astounding rise in the shadow of the Holocaust from a poor socialist country to a technological hub and regional power in less than a century - despite constant attempts by its enemies to destroy it - only strengthens Rabbi Soloveitchik's point.

How can we explain the persistent survival and success of God's people?

Even before the people of Israel left Egypt to receive the Bible at Mount Sinai, God gave them their very first commandment: the Hebrew calendar. "And God spoke to Moses and Aaron in the land of Egypt, saying: 'This month shall be unto you the beginning of months; it shall be the first month of the year to you'" (Exodus 12:1-2).

For the people of Israel, this commandment was the beginning of a new era. From this moment onwards, Israel would live according to its own calendar. Unlike most other nations, Israel would not follow a strictly solar calendar, but rather a lunar calendar tied directly to the moon's monthly cycle of waxing and waning. Whereas the sun is constant in size, rising and setting each day at a predictable time, the moon is in a constant state of renewal. For the first fifteen days of each Hebrew month, the moon grows larger, reaching its peak with a full moon on day fifteen. During the second half of the month, the moon grows smaller and smaller, ultimately disappearing from view - only to emerge anew and begin growing again at the start of the next month.

The symbolism of the sun and moon are found in the Bible itself. "What has been is what will be, and what has been done is what will be done, and there is nothing new under the sun" (Ecclesiastes 1:9). Esau counts time according to the sun; *Edom*, "red," is the color of the sun. The sun determines the yearly calendar. "*Shana*," Hebrew for "year," shares the same root as "*shinun*," meaning review and repetition. In rejecting God and embracing only the physical and material, the people of Esau are destined to live by the rules of the sun - and there is nothing new under the sun. The sun, with its permanence and predictability, represents the laws of nature, creation and science. Without God, there is only nature, and nature inevitably ends with death.

Though there is nothing new under the sun, the moon is a different story. "What profit has man in all his toil that he toils under the sun?" (Ecclesiastes 1:3). The sages explain that under the *sun* there is no profit, but when one is not under the sun - when one lives, like the people of Israel, under the dominion of the moon - there *is* profit;[24] renewal is possible! "*Chodesh*," Hebrew for "month," derives from the same root as "*chadash*," Hebrew for "new." Every month, the moon is born again. If the sun represents nature, the moon symbolizes the God of revelation Who is not bound by the rules of nature. God is fundamentally unpredictable; He performs miracles and reveals Himself anytime He wishes.

"I am the Lord, your God, Who took you out of the land of Egypt from being slaves to them; and I broke the pegs of your yoke and led you upright" (Leviticus 26:13). When God took Israel out of Egypt, He broke their yoke of servitude to the Egyptians. But He also broke their yoke of servitude to nature and transformed them into a nation that would not be bound by nature's laws. Other nations rise and fall; it is the way of the world. But God had different plans for Israel. Israel would be the nation of spring, the season of magical rebirth, when a world that appears to be dead springs back to life. This is why God tells Israel: "*This month*" - the Hebrew month of *Nissan*, the first month of spring - "shall be unto you the beginning of months; it shall be the first month of the year to you." Israel, the people of the moon, are the people of spring - the people who never die.

"The people of Israel merited to draw down a new path in the world from the upper worlds. And this is the path of miracles and wonders that are unique to this nation… God, Who wanted to renew the world through His Bible and commandments, gave Israel the merit to bring this renewal to the world."[25]

This was a gift given exclusively to Israel. "This month shall be unto *you* the beginning of months." Only Israel, alone among the nations, would be able to avoid the natural life cycle of nations. Only Israel would possess the ability to renew itself and return to its land after thousands of years of exile.

Two thousand years after God established Israel's calendar, Muslims would also adopt a lunar calendar. But the Islamic lunar calendar differs radically from that of Israel. The Bible teaches that Passover must always fall during the spring: "Keep the month of spring, and make the Passover offering to the Lord, your God, for in the month of spring, the Lord, your God, brought you out of Egypt at night" (Deuteronomy 16:1). In this verse, the Bible commands Israel to ensure that the Hebrew month of *Nissan*, the month of Passover, always falls in the spring season, when the Exodus took place. This is more difficult than you might think, for the lunar year consists of approximately 354 days - which is about 11 days shorter than the 365.25-day solar cycle that determines the seasons. If no adjustments are made, the 11-day discrepancy means Passover would fall 11 days earlier every year. Within a few years, Passover would take place in the winter, a scenario the Bible forbids. To ensure the lunar-based Jewish year remains synchronized with the solar seasons, Israel's calendar periodically includes an additional "leap month" to compensate for the 11-day discrepancy between the solar and lunar cycles.

Islam, however, makes no attempt to align its lunar calendar with the solar seasons. Each year, its calendar falls further out of sync with the solar calendar. This is why Ramadan, Islam's holiest month, is always "moving" and falls each year 11 days earlier than it fell the year before.

The difference between the Jewish and Islamic calendars reflects the fundamental difference between Ishmael and Israel. Like Israel, the people of Ishmael believe in God, for they too are the children of Abraham. Like Israel, they follow the dynamic lunar calendar, which reflects their belief in God. But like their forefather Ishmael, their faith is "wild"; they do not bind themselves to the Bible and God's will as expressed through His commandments. Unlike Israel's calendar, which balances the moon and the sun, their lunar calendar is not bound by the laws of the seasons. Just as their faith in God is "wild," their calendar lacks all boundaries and control.

"The hand of the Lord came upon me, and carried me out in the spirit of the Lord, and set me down in the midst of the valley, and that was full of bones... So says the Lord God to these bones; 'Behold, I will cause spirit to enter into you, and you shall live!'" (Ezekiel 37:1,5). God knew from the very beginning that His people would sin and be scattered across the world, far from one another, and that the nation itself would appear to be like dry bones. But just as the moon only superficially "disappears" from view, the people of Israel only *seemed* to have died in exile. "Redemption is embedded in the very nature of Israel; it is imprinted deeply upon their souls."[26]

Mark Twain wondered, "The Egyptian, the Babylonian, and the Persian rose, filled the planet with sound and splendor, then . . . passed away. The Greek and the Roman followed. The Jew saw them all, beat them all, and is now what he always was, exhibiting no decadence, no infirmities of age, no weakening of his parts. ... All things are mortal but the Jew; all other forces pass, but he remains. What is the secret of his immortality?"[27] What Mark Twain wondered, we know. It is the secret of "This month shall be unto you the beginning of months," the secret of the moon.[28]

This, in a nutshell, is the history of the Jewish people. After every destruction - and there would be many - God's people would rise up from the ashes to live and thrive again. "This month shall be unto you" was God's promise that Jacob would one day become Israel again. No matter how bad it would get in the future, Jacob's children would rise up and reclaim their status as Israel.

There is no greater fulfillment of God's promise than Israel's miraculous return to nationhood only three years after the destruction of one-third of world Jewry in the Holocaust. In all of human history, there is no other example of a nation that lost its independence and was exiled for two thousand years, only to return to its ancient homeland and be reborn as a nation once again, as if out of thin air. Those with eyes to see can only wonder in awe at God's eternal people, a people who refuse to die.

"'You are My witnesses,' says the Lord, 'and I am God'" (Isaiah 43:12). The sages explain, "If you, the people of Israel, are my witnesses, then 'I am God.' But if you are not my witnesses, then 'I am not God.'"[29] How do the people of Israel testify to the existence of the Creator? Simply by continuing to exist, even as all other nations rise, fall and eventually disappear. When humanity recognizes the Jewish people's unnatural life force, they discover that God is the source of that life. Israel is the porthole through which the nations are drawn to God.[30] "This people I formed for Myself; they shall recite My praise" (Isaiah 43:21).

"So said the Lord, Who gives the sun to illuminate by day, the laws of the moon and the stars to illuminate at night, Who stirs up the sea and its waves roar, the Lord of Hosts is His name. If these laws depart from before Me, says the Lord, so will the seed of Israel cease being a nation before Me for all time" (Jeremiah 31:34-35).

I am a Jew and I give a Jewish Damn

In 1908, forty years before the establishment of the State of Israel, Rabbi Aryeh Leib Kagan, the son of the great Rabbi Israel Meir Kagan, spoke with his father about the nascent Zionist movement. He quoted an article from *HaMelitz*, the first Hebrew newspaper in the Russian Empire and the organ of the progressive and secular Jewish community in Russia. In the article, the author expressed his hope that one day, the Jewish people would declare independence from the Ottoman Empire and establish their own independent country in the holy land, just as Bulgaria had recently done. Hearing this, his father began to cry. "Is this why our blood has been spilled for 1,800 years? So that we can be [an average country] like Bulgaria?"

Rabbi Abraham Isaac Kook emphasized this point. "It is a fundamental mistake to retreat from our unique greatness, to refuse to recognize that God has chosen us from among all the nations. We are not merely different from other nations. Our history is unlike anything ever seen among any nation or language… If we know our greatness we know our true selves, and if we forget our greatness, we forget ourselves… It is only because we have forgotten our unique greatness that we remain small and lowly."[31] "On the day I called out, You answered me; You made me great, putting strength into my soul" (Psalm 138:3). More than anything else, Israel needs "strength of soul." The people of Israel's internal struggle to comprehend their own uniqueness holds the key to their redemption and, ultimately, the redemption of the entire world.

Though the free world could not have won World War II without the United States, the American government's consistent refusal to help European Jewry during the Holocaust is an eternal moral stain upon the nation. After the Kristallnacht pogrom of 1938, President Roosevelt refused to allow 20,000 German Jewish children into the U.S., though he would rush, a few years later, to open America's doors to British children when Germany bombed London. During the Evian conference of 1938 and the Bermuda conference of 1943, the Allies refused to offer even basic assistance like transport and food to Jews who managed to flee the Nazis. On multiple occasions, Western nations deliberately hindered Jews trying desperately to escape from the Nazi butchers.

How did American Jewry respond to Roosevelt's consistent refusal to help endangered Jews? After Kristallnacht, Eleanor Roosevelt warned American Jews to keep a low profile. "I think it is important in this country that the Jews as Jews remain unaggressive and stress the fact they are Americans first and above everything else." Tragically, most Jews, including Roosevelt's friend, Rabbi Stephen Wise, followed her advice. With some notable exceptions, they largely remained silent, refusing to publicly condemn the President.[32]

In the decades following World War II, some young American Jews began to ask themselves why their community had not done more to stop the Holocaust. For them, the slogan "Never Again" was a rebuke. Why had American Jews been so afraid to pressure the White House? Why didn't they demand that the United States accept more Jewish refugees when there was still time to save them? Why did American Jews passively allow their brothers and sisters in Europe to be slaughtered instead of standing up and fighting for their survival?

Disgusted by the passivity of their parents' generation, some of these young people were driven to action on behalf of the over two million Soviet Jews who faced government-led religious persecution, were unable to live openly as Jews and denied the right to emigrate. In 1964, Jacob Birnbaum launched The Student Struggle for Soviet Jewry (SSSJ), a student-led grassroots movement that would galvanize American Jewry to lead an international human rights campaign advocating for the right of Soviet Jews to emigrate.

Rabbi Meir Kahane, one of the most provocative leaders of the movement, repeatedly condemned the older generation of American Jews for their passivity. He speculated on what would have happened if American Jews in the 1940s had sat down in the streets of Washington DC and refused to move until Roosevelt agreed to bomb the crematorium in the concentration camps. In March of 1971, Kahane put his theory to the test, renting a fleet of buses and bringing over a thousand young Jews to Washington. Standing outside of the Soviet embassy, he appealed to his followers. "I'm asking you to do today what Jews didn't do while the gas chambers were burning. Sit down in the streets of Washington!" It was a peaceful protest. As they were arrested, the young Jews sang "One, two, three, four, open up the iron door! Five, six, seven, eight, let my people emigrate!"

Kahane believed the Washington demonstration was proof that something profound was happening among the younger generation of American Jews. Finally! Here were Jews unafraid to stand up for their people and willing to go to jail for a Jewish cause. He wrote, "For the first time, huge numbers of young Jews were beginning to look at themselves not with self-hate or disinterest but with pride and self-respect. From a period of time when young Jews looked at themselves and asked, 'Who am I?' and answered either: 'I don't know,' or, worse, 'I don't care,' we had moved to thousands of young Jews marching off to jail after looking at themselves in the mirror and saying 'I am a Jew and I am beautiful. I am a Jew and Jewish is beautiful, I am a Jew and I give a Jewish damn.'"[33]

Today, Jews across the world are once again waking up from their passivity and fear to "give a Jewish damn." As the children of Ishmael and Esau work together to destroy Israel, Jacob is once again becoming Israel - and Israel's enemies are advised to take note.

"And Haman recounted to Zeresh his wife and to all his friends all that had befallen him, and his wise men and Zeresh his wife said to him, 'If Mordecai, before whom you have begun to fall, is of Jewish stock, you will not prevail against him, but you will surely fall before him'" (Esther 6:13). Haman's wife was no fool. She said, "This nation has been compared to the stars and to the dust. When they descend, they descend to the dust, and when they ascend, they ascend to the sky and the stars."[34] When the sleeping giant of Israel awakens, no enemy can stand before her.

"The shame of His people He shall remove from upon the entire earth" (Isaiah 25:8). The day will come when God's people will leave behind the fear and shame of Jacob forever, when Israel will never again be afraid to stand up to its enemies.

"Awake, awake, O Zion, clothe yourself with strength!... Shake yourselves from the dust, arise!" (Isaiah 52:1-2).

PART III:

PROPHECIES OF TODAY

PROPHECIES OF
Ishmael

CHAPTER 7:

PRISONERS OF HOPE: ZECHARIAH'S PROPHECY OF OCTOBER 7

When seeking signs of current events in the Bible, it's important to do so with care and humility. History is littered with exciting yet false interpretations of scripture. The Book of Zechariah, in particular, contains many cryptic visions, and Biblical commentators have struggled to understand its meaning. "The prophecy of Zechariah is extremely enigmatic, because it contains visions resembling a dream that requires an interpretation. We cannot ascertain the truth of its interpretation until the teacher of righteousness comes."[1]

Nevertheless, the Bible is not a book of history, but an eternal book that speaks to every generation. And so we must, despite the dangers, seek to understand our tumultuous times through the lens of the Bible. Zechariah's prophecies were meant for our generation, and specifically for this painful time. The prophecies that baffled our forefathers are today's front-page news.

On October 7, Hamas terrorists brutalized, raped and murdered over 1,200 Jews, the worst and most sickening massacre of Jews since the Holocaust. Hamas also abducted 242 hostages, including babies, children, and elderly

Holocaust survivors. Hezbollah, another radical terrorist group sponsored by Iran and based in Lebanon on Israel's northern border, soon joined Hamas in attacking Israel. In response, Israel launched a full-scale war against Hamas in Gaza, while simultaneously engaging with Hezbollah in the north. Soon after, the Iran-backed Houthi rebels of Yemen joined the attack on Israel, launching missile and drone attacks at Eilat, Israel's southernmost city.

A close study of the 9th chapter of Zechariah strongly suggests that this war was prophesied by Zechariah. His words are chilling - but also contain a profound message of hope.

A Messianic Prophecy

Interpreting prophecy is challenging, particularly when trying to pinpoint the historical era to which the prophet's words apply. The words of the prophets are often opaque and difficult to interpret clearly. Some prophecies were meant for the near term - such as when Jeremiah prophesied the destruction of the first Temple - while other prophecies concern the distant future.

Chapter 9 of Zechariah begins with a reference to the land of "*Hadrach*." "The prophecy of the word of the Lord in the land of *Hadrach*" (Zechariah 9:1). But where is this mysterious land of "*Hadrach*"?

The sages explain that "*Hadrach*" is not a country, but rather hints to the time period addressed in this chapter. In Hebrew, the word "*Hadrach*" can be broken into two separate words: "*Had*," meaning "sharp," and "*rach*," meaning "soft." "This refers to the Messiah, who is sharp against the nations and soft to Israel."[2] When the Messiah arrives, he will inaugurate an era that will be very "sharp" and painful for Israel's enemies, but "soft" and joyous for Israel. This is the era of turmoil and redemption that will unfold in the generations preceding the Messiah's arrival - the great war of Gog of Magog against the people of Israel.

Another key verse makes clear that this entire chapter speaks of the messianic age. "Be exceedingly happy, O daughter of Zion; Shout, O daughter of Jerusalem. Behold! Your king shall come to you. He is just and victorious; humble, and riding a donkey and a foal, the offspring of she-donkeys" (Zechariah 9:9). The sages agree that this verse can only be referring to the Messiah. "We do not find that Israel had such a ruler during the days of the second Temple, and so this chapter must be referring to the Messianic age."[3]

We are currently living in the "Messianic age," the generations leading up to the arrival of the Messiah, when the people of Israel have returned to their land and the prophecies of the Bible are being fulfilled.

Hamas, Hezbollah and the Houthis

Zechariah first speaks of an enemy in the north: "And Tyre built a fortification for herself, and she gathered silver like dust and gold, like the mire of the streets. Behold, the Lord shall impoverish her, and He shall smite her wealth in the sea, and she shall be consumed by fire" (Zechariah 9:3-4).

Ancient Tyre was located on the southern coast of Lebanon, 83 kilometers south of Beirut - precisely where the Iranian-backed terror group Hezbollah is currently fortified. Receiving billions of dollars in funding from Iran, Hezbollah has "gathered silver like dust and gold like the mire of the streets," money it used to stockpile 150,000 deadly rockets that it is currently using against Israel. Immediately following the horror of October 7, Israeli towns near the northern border were evacuated as Hezbollah began bombing northern Israel.

Despite their great power, God has promised that "He shall smite her wealth in the sea, and she shall be consumed by fire." Hezbollah is destined to be destroyed.

"Ashkelon shall see and fear, and Gaza - and she shall quake violently - and Ekron, for the one to whom she looked was ashamed. And a king was lost from Gaza, and Ashkelon shall not be inhabited. And the strangers shall dwell in Ashdod, and I will cut off the pride of the Philistines" (Zechariah 9:5-6).

The modern-day cities of Ashkelon and Ashdod, on Israel's southern Mediterranean coast, are Jewish cities under Israeli control. In ancient times, however, the cities of Ashkelon, Ashdod, Gaza, Ekron, and Gath were the strongholds of the Philistines in Gaza.

To be clear, the "Palestinians" of today do not descend from, and bear no relation to, the ancient Philistines who dwelled along Israel's coast in Biblical times. It was only on May 28, 1964, the date on which the PLO was established,[4] that the Arabs in Israel began using the name "Palestinian."

Nevertheless, it is no accident that today's Arabs of Gaza have taken on the name "Palestinian," for they share something in common with the Philistines of old. The Philistines of the Biblical era were the Israelites' most persistent and terrible adversary. Beginning with the era of Samson and continuing through the generations of Samuel, Saul and David, the Philistines were consistently the most dangerous foe of the twelve tribes of Israel, causing Israel great suffering and preventing them from being sovereign in their own land.[5]

When Zechariah tells us that God will "cut off the pride of the Philistines," he can only be referring to the "Palestinians" of our time, the spiritual descendants of the ancient Philistines, for the ancient Philistines no longer exist.[6] Today's "Palestinians" have proven that their society is at least as cruel and despicable as that of the ancient Philistines.

Hamas terrorists don't fall from the sky. They were raised and educated in a society of men, women, and children that is obsessed with murdering Jews and erasing Israel from the map. What kind of culture produces hundreds of men who proudly video themselves raping teen girls before executing them? What kind of society glorifies baby killers who burn the bodies of their infant victims, crowning them as heroes? Hamas terrorists are not a guilty minority terrorizing an innocent majority. They are not "lone actors," but rather the messengers and representatives of their people, a fact that survey after survey has made clear. In December 2023, just two months after the Hamas massacre of October 7, the Palestinian Center for Policy and Survey Research released results of a poll showing that over 70% of Arabs in Judea, Samaria and Gaza support Hamas' decision to carry out the October 7 massacre and that the vast majority do not believe that Hamas carried out atrocities during the massacre.[7] This unbelievable arrogance, "the pride of the Philistines," will soon be "cut off."

"And I will remove his blood from his mouth, and his detestable things from between his teeth. And it, too, shall remain to our God: and it shall be like a study hall in Judah; and Ekron, like Jebusi" (Zechariah 9:7).

God will remove the blood from the mouths of the Palestinians, a people that glorifies death and celebrates the murder of Jewish children with parties and fireworks. But Israel's victory over Gaza will not merely prevent the Palestinians from committing any further murders. Ekron, the great Palestinian city, will become like "Jebusi." What does this mean?

The Jebusites were a Canaanite tribe that dwelled in the Jerusalem area. Even after Joshua conquered much of the land of Israel, the Jebusites continued to control Jerusalem. It was only David, 400 years later, who conquered the Jebusites and finally transformed Jerusalem from a pagan Jebusite city into the capital of Israel and the seat of God's glory.

Zechariah prophesies that the Philistine cities of Gaza will be transformed into Jewish cities, just as David recast the city of Jerusalem into God's holy city. The day will come when the streets of Gaza City will not be used to train terrorists, but rather as "a study hall in Judah." "And they shall fly of one accord against the Philistines in the west" (Isaiah 11:14). Israel will overrun the Philistines and conquer Gaza for itself.[8]

"And it shall be a possession for the remnant of the house of Judah" (Zephaniah 2:7). Gaza will one day - hopefully sooner than later - become a destination for Jews returning from exile. "For the lands of the Philistines [Gaza] are among the lands that fell within the portion of the tribe of Judah during the conquest of Joshua the son of Nun, and it will once again be a Jewish land, where Jewish shepherds shall bring their flocks to graze and where they will sleep soundly at night."[9]

The terrorists of Gaza will pay for their brutality. "For Gaza shall be deserted… At noon they shall drive her out, and Ekron shall be uprooted. Woe to the inhabitants of the seacoast, the nation of Cherethites! The word of the Lord is against you, Canaan land of the Philistines, and I will destroy you so that there shall not be an inhabitant" (Zephaniah 2:4-5). As Israel systematically uproots Hamas from Gaza, whole swaths of that strip of land lie empty and deserted, just as Zephaniah prophesied.

In these verses, the people of Gaza are referred to as the "nation of *Cherethites*." There is no nation, in the Bible or throughout history, called the *Cherethites*. The word derives from the Hebrew word "*kareit*," meaning "to be cut off." In biblical law, one who is punished by God with *kareit* has no future; his soul is cut off from God. This, ultimately, will be the fate of the people of Gaza, who overwhelmingly support the murder of innocent Jews.

"And I will encamp beside My house against a garrison of those passing by and of those returning. And no oppressor shall overrun them, for now I have seen with My eyes" (Zechariah 9:8). On October 7, Hamas terrorists overran Israel's southern border. In this verse, God promises that Israel will not be overrun again, that despite Hamas' threats to "repeat October 7 again and again,"[10] God will not allow Israel's borders to be overrun a second time. "I will encamp beside My house to protect it from those who set up a garrison and raiders, that they should not set these up against it."[11]

What has changed? On that terrible day, God hid His countenance from His people. Since October 7, Israel has cried out to God - and now God's eyes are open, "for now I have seen with My eyes." He is once again actively protecting the borders of Israel. "Behold the Guardian of Israel will neither slumber nor sleep" (Psalm 121:4).

"You, too - with the blood of your covenant I have freed your prisoners from a pit in which there was no water." When I read this verse after October 7, my heart stopped. On that fateful day, Hamas terrorists took 242 innocent men, women and children as hostages. They imprisoned these hostages deep underground among the 500 miles of terror tunnels that Hamas built underground in Gaza. For the last 17 years, Hamas has used billions of dollars of international aid to build these tunnels and buy weapons, instead of using the money to build the Gazan economy.

As I write, Hamas is still holding over 100 hostages, though many are believed to have been murdered. "I have freed your prisoners from a pit in which there was no water." Please, God, may these words come true today! Free our hostages, who are hidden in a pit, deep beneath the earth. Bring them home to us now!

"And the Lord shall appear over them, and his arrows shall go forth like lightning. And the Lord God shall sound the shofar, and He shall go with the whirlwinds of Yemen" (Zechariah 9:14).

On October 19, 2023, less than two weeks after the Hamas attack of October 7, Iranian-backed Houthi rebels in Yemen launched missile and drone attacks against Israel from the south. In this verse, God promises that "His arrows shall go forth like lightning," that He will bring retribution upon Yemen from the air.

Days are coming when Israel, the United States and others will be forced to take retribution against the Houthis. Yemen will not be spared.

Prisoners of Hope

God has promised that Israel will defeat its enemies, both in the north and the south. But how will this small and diplomatically isolated nation, surrounded by enemies, succeed against all odds? The answer is found in this chapter's most powerful verse: "Return to the stronghold, you prisoners of hope" (Zechariah 9:12).

What is the "stronghold" of Israel, and why are the people of Israel "prisoners of hope"?

When Israel is under attack, when it has suffered painful losses and terrible blows, the prophet reminds her: "Return to your strength and to your glory,"[12] to the root of your unique greatness! The "stronghold" of Israel is nothing other than the gift God gave His people in Egypt - the gift of *renewal*. "This month shall be unto you the beginning of months; it shall be the first month of the year to you" (Exodus 12:1-2). God promised Israel that she would be like the moon - a nation that is not bound by nature or realpolitik, a nation that constantly renews itself and never dies!

Zechariah tells us to remember the beginning of our history. "Remember how bad things were in Egypt, when you were slaves with no realistic hope of salvation? Remember what God told you then? You are *not* a normal nation, but a people who constantly renew themselves, a people who come back from every defeat stronger than you were before!" The gift of renewal, which Israel received at the very beginning of its national birth, is the "stronghold" to which God's people must return.

From the moment God gave Israel the gift of renewal, the promise that they would never be destroyed, His people were destined to forever be "prisoners of hope" - for they would always find a path to salvation. From the time of the Exodus until today, through thousands of years of exile and persecution, they never gave up on the dream of returning to their homeland. If there was ever a nation that could recover from the horrors committed by Hamas on October 7, it is Israel, the "prisoners of hope."

Israel's Greatest Generation

Shortly after October 7, I met with a mission of American Christians in their 50s and 60s who came to Israel to express their love of Israel. They called it "the ministry of presence"; sometimes, simply showing up and being present makes all the difference. Still, I couldn't help but notice that there was not one young Christian participating in the mission, reflecting the sad reality that the vast majority of Christians who support Israel are older.

I asked the group's pastor about the younger generation of American Christians. "Will they also support Israel?" With a pained expression, he said, "We're not confident that America will make it, that America will be there in the end. We're a country that no longer loves the Bible and God's word. There are no guarantees."

The pastor has good reason to worry. By all accounts, young Americans are turning away from the Church in droves. According to the Pew Research Center, people who say they do not have a religious identity are projected to rise from about 30% of Americans today to over 50% in the coming decades. The main reason for this shift is "switching" – Christians deciding to no longer be Christian. Millions of young Americans are turning away from God.

This is hardly an internal Christian problem. As G.K. Chesterton wrote, "When men choose not to believe in God, they do not thereafter believe in nothing, they then become capable of believing in anything." Young Americans are radicalizing in ways previously unimaginable. A recent Harvard–Harris poll found that 51 percent of Americans between the ages of 18-24 believe that Hamas' slaughter of Israeli civilians "can be justified and that Israel should "be ended and given to Hamas."[13] Given the frightening growth of antisemitism at America's top universities, it is reasonable to assume that radical anti-Israel beliefs are even more prevalent among the future leaders of the nation. "The road to hell," Thomas Sowell prophetically said, "is paved with Ivy League degrees."

But the moral collapse of the "Tiktok generation" is not inevitable, as Zechariah prophesied: "For I bend Judah for Me like a bow; I filled [the hand of] Ephraim, and I will arouse your children, O Zion, upon your children, O Javan; and I will make you as the sword of a mighty man" (Zechariah 9:13). "I will arouse your children, O Zion." God promises that the young people of Israel will awaken - a prophecy that has come true before our eyes.

Young Israelis are on an entirely different trajectory from their American counterparts. During Israel's darkest hour, they have proven themselves to be the Jewish people's "greatest generation," selflessly fighting to protect the nation and avenge the atrocities of October 7. Filled with Jewish pride and love for one another, they are not only heroes, but also role models for young people across the world.

"For how [great] is their goodness and how [great] is their beauty! Corn [will give strength to] young men, and new wine will cause maids to speak" (Zechariah 9:17). The young men and women of Israel will rise up and reveal to the world their goodness and beauty, which had heretofore been hidden from sight.

Since October 7, young Jews in Israel and throughout the world are standing up with pride and strength, and they are returning to the God of Israel. Tens of thousands of young "secular" Israeli soldiers have requested *tzitzit*, the tassels Jews are commanded to wear on the corners of their garments. Thousands of videos are circulating of Israeli soldiers of all religious backgrounds praying intensely before heading into battle.

"Days are coming, says the Lord, when I will send famine into the land, not a famine for bread nor a thirst for water, but to hear the word of God" (Amos 8:11). Israel's young people are thirsty for God's word. "This tangible living thirst, which fills the practical lives [of the people of Israel] with its light… calls out to the nation to wake up, rise up and shake off the dust of humiliation."[14]

"Be exceedingly happy, O daughter of Zion; Shout, O daughter of Jerusalem. Behold! Your king shall come to you. He is just and victorious; humble, and riding a donkey and a foal, the offspring of she-donkeys. And I will cut off the chariots from Ephraim, and the horses from Jerusalem; and the bow of war shall be cut off. And he shall speak peace to the nations, and his rule shall be from the sea to the west and from the river to the ends of the earth" (Zechariah 9:9-10).

The Messiah, Israel's king, will not be like the kings of our enemies. He will not be an arrogant dictator like Vladimir Putin or Ayatollah Sayyid Ali Khamenei of Iran. The king of Israel will be just and humble, and inaugurate an era of peace. And yes - he is on his way.

CHAPTER 8:

ARE WE LIVING THE GOG OF MAGOG WAR?

This is not business as usual. Though Israel has fought many small wars against Hamas, everyone understands that the October 7 war is different. After Hamas slaughtered 1,200 innocent Israelis on that terrible day, nations throughout the world immediately felt the reverberations. This is a war with global implications, pitting Jews and Christians, the people of the Bible, against Muslims and secular progressives, who reject the Bible and all that it stands for.

Could this finally be the war of Gog and Magog?

In two of the most famous chapters of the Bible, the prophet Ezekiel describes a great war that will take place at the end of days. Gog of the land of Magog from the north will lead a host of nations in battle against Israel and God. God's wrath will come down upon the invaders, who will die in a series of supernatural plagues, and then the final redemption will arrive.

"Son of man, set your face toward Gog, of the land of Magog, the chief prince of Meshech and Tubal… And you will come from your place, from the utmost north, you and many peoples with you, all of them riding horses; a great assembly and a mighty army. And you will ascend upon My people Israel like a cloud to cover the earth; at the end of days it will be, and I shall bring you upon My land in order that the nations recognize Me when I am sanctified through you before their eyes, O Gog" (Ezekiel 38:1, 15-16).

For thousands of years, rabbis, pastors and Bible scholars have made confident claims about the identity of Gog and Magog, assuming that the great wars of their generation must be the fulfillment of this prophecy. But with the passage of time and the stubborn refusal of the final redemption to arrive, their speculations fell flat.

"So said the Lord God: Are you he about whom I spoke in ancient days through My servants, the prophets of Israel who prophesied in those days many years ago, to bring you upon them?" (Ezekiel 38:17). Ezekiel himself tells us that this prophecy will be fulfilled in such a distant future that the identity of Gog and Magog will be uncertain. Only "at the end of days" when God will "bring [Gog] upon [His] land" (38:16) will the identity of Gog and the land of Magog become clear to all.[1]

Though we cannot make predictions with any certainty, I believe that *our* generation is the distant future of which Ezekiel speaks. Gog and his evil minions have indeed come upon God's land in a cruel and brutal fashion. The war of the Muslim nations against Israel aligns with the Gog and Magog prophecies in ways that are truly eye-opening. The connections are hard to ignore.

Identifying the Enemy: The Land of Magog

"Son of man, set your face toward Gog, of the land of *Magog*, the chief prince of *Meshech* and *Tubal*, and prophesy against him, and say: 'Thus says the Lord God: Behold, I am against you, O Gog, chief prince of Meshech and Tubal... *Persia*, *Cush*, and *Put* are with them; all of them with buckler and helmet. *Gomer* and all its wings, the house of *Togarmah*, the utmost parts of the north and all its wings, many peoples with you.'" (Ezekiel 38:2-3, 5-6)

What is the identity of the land of Magog? And who are these other nations that are destined to participate in this monumental war against Israel?

Interestingly, Israel's traditional Biblical enemies are not included in these verses. There is no mention of the Moabites, Ammonites, Egyptians, Philistines, Midianites, or Amalekites. These ancient adversaries are replaced by new enemies, who will invade the ingathered nation of Israel from afar.

This is a very significant shift. In earlier times, Israel battled neighboring tribes and peoples in conventional struggles for land and resources. But the final battle against Gog will be a global war of far greater significance.

The sages identify the Land of Magog as "*Germanya.*"[2] Yechiel Zvi Hirschenson, a 19th-century scholar, asserts that "*Germanya*" refers to Kerman or Kermania, the second largest province in modern Iran, whose main city is called Kerman to this day. This identification follows the rules of ancient Hebrew, in which the letters G and K are interchangeable.[3]

On January 3, 2020, the United States assassinated the infamous Lt. General Qassem Soleimani, commander of Iran's Islamic Revolutionary Guards Corps Quds Force. Soleimani, an arch-enemy of both Israel and the United States, was from the city of Kerman. Could this be merely a coincidence? Given modern Iran's genocidal stance toward the State of Israel and its sponsorship of the three groups currently attacking Israel - Hamas, Hezbollah, and the Yemenite Houthis - the identification of the land of Magog with the Islamic Republic of Iran is compelling.

What about the other nations that join with Gog in the war against Israel? Persia, of course, is Iran, which corresponds with the identification of Magog as an Iranian province. *Put* is traditionally identified with northern Africa, while *Kush* usually refers to the lands south of Egypt, including Sudan, Yemen and the entire Arabian peninsula. Historically, *Meshech* and *Tubal* were Scythian tribes from Asia Minor, which is modern-day Turkey.

Based on rabbinic tradition and historical research, it is reasonable to conclude that "Gog of the Land of Magog" is an Iranian leader who will attack Israel together with many Arab allies and Turkey. This aligns closely with today's political reality, in which all of these nations and terror groups seek the destruction of Israel.

Gog, Magog and Ishmael

Ethnically and historically, the Iranian (Persian) and Arab peoples are separate and distinct groups. While both peoples share Islam as a common religion, Iran is predominantly Shia Muslim, while most Arabs are Sunni Muslims. Since Iran's Islamic Revolution in 1979, its Shia theocracy has worked to assert itself as the dominant leader of all Muslims, in opposition to the Sunni-dominated Saudi Arabia. Through its proxies, Iran has launched many attacks on Saudi Arabia, directly challenging the Saudis' status as the world's leading Muslim power.

How can Iran's identity as the "Land of Magog" be understood within the biblical framework of the end times? Is Iran considered part of "Ishmael," or is it a distinct nation? How does the Gog of Magog prophecy align with Daniel's prophecy concerning the four kingdoms that will oppress Israel[4] - and particularly the fourth kingdom of Ishmael and Edom that will work together to persecute Israel at the end times?

Over 400 years ago, Rabbi Judah Loew of Prague argued that the precise identification of the four distinct kingdoms does not necessarily require historical and numerical accuracy. When taking this more flexible approach, it is possible to consider several empires collectively as one "kingdom."

Unlike Saadia Gaon,[5] Rabbi Loew did not count the people of Ishmael as a separate and distinct "kingdom,"[6] but rather *as part of* the second kingdom - the kingdom of Persia.[7] Though ethnically separate peoples, the Persian and Arab peoples are bonded together through common national character traits.[8] Both Arabs and Persians are "prepared to violently attack others"[9] and "constantly seek to swallow up other nations."[10] The sages write that at the end of times, "The Holy One, blessed be He, will ask of the Persians: 'How have you occupied yourselves?' And they will reply 'Master of the Universe… we have captured many cities, we have waged many wars.'"[11]

Despite their ethnic differences, Ishmaelites and Persians are spiritually united through their allegiance to Islam, their shared character traits and their hatred of Israel. According to Rabbi Loew, the Persian-Ishmaelite axis, representing the second great kingdom of Daniel's dream, will join with the Edom, the fourth kingdom, in the war against Israel at the end of days.

Today, Iran has successfully united hundreds of millions of Persians and Arabs, both Shia and Sunni, in an "axis of resistance" against Israel. Iran's proxies include Shia terror groups like Hezbollah and the Yemenite Houthis, as well as the Sunni terror group Hamas. And despite their historic Shia-Sunni differences, Iran has grown increasingly closer to Erdogan's autocratic regime in Turkey. United by their genocidal hatred of Israel and the West, the "Gog of Magog" Iranian regime and its allies have joined forces to battle the State of Israel, conquer other Arab nations and launch a jihad against the West.

The sages taught: "The year the Messiah is revealed, all the nations of the world will antagonize each other and threaten each other with war. The king of Persia will antagonize the King of Arabia. The King of Arabia will go to Edom for advice. Then the King of Persia will destroy the entire world. And all the nations of the world will panic and be afraid and fall on their faces and be overcome with pain like the pain of labor. And Israel too will be afraid and in a tumult and say: 'Where can we go? What can we do?' God will say to them: 'My children, do not be afraid! Everything that I have done I only did for your sake! Why are you afraid? Do not fear, the time of your redemption has arrived. This final redemption will not be like the first redemption [from Egypt], for the first redemption was followed by pain and servitude to other nations, but the final redemption will not be followed by any pain or servitude.'"[12]

From Pregnancy to Birth

At the very end of the Book of Isaiah, the prophet speaks of the final days in coded language: "There is a sound of stirring from the city, a sound from the Temple, the voice of the Lord, recompensing His enemies. When she has not yet travailed, she has given birth; when the pang has not yet come to her, she has been delivered of a male child. Who has heard [anything] like this? Who has seen [anything] like these? Is a land born in one day? Is a nation born at once, that Zion both experienced birth pangs and bore her children?" (Isaiah 66:6-8).

These verses provide a timeline for Israel's redemption and the Gog of Magog war. Some time before the coming of the final redemption, a portion of the exiles will gather in the land and resettle Jerusalem. This is the meaning of "When she has not yet travailed, she has given birth." The renewed State of Israel will be born *before* the travails of the war against Gog. "When the pang has not yet come to her, she has been delivered of a male child." Before the final war against Gog, Israel will deliver a "male child"; there will be a partial deliverance of one 'child,' but not the complete deliverance of many 'children.' At this early stage of redemption, millions of Jews will remain in exile.

The prophecies of the first two of these verses have already been fulfilled. A minority of Jews returned to the holy land and with heroic efforts and God's help, they built the modern State of Israel. This is the "male child" that Isaiah prophesied, the partial redemption that would take place before the final war against Gog of Magog. But the third verse, which speaks of the birth of many "children," is yet to come.

Only after Israel is redeemed from servitude and is once again sovereign in her land will Gog attack the people of Israel,[13] as the commentators explain: "Then, after many years of living there, the 'birth pangs' of the war of Gog of Magog will descend upon them and the great ingathering of Israel will begin… and then, when the time of redemption arrives, when the woman giving birth will sit upon the birthing stool, she will experience crises and pain, which is the war of Gog."[14]

"From many days you will be remembered; at the end of the years you will come to a land [whose inhabitants] returned from the sword, gathered from many peoples, upon the mountains of Israel, which had been continually laid waste, but it was liberated from the nations, and they all dwelt securely" (Ezekiel 38:8).

This verse tells us the timing of Gog's attack. The attack will not occur when Israel has lived comfortably in the land for centuries, but rather at the "end of years," shortly after Israel "returned from the sword, gathered from many peoples," following a time when mass numbers of Jews are murdered by the sword after which the survivors will return from many other nations to the holy land. This is an allusion to the founding of the modern State of Israel, reborn when thousands of survivors gathered in the land in the aftermath of the Holocaust.

A close reading of the verses in Ezekiel and Zechariah reveals that Gog and his allies will attack Israel on three separate occasions;[15] after each failure, they will regroup and attack the people of Israel again.[16] The three battles are likely to play out over many years - a prophecy that clearly aligns with the history of the modern State of Israel, in which the nations of Ishmael have continuously attacked Israel despite their many losses.

"Upon the mountains of Israel, which had been continually laid waste, but it was liberated from the nations, and they all dwelt securely." Gog will attack after a reborn Israel is "liberated from the nations" and has rebuilt the devastated cities of the land and "dwells securely." This was precisely Israel's situation when Hamas attacked southern Israel on October 7, 2023.

While the early stages of redemption, the 'pregnancy' of Israel - the reestablishment of the people of Israel in the land of Israel - will happen slowly over time, the painful "birth" itself, the final war against Gog, will unfold more rapidly in wondrous fashion. "Who has heard [anything] like this? Who has seen [anything] like these? Is a land born in one day? Is a nation born at once?"

After 75 years of independence, events are unfolding with extraordinary speed. Israel is under attack on multiple fronts, while the United States changes decades of foreign policy on an almost daily basis to pressure Israel to capitulate to terrorism. Meanwhile, the evil axis of Iran, Hezbollah and Hamas grows ever bolder, preparing for the final war against God's people.

A War of Pure Destruction

"And you will ascend; like a storm you will come; like a cloud to cover the earth you will be; you and all your wings and many peoples with you... And you will say, 'I shall ascend upon a land of open cities; I shall come upon the tranquil, who dwell securely; all of them living without a wall, and they have no bars or doors. To take spoil and to plunder loot, to return your hand upon the resettled ruins and to a people gathered from nations'" (Ezekiel 38:9,11-12).

Gog and his allies will overwhelm the communities of Israel "like a storm," like "a sudden loud and crushing rush of water" that terrifies the populace.[17] The Hebrew word for "storm" in this verse, *shoah*, is the Hebrew word used for the Holocaust. On October 7, Hamas terrorists descended upon "tranquil" Israeli communities with few defenses and weapons,[18] suddenly, like a storm, perpetrating the greatest massacre of Jews since the Holocaust.

"For in My jealousy and in the fire of My wrath I have spoken; Surely there shall be a great noise on that day in the land of Israel" (Ezekiel 38:19). What is this great noise? "The war at the end of days will be intense and the sound of weapons and cannon shall be heard throughout the land, bombs that will destroy hills and fortified gates with a loud and powerful noise."[19] Since October 7, the sound of rocket fire from Gaza and Lebanon can be heard all throughout Israel, followed by the powerful booms of Israeli fighter jets destroying enemy strongholds.

What motivates the evil coalition of Gog of Magog to attack the people of Israel? Why does Gog send forth his "hand upon the resettled ruins," to "destroy the land and make it as desolate as it was"[20] before the people of Israel returned to the land? What drove Hamas to destroy the beautiful southern Israeli communities on the Gaza border?

Gog and Magog's motivations for attacking Israel are different from those of other nations that have attacked Israel throughout history. "All of the opposition of earlier enemies who attacked Israel derived from self-serving motives: to advance themselves through Israel's destruction, to prevent Israel from succeeding at their expense, or to prevent the weakening of their strength as Israel grows spiritually stronger. But the war of Gog of Magog will derive purely from a desire to cause harm and destruction... It will come at a time when Israel is back in its land and seeks peace with its neighbors. But [Gog and Magog] will desire only to cause evil and will be jealous of the glory of God that will be increased through Israel."[21]

Iran, Hamas and Hezbollah are not afraid that Israel will conquer their lands, nor do they seek economic benefits from attacking Israel. Hamas' attacks have only brought death and destruction upon the Gaza Strip. They are driven by pure hatred of Israel, seeking only to murder and destroy. As Yahyah Sinwar, leader of Hamas in Gaza said, "The leaders of Israel should know this. October 7 was just the general rehearsal."[22] His goal is simple and frightening: to murder as many Jews as possible and to eradicate them from the land.

God's Vengeance

Gog and his allies believe they can uproot the people of Israel and send them, once again, into the darkness of exile. But God has different plans. "'For, as the new heavens and the new earth that I am making, stand before Me,' says God, 'so shall your seed and your name stand'" (Isaiah 66:22). The prophet refers to the heavens and earth as "new," for even as generations of men come and go, they remain unchanged, as "new" as they were the day they were created. "So shall your seed and your name stand." The commentators explain: "Do not think that though you have been redeemed, your seed after you will be exiled from their land and their name lost in exile, as… Gog of Magog who fights for Jerusalem to exile Israel and wipe out their name. For the seed of Israel will stand forever, like the heavens and earth."[23]

God will save His people, and the enemies of Israel will pay for their evil deeds: "So says the Lord God: 'Lo! I am against you, O Gog, prince and head of Meshech and Tubal. And I will unbridle and entice you and lead you up from the utmost parts of the north and bring you upon the mountains of Israel… Upon the mountains of Israel shall you fall, you and all your hordes, and the people that are with you; to the birds of prey, to all the winged creatures and the beasts of the field have I given you to be devoured'" (Ezekiel 39:1-2,4).

Not only will Gog and the people of Ishmael suffer for their sins, but so will Edom, the Western nations that support them. Initially, the Edomites will join the Ishmaelites in an alliance against Israel. But ultimately, the Ishmaelites will turn on the Edomites, who will be forced to fight back. "And I will call the sword against him upon all My mountains, says the Lord God: every man's sword shall be against his brother" (Ezekiel 38:21). The 15th-century scholar, Don Isaac Abarbanel, identifies the "brothers" who will turn on one another at the end times: "This verse alludes to Edom and Ishmael, for they are brothers through their original forefathers."[24] Though at first they will join together in their attacks on Israel, Ishmael and Edom will ultimately declare war on each other.[25]

The Western nations trying so hard to appease the Ishmaelites will inevitably have no choice but to battle the Islamic jihadists of Iran and their allies and proxies. When the Ishmaelites go too far and directly attack the West, the Edomites will be forced to declare war against them. This will lead to the great war between Ishmael and the West, when "every man's sword will be against his brother."[26]

This is the meaning of Zechariah's prophecy concerning the splitting of the Mount of Olives. "And the Mount of Olives shall split in the midst thereof, toward the east and toward the west, a very great valley. And half the mountain shall move to the north, and half of it to the south" (Zechariah 14:4). The "splitting" of the Mount of Olives represents the breakdown of the Ishmael-Edom alliance and the war that will break out between them, between "east" and "west." "The war between Edom and Ishmael will be extremely intense. It will be as if the Mount of Olives had split while they were fighting there."[27] Zechariah uses the Mount of Olives in Jerusalem as the symbol for the war between Ishmael and Edom for Israel will be at the center of the great war at the end times.

Even Gog's allies who live far from Israel will pay for their treachery. "And I will send fire on Magog and on those who dwell in safety in the islands, and they will know that I am the Lord" (Ezekiel 39:6). "Behold, they may gather together, but not by Me; whoever mobilizes against you shall fall because of you" (Isaiah 54:15). The commentators explain: "These are the nations that gather against you... God has caused them to turn against you, but this is not to bring evil upon Israel but rather to help them. For Israel will take vengeance upon all of them... for the glory of God and the glory of Israel."[28]

"For with fire will the Lord contend and with His sword with all flesh, and those slain by the Lord shall be many. 'Those who prepare themselves and purify themselves to the gardens, [one] after another in the middle, those who eat the flesh of the swine and the detestable thing and the rodent, shall perish together,' says the Lord" (Isaiah 66:16-17).

In the war of Gog of Magog, Edom and Ishmael "shall perish together."[29] Many will be destroyed "with His sword" as Ishmael and Edom turn on one another, while others will die "with fire" at the hands of heaven, as is written: "And I will judge against him with pestilence and with blood, and rain bringing floods, and great hailstones, fire, and brimstone will I rain down upon him and upon his hordes and upon the many peoples that are with him" (Ezekiel 38:22).[30]

The vengeance against Gog and his allies will be a comfort to Israel,[31] for it will restore Israel's faith in God's justice. "He sent me to bind up the brokenhearted… To declare… a day of vengeance for our God, to console all mourners" (Isaiah 61:1-2).

The Birth of Redemption

Ezekiel and Isaiah emphasize that the nations of the world will see God's judgment with their own eyes.

"And I shall publicize My glory among the nations, and all the nations will see My judgment that I performed and My hand that I place upon them" (Ezekiel 39:21). God will spare a remnant of Gog's army so that they can travel across the world and share their eyewitness testimony of God's judgment with all the other nations.[32] Then the nations will be inspired by these witnesses to come to the holy land and see God's judgment for themselves. "'All flesh shall come to prostrate themselves before Me,' says the Lord. 'And they shall go out and see the corpses of the people who rebelled against Me, for their worm shall not die, and their fire shall not be quenched, and they shall be an abhorring for all flesh'" (Isaiah 66:23-24).

After the destruction of Gog and his allies, the nations who come to worship God in Jerusalem will first go to the Valley of Jehoshaphat to see the corpses of the camp of Gog of Magog who sinned against God and sought to expel the people of Israel from their land.[33] "Therefore shall a strong people honor You; a city of tyrannical nations shall fear You" (Isaiah 25:3). After witnessing the destruction of Gog and his allies, the most powerful nations throughout the world will fear and honor God's people.[34]

"'Will I bring to the birth stool and not cause to give birth?' says the Lord. 'Am I not He who causes to give birth, now should I shut the womb?' says your God" (Isaiah 66:9). From the birth pangs of Gog and Magog, the redemption of Israel will be born. Every word and every prophecy will be fulfilled. For God will not bring only part [of the salvation], but the salvation in its entirety.[35]

CHAPTER 9:

ISHMAEL'S RESENTMENT: THE AL-AQSA FLOOD

When approximately 3,000 of its terrorists invaded Israel on October 7, 2023, massacring over 1,200 innocent people, Hamas launched the opening salvo of its war against the Jewish state. Israel has called this war "The Swords of Iron War," a banal and meaningless name that will likely soon be forgotten. Hamas, however, gave the war a far more interesting name: "The Al-Aqsa Flood."

Al-Aqsa is the name of the mosque that sits atop the Temple Mount in Jerusalem - the holiest site of the Jewish people - about 50 miles away from the Gaza border. Though Israel liberated the Old City of Jerusalem after Jordan invaded the Jewish state in 1967, Israel allowed Jordan to maintain control over the day-to-day administration of the Al-Aqsa Mosque through the Jordanian Waqf, a branch of Jordan's Ministry of Awqaf Islamic Affairs and Holy Places.

After its brutal attack, Hamas leaders issued a document listing its many grievances against Israel and justifying the October 7 slaughter. The first reason listed is "The Israeli Judaization plans to the blessed Al-Aqsa Mosque, its temporal and spatial division attempts, as well as the intensification of the Israeli settlers' incursions into the holy mosque."[1] On its face, this is a complete fabrication; neither the Israeli government nor "Israeli settlers" interfere with Al-Aqsa Mosque in any way. In recent years, many Israelis have argued for the right to Jewish prayer on the Temple Mount, but no one has interfered with the Al-Aqsa Mosque itself or tried to remove Muslims' access to Al-Aqsa.

When an IDF soldier who finished his tour of duty in Gaza returned home, his mother asked what he planned to do first. He said "I'm going to hang a picture of the Temple in Jerusalem on my wall." Surprised, his mother asked "Really? Not a shower or eating your favorite food?" Her son explained: "You don't understand. In Gaza, there isn't a home, government office, or school without a picture of the Al-Aqsa Mosque hanging on its walls. If they are so committed to Al-Aqsa, we must be even more committed to building the Temple. The verse says 'Zion, whom no one seeks' (Jeremiah 30:17), teaching us that we have an obligation to seek out the Temple!"[2] With this in mind, thousands of Israeli soldiers have sewn patches depicting the Temple in Jerusalem to the shoulders of their uniforms since the beginning of the war.

If Muslims already control Al-Aqsa, why are Hamas and Gazan Arabs obsessed with "protecting" Al-Aqsa from non-existent Israeli aggression? And what does Al-Aqsa have to do with their slaughter of Jewish women and children in southern Israel?

A Holy City for Muslims?

Following the painful years of the Napoleonic wars, Germans sought a scapegoat for their suffering. As usual, they blamed the Jews. In October 1819, Germans perpetrated a series of pogroms against Jews in Bavaria called the "Hep-Hep riots," for when the antisemites saw a Jew in the street, they would scream "Hep-Hep!" "Hep" is an acronym for "Hierosolyma est perdita," Latin for "Jerusalem is lost." Essentially, they were telling the Jews: "You are finished, you have no hope of returning to Jerusalem!"[3]

What did Jerusalem have to do with German Jews in 1819? Whether or not they consciously understood the deeper meaning of their antisemitic cry, these Germans were onto something. The Jewish people, wherever they might be in the world, are synonymous with Jerusalem. Though the Romans destroyed the Second Temple and much of the city in 70 CE, the Temple Mount and Jerusalem, the city of David, remain holy forever. As Maimonides wrote, "Why do I say that the original consecration sanctified the Temple and Jerusalem for eternity?... Because the sanctity of the Temple and Jerusalem stems from God, and God's will can never be nullified."[4]

Since the Temple was destroyed and most Jews were exiled from Israel, the Jewish people have remained steadfast to it. Jews pray in the direction of Jerusalem, beseech God for its rebuilding three times each day, and finish the Passover service by singing "Next year in Jerusalem." The grace after meals, recited regularly by faithful Jews, says more about the future return to Jerusalem than about the food we eat.

"If I forget you, O Jerusalem, may my right hand forget its skill. May my tongue cling to my palate, if I do not remember you, if I do not bring up Jerusalem at the beginning of my joy" (Psalm 137:5-6). The memory of the Temple's destruction holds immense significance in Jewish consciousness. It is commemorated through the fast of the 9th of Av, by leaving homes partially unfinished, and by breaking a glass during wedding ceremonies. Every Sabbath morning, after reciting a portion from the prophets, the reader prays: "Have pity on Zion which is the home of our life... Blessed are you God, who makes Zion rejoice in her children."[5]

The Jewish people's attachment to Jerusalem goes far deeper than ritual. "We did not enter the city of Jerusalem on our own in 1967. Streams of endless craving, endless praying, clinging, dreaming, day and night, midnights, years, decades, centuries, millenia, streams of tears, pledging, waiting - from all over the world, from all corners of the earth, carried us of this generation to the [Western] Wall, to the city of Jerusalem."[6] As Nobel Prize winning author Shmuel Agnon put it, "As a result of the historic catastrophe in which Titus of Rome destroyed Jerusalem and Israel was exiled from its land, I was born in one of the cities of the exile. But always I regarded myself as one who was born in Jerusalem."[7]

The sages teach that "a true Jew is one who thinks about Jerusalem every moment of his life,"[8] and "Jerusalem will be rebuilt when we covet it with the full intensity of our desire."[9] The aspiration to return to Jerusalem and reconstruct the Temple is not confined to the world of pietists or mystics. "You, who forsake God, who forget My holy mount... Behold, My servants shall sing from joy of heart, but you shall cry out from sorrow of heart, and from a broken spirit you shall wail" (Isaiah 65:11,14). Every Jewish man, woman and child must yearn for Jerusalem, for forgetting God's holy mount is tantamount to forsaking God Himself.

"Rejoice with Jerusalem and exult in her all those who love her: rejoice with her a rejoicing, all who mourn over her. In order that you suck and become sated from the breast of her consolations, in order that you drink deeply and delight from her approaching glory" (Isaiah 66:10-11). Jews mourn for her "in order that you suck and become sated from the breast of her consolations," for they know that this will be their reward.[10] A Jew mourns for the Temple knowing with *certainty* that it will one day be rebuilt and that Israel will be comforted.

No nation in history is more attached to a particular place than the Jewish people are to the Temple Mount, the site of both the first and second Temples. Nevertheless, Muslims consistently deny the clear connection between the Jewish people and the Temple Mount.

A few examples: In 1967, a top Islamic official of the Temple Mount depicted Jewish attachment to the Western Wall, the only part of the Temple that still stands today, as an act of "aggression against al-Aqsa mosque."[11] Decades later, during the July 2000 negotiations at Camp David, Yasir Arafat refused to recognize any Jewish connection to the Temple Mount, asserting that no Jewish Temple had ever stood there. When discussions resumed in Taba later that year, the Israelis consented to full Muslim sovereignty over the Temple Mount but asked the Arabs to acknowledge the site's significance to Judaism. They refused.[12]

The supposedly "moderate" Palestinian Authority's website continues to deny the Jewish people's connection to the Western Wall. "Some Orthodox religious Jews consider it as a holy place for them, and claim that the wall is part of their Temple which all historic studies and archeological excavations have failed to find any proof for such a claim."[13] More recently, Palestinian Authority President Mahmoud Abbas made news at the United Nations when he denied any Jewish connection to the Temple Mount. "They dug everywhere, and they couldn't find anything."[14] Along these lines, Islamic institutions pressure Western media outlets, urging them to refer to the Temple Mount and the Western Wall with their Islamic designations - Al-Haram ash-Sharif and Al-Buraq - rather than their significantly older Jewish names.

Abbas and others hope that by repeating their lies over and over, ignorant people will believe them. Archaeological evidence indisputably proves otherwise. In the late 1990s, the Waqf used heavy machinery to bulldoze a massive area in the southeastern corner of the Temple Mount, dumping the soil in the Kidron Valley to the north east of the Old City of Jerusalem. In response to this purposeful destruction of archaeological evidence, Israeli archaeologists launched a systematic project to sift the soil, utilizing thousands of volunteers. What they found was astounding. They discovered hundreds of thousands of artifacts of every kind, from stone vessels to frescoes. Approximately 15 percent of the diagnostic pottery fragments found were traceable to the First Temple era (10th century B.C.E. to the Babylonian destruction of the Temple in 586 B.C.E.). The discoveries included artifacts dating back to the 10th–9th centuries B.C.E., coinciding with the reigns of kings David and Solomon.[15]

Muslim denial of Jewish history at the Temple Mount is new. In 1925, the Supreme Moslem Council published a nine-page English-language tourist guide entitled "A Brief Guide to al-Haram al-Sharif" - the Arabic name for the Temple Mount. The pamphlet states: "The site is one of the oldest in the world. Its sanctity dates from the earliest (perhaps from pre-historic) times. Its identity with the site of Solomon's Temple is beyond dispute. This, too, is the spot, according to universal belief, on which 'David built there an altar unto the Lord, and offered burnt offerings and peace offerings' (II Samuel 24:25)."[16]

What has changed since 1925? Why are Muslims today so intent on denying any Jewish connection to the Temple Mount?

The question is only strengthened by the relatively low status of Jerusalem in Islamic thought and practice. Muslims do not pray to Jerusalem, nor is Jerusalem ever explicitly named in their prayers. Throughout history, the city has never been the capital of a sovereign Muslim state nor has it evolved into a hub of cultural or scholarly activities. Historians agree that the Prophet Muhammed was never in Jerusalem.[17] Few politically significant events for Muslims have originated from there. As Daniel Pipes writes, "Jerusalem appears in the Jewish Bible 669 times and Zion (which usually means Jerusalem) 154 times, or 823 times in all. The Christian Bible mentions Jerusalem 154 times and Zion 7 times. In contrast… Jerusalem and Zion appear as frequently in the Koran as they do in the Hindu Bhagavad-Gita, the Taoist Tao-Te Ching, the Buddhist Dhamapada and the Zoroastrian Zend Avesta - which is to say, not once."[18]

The Islamic connection to Jerusalem is based on an interpretation of a passage in the Koran. "Praise be to Allah who brought his servant at night from the Holy Mosque to the Remote Mosque, the precincts of which we have blessed."[19] Some Muslim scholars interpret this to mean that the Prophet Mohammad was miraculously transported from Mecca to Jerusalem, from where he then made his ascent to heaven. The events of this journey were embellished over the generations with many legends. With this interpretation, Islam was able to link itself, however tenuously, to the traditional holiness of Jerusalem established by Judaism and Christianity.[20]

The difference between Islam's connection to Jerusalem and that of Judaism and Christianity is significant. For Jews and Christians, Jerusalem is holy because real, tangible and historic events took place in Jerusalem. Both Temples stood in Jerusalem, where Jews would gather for pilgrimage festivals three times each year. Jesus lived and died in Jerusalem. The opposite is true of Islam. Nothing of consequence to Islam took place in Jerusalem. For Muslims, Jerusalem only matters to them because they insist that it matters; they chose to make Jerusalem holy, and so it became holy.

For most of history, Muslims were indifferent to Jerusalem. During the many centuries of Muslim rule - with the brief exception of the Crusader kingdom, Muslims ruled Jerusalem from 638 to 1917 - the city was ignored and left in terrible condition. In 1611, the English traveler George Sandys found that "Much lies waste; the old buildings (except a few) all ruined, the new contemptible."[21] In 1867, Mark Twain described the holy city in similar terms. "Renowned Jerusalem itself, the stateliest name in history, has lost all its ancient grandeur, and is become a pauper village; the riches of Solomon are no longer there to compel the admiration of visiting Oriental queens; the wonderful temple which was the pride and the glory of Israel, is gone."[22]

Why has Jerusalem become a focal point of fundamentalist Islam and the rallying cry for Hamas? Why do passionate imams regularly whip their followers into an angry frenzy over the supposed evils Israel is committing against Al-Aqsa, after 1,300 years of indifference?

An Ancient Resentment

In Jewish tradition, the unique holiness of the Temple Mount far predates the Temple itself. After the awesome drama of the binding of Isaac, Abraham named the mountain where he and Isaac stood. "And Abraham named that place, 'The Lord will see (*Yireh*)' as it is said to this day: 'On the mountain, the Lord will be seen' (Genesis 22:14)." What, exactly, will the Lord see in this place? The sages explain: "The Lord will choose and see for Himself this place, to cause His Divine Presence to rest therein and for offering sacrifices here. Future generations will say about it, 'On this mountain, the Holy One, blessed be He, appears to His people.'"[23] The mountain where Abraham was prepared to sacrifice Isaac for God was none other than the Temple Mount itself.

The biblical story of the binding of Isaac is a uniquely important story for Muslims, even though Islam does not accept the Hebrew Bible. The Koran contains its own version of the binding story, but unlike the Bible, it does not mention the name of the sacrificial son. Shaykh Muhammad ibn Abd al-Wahhab, an 18th century Sunni Muslim scholar, concluded that the sacrificial son must have been Ishmael, for the Koran describes the sacrificial son as Abraham's "unique son," which could only have been Ishmael, the forefather of Mohammed.[24]

Who was the beloved and chosen son of Abraham who was bound up as an offering to God? Was it Isaac, the forefather of Israel, or Ishmael, the forefather of Islam?

God said to Abraham, "Please take your son, your only one, whom you love, yea, Isaac, and go away to the land of Moriah and bring him up there for a burnt offering on one of the mountains, of which I will tell you" (Genesis 22:2). The contrast between Isaac, the chosen son, and Ishmael, banished from Abraham's home, could not be clearer. It was inevitable that Islamic tradition, while keeping the basic framework of the story, would replace Isaac with Ishmael.

Against the background of this ancient rivalry, today's struggle over the Temple Mount becomes clearer. The Temple Mount is not simply a contested holy site; it is the root of Ishmael's age-old resentment of Israel and the passionate hatred that fuels Iran, Hamas and Hezbollah. If the Bible is true, if the Temple Mount is the place where Isaac willingly allowed his father to bind him and offer him as a sacrifice, it serves as a constant reminder of Ishmael's humiliation and secondary status. And so Muslim leaders constantly deny the Jewish people's historical ties to the city and Temple Mount, assuming that if they repeat the lie for long enough, the international community will accept their position.

For 1,300 years, Muslims showed little interest in the Temple Mount or Al-Aqsa because the Jews, the descendants of Isaac, were downtrodden and posed no threat to Islamic supremacy. When Jews were a poor and tiny minority and subject to Muslim authority, Muslims ignored the city. Jerusalem only became the focus of Muslim religious passion once the Jewish people began returning to their ancient homeland. During the British Mandatory period (1917 - 1948), as the Jewish presence in the holy land grew rapidly, Arab politicians elevated Jerusalem to a significant destination. Visiting leaders from the Arab world often made appearances in Jerusalem, publicly praying at Al-Aqsa and delivering impassioned speeches. When visiting Jerusalem to great fanfare in 1926, King Faisal of Iraq ceremoniously entered the Temple Mount through the same gate utilized by Caliph 'Umar during the initial conquest of Jerusalem in 638.

When the Jordanians ruled over the Old City of Jerusalem from 1948 to 1967, Muslim interest in it noticeably waned, mirroring a broader trend of neglect. Jordanian policies effectively relegated Arab Jerusalem to the status of an isolated provincial town, overshadowed even by cities like Nablus. Economic stagnation prompted a mass exodus of Arab Jerusalemites, a sharp contrast to the rapid growth experienced by Amman during the same period. Mosques struggled with financial constraints, and the Friday prayers, traditionally held at Al-Aqsa Mosque, were broadcast from a lesser-known mosque in Amman instead.

Only following Israel's victory and its liberation of Jerusalem in the Six-Day War did Muslims make Jerusalem the object of their yearning and dreams. Beginning in 1967, Arabs in Judea, Samaria and Gaza began hanging pictures of Al-Aqsa and the Dome of the Rock in their homes and grocery stores. Jerusalem and the Temple Mount soon became the most emotional issue of the Israeli-Arab conflict.

As Daniel Pipes wrote, "Muslim interest lies not so much in controlling Jerusalem as it does in denying control over the city to anyone else."[25] But it is particularly the Jews, and their control over the city, which enrages the descendants of Ishmael. Every Jew who prays at the Western Wall or, even worse, dares to pray on the Temple Mount itself, is a slap in the face to Muslims everywhere.

It does not matter that the Temple Mount compound remains under Muslim control, or that the primarily secular Jews in southern Israel who were brutally butchered by Hamas on October 7 lived fifty miles away from Jerusalem. The people of Israel's ancient bond with the Temple Mount lies at the heart of all Muslim grievances towards Jews. This time, they are certain, Ishmael will finally kill his younger brother, and Jerusalem will be theirs forever.

Zechariah's Prophecy - Jerusalem and the End Times

In chapters 12 and 14 of the Book of Zechariah, the prophet makes clear that the redemption at the end of days will arrive after a great war whose focus will be Jerusalem.

"And I will gather all the nations to Jerusalem to wage war" (Zechariah 14:2). All of the nations are obsessed with Jerusalem. Zechariah makes clear that he does not speak of a battle waged by a particular Arab army against Israel, but rather a world war against Israel whose focal point will be Jerusalem. In the final series of wars before redemption, the people of Israel will be forced to fight, physically and spiritually, for Jerusalem.

What form will the battle take? Which elements of Zechariah's prophecy will be fulfilled in a real and physical way, and which aspects constitute a spiritual vision? Will there be a physical battle against Jerusalem, or an international coalition arrayed against the Jewish state? It is impossible to know with certainty. But one thing is clear - Jerusalem will be at the center of the world's attention at the end of days.

Prophecies that seemed fantastical for most of history are being fulfilled before our eyes. As one scholar wrote in the wake of the Six-Day War of 1967, "Zechariah prophesied about the events of our time... We have seen the nations unite in their efforts to remove Jerusalem from the hands of Israel. It is possible that the many prophecies describing the nations' wars against Jerusalem are referring to the war against Israel in the United Nations, where the nations use threats, blasphemies and insults in their attempt to steal Jerusalem, the holy city, from the people of Israel. Standing against the entire world, Israel's representative 'dwells alone' (Numbers 23:9), without any other nation willing to help him."[26] The nations' attempts to take Jerusalem from the people of Israel continue to this day.

"Behold! I am making Jerusalem a cup of weakness for all the peoples around... And it shall come to pass on that day that I will make Jerusalem a stone of burden for all peoples; all who bear it shall be gashed, and all the nations of the earth shall gather about it." (Zechariah 12:2-3). Jerusalem is a "stone of burden" for the nations. They set aside their other activities to focus only on trying to take Jerusalem away from Israel, as if it were a heavy and painful burden to them to leave Jerusalem in Jewish hands.[27]

Why has Jerusalem, a relatively small city compared to the great metropolises of New York and London, become the center of the world's attention? Why did the entire world weigh in on President Trump's decision to move the US embassy from Tel Aviv to Jerusalem? There is no rational reason for the international obsession with Jerusalem; it can only be the work of God.

The enemies of Israel are obsessed with Jerusalem, but it will be "a cup of weakness" and "a stone of burden" for them that will lead to their destruction. With the Al-Aqsa Flood, Hamas and other jihadists have made Jerusalem the center of their longing, even more than Mecca and Medina - but the "stone of burden" will come crashing down upon their heads.

Marina Sokol, whose son Israel fell in battle in Gaza in January 2024, ascended the Temple Mount with her family at the end of the seven days of mourning. Explaining why she went there, she said, "I lost my son in this war, and this war is over the Temple Mount. We must bring sacrifices to God in this place. Because we are not doing so, we are forced to sacrifice the very best of our sons instead. Look at our fallen soldiers - they are the very best of our people, because we are forbidden to bring flawed sacrifices to God. The connection between this war and the Temple Mount is clear. It is a religious war, a war between Islam and Judaism... If their goal is the Dome of the Rock, our goal must be the Temple. As in the binding of Isaac, instead of tying up our sons, we must tie up a ram [and offer sacrifices to God in a rebuilt Temple]. If we bring sacrifices to God in this place, our enemies will no longer be here."[28]

Those who believe the status of Jerusalem can be negotiated with the Muslims, or that it will one day serve as the capital to both Jewish and Arab states, have never read the words of the prophets. "Judah shall remain forever, and Jerusalem throughout all generations" (Joel 4:20). Israel will be the only victor in this war.

As the nations plot to take Jerusalem from the Jews, gentile lovers of Israel are flocking to Jerusalem from all over the world to dance in the streets of the holy city. Only three days before Hamas jihadists launched its brutal invasion on October 7, 2023, thousands of Christians from around the world gathered in the streets of Jerusalem for the annual "March of the Nations." It was an impressive show of unity, bringing together over 3,000 Christians from 90 different countries who donned their traditional garb and proudly displayed their national flags. Their purpose was to honor Jerusalem and express their steadfast backing for Israel, rooted in their common faith.[29] The day is coming when "the mountain of the Lord's house shall be firmly established at the top of the mountains, and it shall be raised above the hills, and all the nations shall stream to it" (Isaiah 2:2).

"Three commandments were given to Israel when they entered the land: to appoint a king, to cut off the seed of Amalek, and to build the 'chosen house' [the Temple in Jerusalem]."[30] After Israel destroys its enemies and God's judgment is brought down upon the nations, the time will come to rebuild God's Temple in Jerusalem.

"And the Lord shall roar from Zion, and from Jerusalem He shall give forth His voice, and the heavens and earth shall quake, and the Lord is a shelter to His people and a stronghold for the children of Israel. And you shall know that I, the Lord your God, dwell in Zion, My holy mount, and Jerusalem shall be holy" (Joel 4:16-17).

PROPHECIES OF
Edom

CHAPTER 10:

OBADIAH'S WARNING TO THE WEST

A mere 21 verses long, the Book of Obadiah is the shortest book in the Hebrew Bible. But boy, do those 21 verses pack a punch!

Obadiah's prophecy speaks of the end of days, about the time of the wars of Gog of Magog.[1] But while the prophets Ezekiel and Zechariah address the evil Gog of Magog and his allies - the Islamic nations who will actively attack the people of Israel - Obadiah addresses the people of Edom, the Western nations that will support and encourage the Ishmaelites who attack Israel.

More than any other prophet, Obadiah understood the evil character of Esau and Edom, for he himself was an Edomite convert to Judaism.[2] As the sages so aptly said, "From the very forest itself comes the handle of the ax that fells it."[3] In one short chapter, Obadiah diagnoses the internal corruption and collapse of the West - prophecies whose fulfillment we are witnessing today.

An Unholy Alliance

"So Esau went to Ishmael, and he took Mahalath, the daughter of Ishmael, the son of Abraham, the sister of Nebaioth, in addition to his other wives as a wife"

(Genesis 28:9). The sages explain that "Esau went to Ishmael to learn his evil ways and to increase his number of wives."[4]

This same dynamic is all too common on American college campuses today, in which young, naive and spiritually lost Americans, the people of Edom, turn to radical Muslim professors and student groups, the people of Ishmael, to find direction and purpose in their lives. Tragically, hundreds of thousands of university students, many of them raised in Christian and Jewish homes, have been radicalized in this way.

These young "revolutionaries," who serve as the foot soldiers of the antisemitic pro-Hamas movement overtaking college campuses all over America, are the Ishmaelites' useful idiots. Suffering from "white-guilt syndrome," they unquestioningly imbibe the lies of their radical Muslim professors and demonize Israel and America for their supposedly racist and colonialist policies, while ignoring the genocidal acts of the jihadists. The LGBTQ+ activists who so passionately support Hamas terrorists would be butchered by Hamas if they dared to step foot in the Gaza Strip. Yet they, and millions of other fools, support the jihadists who despise them.

"The vision of Obadiah; So said the Lord God concerning Edom; We have heard tidings from the Lord, and a messenger has been sent among the nations, 'Arise and let us rise up against them in war!'" (Obadiah 1:1). Who is this messenger calling the nations to rise up and attack Edom? The commentators explain that this refers to the children of Ishmael who will encourage each other to rise up and destroy the West.[5] Since October 7, jihadists have increased their calls for attacks on Western nations. In November 2023, the al-Qaeda General Command called for attacks against US interests around the world. "O sons of the Ummah from the Muslim communities amongst the arrogant West: Your opportunity today to support your brothers is great."[6]

"And at the time of the end, the king of the south will clash with him, and the king of the north will storm over him with chariots, with horsemen, and with many ships, and he will come into the lands and inundate and pass" (Daniel 11:40). At the end of days, the king of the south, the leader of the Ishmaelites, will rise up and fight against Edom, the king of the north, as if goring him with the horn of a beast. Edom will respond to Ishmael's attack by fighting fiercely against him with great force, like a windstorm. Edom will have many ships and soldiers, and will bring his armies to fight Ishmael in the south.[7] In other words, today's Muslim Jihadists will call their people to war against the secular nations of the West - and they will ultimately provoke a furious response.

This is precisely what is occurring today, as imams throughout Europe teach their followers to embrace jihad, hate Jews and to overthrow the Judeo-

Christian culture of the West. They are openly declaring their true goal - to topple and take over the West from the inside. How long will it take for the West to awaken and respond?

On Friday night, November 13, 2015, ISIS jihadists entered the Bataclan theater in Paris, where they murdered 90 young people attending a concert. Nine years later, on February 10, 2024, young people gathered at that very same theater to chant "Free Palestine" and protest Israel's decision to eradicate the jihadist terror group Hamas. Incredibly, thousands of people gathered at a venue where Islamic terrorists massacred non-Muslims to cheer and support Islamic terrorists. Can there be any greater example of people not learning from history?

As Obadiah explains, the people of the West are foolish and asleep. They do not realize that by helping Ishmael in its war against Israel, they are sowing the seeds of their *own* destruction. Their erstwhile Ishmaelite "allies" do not only hate the Jews. Their ultimate goal is to topple the entire West and bring it under the dominion of Islam. As the jihadist terrorists proudly say, "First we kill the Saturday people, then we kill the Sunday people."[8]

The Downfall of the West

"If you go up high like an eagle, and if you place your nest among the stars, from there I will bring you down, says the Lord" (Obadiah 1:4).

The Western nations of Edom, who for so long were the world's dominant powers, will crash down from their great heights. One who falls from a low place is not seriously in danger. Therefore God placed the "nest" of Edom high up among the "stars," giving the Western nations dominance over the world, in order to increase the impact of their ultimate demise.

From their heights of power, the Western nations will be brought down to the Valley of Jehoshaphat for divine judgment: "For behold, in those days and in that time when I return the captives of Judah and Jerusalem, I will gather all the nations and I will take them down to the Valley of Jehoshaphat, and I will contend with them there concerning My people and My heritage, Israel, which they scattered among the nations, and My land they divided" (Joel 4:1-2).

When God "returns the captives of Judah," when the Israeli hostages are returned to their families, God will judge the nations for their treatment of Israel. God will ask every nation: "When Islamic terrorists raped, tortured and slaughtered over 1,200 of My beloved children on October 7, how did *you* respond?" Those nations that supported Hamas and Iran in their goal of dividing the holy land and taking it away from the people of Israel will be judged and punished for their betrayal.

"Did thieves come upon you, did plunderers of the night? How were you silent? Will they not steal till they have enough?" (Obadiah 1:5). The downfall of the West will not occur overnight or in spectacular fashion. Rather, the enemies of Edom - the Muslim Ishmaelites - will sneak up on the West like thieves who take everything you own as you sleep.

One of America's most astute commentators wrote, "We must not wait and watch as Arab propaganda floods the campuses... We must not wait for leftists to flood the campuses with their siren songs that rip away Jewish youth with their attacks on Israel as a 'lackey of imperialism,' 'aggressor,' and 'fascist, racist state.' We must not wait for an Arab or a leftist teach-in against Israel before we panic and seek solutions... [It is] a myopia that hovers over us and blinds us to problems until they are upon us, ready to devour us. Only then do we suddenly wrench ourselves free from our paralysis. Only then do we begin rushing about in a frenzied panic seeking a solution."[9] Rabbi Meir Kahane wrote these words over 50 years ago, in 1971. But America was sleeping.

Everyone will ask: "Why did you not awaken from your slumber to expel these Ishmaelite enemies from your midst?"[10] This is the question that should be asked today, as Europe's radical Muslim population grows by leaps and bounds. Projections show that Muslims will make up 19.7% of Germany's population by 2050, with similar numbers in England and France. Meanwhile, leaders who dare call out the obvious danger of Europe's rising Muslim population, like Geert Wilders of the Netherlands, are marginalized as bigots and "Islamophobes."[11]

In May, 2024, over a thousand Islamic extremists paraded through the streets of Hamburg, Germany's second-largest city, calling for the country's transformation into an Islamic state governed by sharia law. The event proceeded after left-wing parties in Hamburg's legislature dismissed a petition from right-wing parties to ban it. Incredibly, the German government downplays and even shows support for the authoritarian threat to democracy posed by radical Muslims, who openly aim to dismantle Germany's constitutional framework. Meanwhile, the government is preoccupied with the perceived threats to democracy from the anti-immigration Alternative for Germany (AfD), whose popularity is largely driven by voters frustrated with the government's reluctance to take a firm stance against these very same Islamists.[12]

"Shall I not on that day, says the Lord, destroy wise men from Edom and discernment from the mountain of Esau?" (Obadiah 1:8). The Western nations, once led by wise leaders, will lack wisdom at the end of days. Oblivious to the Muslim terrorists infiltrating the borders of the United States and planning to overthrow the US government from the inside, President Biden focused on advocating for transgender rights and foolish debates about who qualifies as a "woman." "Now, therefore, I, Joseph R. Biden Jr., President of the United States of America, by virtue of the authority vested in me by the Constitution and the laws of the United States, do hereby proclaim March 31, 2024, [Easter Sunday], as Transgender Day of Visibility."[13]

"Your food they lay as a wound under you; there is no discernment in them (Obadiah 1:7). Edom foolishly gives its "bread," its foreign aid, to evil Ishmaelites who seek their destruction. For decades, the European Union and United States have gifted billions of dollars of "humanitarian aid" to Gazan Arabs, even as their terrorist government, Hamas, used that money to finance their terror operations against Israel and the West.[14] Similarly, President Obama's nuclear deal released $150 billion to the Iranian Mullahs, who promptly used the money to finance terror operations against American targets.[15] The "lack of discernment" among Western leaders is astounding. As Congressman Louie Gohmert once said, "We don't need to pay our enemies to hate us. They'll do it for free!"

As the West drifts further and further from belief in God and the Bible, its leaders lack the discernment to differentiate between ally and adversary. No longer possessing the Judeo-Christian values of truth, honesty and loyalty, Western governments are willing to support Iranian mullahs and other terrorist regimes dedicated to their own destruction, so long as it brings them short term political or financial gain. In November 2023, the Biden administration released $10 billion in frozen assets to the mullahs of Iran - the world's greatest sponsor of terrorism that bankrolled the slaughter of October 7 - hoping to bribe its leaders to avoid causing disruptions in the Middle East until after the U.S. presidential election in November 2024. Unsurprisingly, Biden's appeasement only emboldened the terrorist regime. Attacks by Iranian proxies on American forces in the Middle East immediately increased. On January 28, 2024, three U.S. service members were killed and at least 34 wounded in a drone attack by Iran-backed terrorists in northeastern Jordan, and on April 14, 2024, Iran launched a massive direct missile and drone attack on Israel.

During the State of Israel's early years, when the majority of the population was secular and dedicated to socialist ideals, some Western nations were supportive of Israel. But as young Israelis embrace their biblical heritage and become more traditional, religious and politically conservative, the West is moving in the opposite direction, growing increasingly secular and distant from God. Western leaders vilify religious politicians in Israel like Betzalel

Smotrich and Itamar Ben Gvir as "right wing extremists" because of their biblical worldview,[16] even as they cozy up to Palestinian Authority Chairman Mahmoud Abbas,[17] a Holocaust denier[18] and terror supporter.[19] The utter lack of "discernment from the mountain of Esau" is breathtaking.

The foolishness of Edom will be its undoing. Though the Western nations of Edom are extraordinarily powerful, their walls are crumbling. "And the fortress of the strength of your walls He humbled. He brought it low; it reached the earth down to the dust" (Isaiah 25:12). The Hebrew word for "fortress," "*botzrah*," is also the name of an Edomite city. God is warning Edom: "*Botzrah*, city of Edom - do not be arrogant because of the great height of your walls, for your walls are crumbling and you will soon be humbled!"[20]

Silence in the Face of Evil

"On that day you stood from afar, on the day strangers captured his possessions, and foreigners came into his cities, and on Jerusalem they cast lots; you, too, are like one of them" (Obadiah 1:11).

After Hamas murdered, raped and tortured over 1,200 Israelis on October 7, most of the Western nations of Edom either remained silent, ignoring the horrors perpetrated by Ishmael against God's people, or actively supported the terrorists. In the wake of October 7, international women's organizations like U.N. Women refused to condemn the brutal sexual crimes perpetrated by Hamas terrorists against hundreds of Israeli women. And where is the global outcry over the Israeli hostages taken by Hamas? The silence is deafening.

Obadiah could not be clearer. Those who remain silent in the face of evil "are like one of them." God will hold the cowardly nations of Edom accountable together with the Ishmaelite Muslims.

"You should not have rejoiced about the children of Judah on the day of their destruction, and you should not have spoken proudly on the day of their distress" (Obadiah 1:12).

Many in the West, like the mealy mouthed UN Secretary-General António Guterres, did not merely remain silent in the face of evil, but also aided and abetted it. Guterres justified the monstrous actions of Hamas, saying their barbaric slaughter "did not happen in a vacuum."[21] As Israel's war against Hamas drags on, Western political leaders like Elizabeth Warren[22] and many others absurdly accuse Israel of genocide, while rarely mentioning the actual acts of genocide perpetrated by Hamas.

"For the day of the Lord over all the nations is close; as you have done shall be done to you; your recompense shall be returned upon your head" (Obadiah 1:15). Obadiah prophesies that the time will come when the hundreds of thousands who celebrated the murder of Israelis on the streets of London will pay for their callousness. The day will come when American professors who called the slaughter of October 7th "heroic" and a "great achievement" will be held to account.

Soon enough, the hypocritical nations of the West will lament their evil doings, but by then it will be too late. "You should have thought about the day when you would receive payment from God for your evil deeds, for that day is coming sooner than you think."[23]

Whither America?

The reckoning for the West is approaching. Most European nations have already caved to Islamicism, cowering helplessly as brazen Muslims and their supporters take over the streets of London and Paris.

What about the ostensible leader of the West, the United States of America? Will the world's leading democracy join the ranks of Edom, turn its back on Israel and surrender to the tyranny of Islam?

In his Holocaust commemoration speech on May 7, 2024, President Biden spoke about the six million Jews slaughtered by the Nazis, saying "This ancient hatred of Jews didn't begin with the Holocaust. It didn't end with the Holocaust either. Or after - even after our victory in World War II. This hatred continues to lie deep in the hearts of too many people in the world and requires our continued vigilance and outspokenness. That hatred was brought to life on October 7th of 2023... People are already forgetting. They are already forgetting. That Hamas unleashed this terror. It was Hamas that brutalized Israelis. It was Hamas who took and continues to hold hostages. I have not forgotten nor have you. And we will not forget."[24]

Beautiful words. The only problem is that, like Esau once lied to his father Isaac, Biden lied to the Jews applauding him that day. His promise, "we will not forget," is contradicted by the entire thrust of his administration's policies.

After October 7, Biden did everything in his power to delay and blunt the IDF's war against Hamas. His administration cut off key military weapons from Israel, used diplomatic maneuvers at the United Nations to undermine

Israel and worked with Hamas' ally, Qatar, to pressure Israel to cave to Hamas' demands and accept defeat. His foreign policy team smeared Israel's efforts to destroy Hamas as "over the top" and arrogantly blamed Israel for civilian deaths in Gaza. Meanwhile, Biden did little in response to the antisemitic, pro-Hamas protests that broke out on college campuses in America. Only his Republican opponents pushed for accountability in universities.

President Biden's feigned virtuousness and betrayal of Israel would make Esau proud. It's a skill he honed for several decades, as Justice Clarence Thomas could attest. At the justice's Supreme Court confirmation hearings in 1991, Joe Biden promised to treat him fairly and honestly, just as he would later promise to stand by the Jewish state. Looking back, Thomas captured Biden's Edomite qualities perfectly: "Throughout my life I've often found truth embedded in the lyrics of my favorite records. At Yale, for example, I'd listened often to 'Smiling Faces Sometimes,' a song by the Undisputed Truth that warns of the dangers of trusting the hypocrites who 'pretend to be your friend' while secretly planning to do you wrong. Now I knew I'd met one of them: Senator Biden's smooth, insincere promises that he would treat me fairly were nothing but talk."[25]

Though the majority of Americans support Israel in spite of the Biden administration, over 50% of young people support the Hamas rapists and murderers who gleefully tortured Jewish women and children, "swept up by the pestilence of a false doctrine."[26] Tens of thousands of these young people rioted on college campuses across America in the spring of 2024, calling for "death to the Jews" and the destruction of Israel while physically assaulting Jewish students. As these young people grow older and assume the leadership of the nation, what kind of country will America become? Can these trends be reversed? Will they abandon the false gods they have been taught to worship?

Over a century ago, G. K. Chesterton described the way great nations and empires collapse from within. "For madness is a passive as well as an active state: it is a paralysis, a refusal of the nerves to respond to the normal stimuli… There are commonwealths… which pass from prosperity to squalor, or from glory to insignificance, or from freedom to slavery, not only in silence, but with serenity."[27] Will Americans awaken in time to rise up and reclaim their nation's future from the Edomites who are pushing this once great nation to the cliff's edge?

"Saviors shall ascend Mt. Zion to judge the mountain of Esau." One day, Israel will sit in judgment over Esau, and "the Lord shall have His kingdom" (Obadiah 1:21). How will America be judged? That remains to be seen.

CHAPTER 11:

DIVIDING GOD'S LAND: THE VALLEY OF JEHOSHAPHAT AND THE TWO-STATE SOLUTION

Imagine that a genocidal Mexican regime attacked the United States, overwhelming US border patrol with thousands of terrorist fighters, who then raped, tortured and murdered over 1,200 innocent American men, women and children throughout southern Texas, while also taking hundreds of Americans hostage. Imagine that 83% of Mexican-Americans living in Texas proudly told US pollsters that they approved of the attack on the United States, saying "violent American oppression of Mexicans will inevitably lead to resistance." And imagine that the President of the United States responded to this by calling for a "two-state solution," in which parts of Texas would be separated from the United States and become a new, independent country, a "Mexico 2.0," claiming that this will bring peace and stability to the region.

If what I'm saying sounds implausible, you haven't been paying attention to the war in Israel. After Hamas terrorists raped, tortured and murdered over

1,200 Jews on October 7, 83% of Arabs in Judea and Samaria stated that they support the atrocities that Hamas committed on that dark day. Yet in the wake of the slaughter, President Biden repeatedly declared that Israel must go forward with a "two-state solution," in which the Arabs of Judea, Samaria and Gaza - whose goal is the genocide of Israel - will be given an independent state in Judea and Samaria, the biblical heartland of Israel. On November 26, 2023, only six weeks after the worst slaughter of Jews since the Holocaust, the President said: "A two-state solution is the only way to guarantee the long-term security of both the Israeli and Palestinian people," adding that his administration "will not give up on working towards this goal."[1]

The President's two-state "delusion" would bring unspeakable horror and destruction upon the people of Israel. It would also directly violate God's will that the land of Israel belong to the people of Israel - a sin foretold thousands of years ago by the prophet Joel.

A Prophecy for Our Time?

At first glance, the Book of Joel awkwardly combines two completely disconnected prophecies. In the first two chapters, the prophet speaks of a plague of locusts that God would bring upon Israel in the immediate future, during Joel's lifetime. But in the last two chapters, Joel looks to the distant future, to the era of Gog of Magog, when God would bring His people back to the land of Israel after millennia of exile - in other words, about *our* generation. "For behold, in those days and in that time when I return the captivity of Judah and Jerusalem" (Joel 4:1).

Why is Joel's prophecy about the locust plague recorded in the Bible for posterity if it was already fulfilled thousands of years ago? What relevance does it have for us today? And how is it connected to chapters 3 and 4, which speak of the end of days? Clearly, there is more to the prophecy of the locusts than meets the eye.

The commentators explain that the prophecy of the locusts carries a hidden message that is critical to understanding the events at the end of time. "The first prophecy [of the locusts] refers to the four kingdoms [that will oppress the people of Israel throughout history]. The four types of locusts described by the prophet represent the four kingdoms that will devour Israel like locusts. For this reason, the prophet uses [military] language to describe the locusts, such as 'For a nation has ascended upon my land, mighty and innumerable' (Joel 1:6), comparing the locusts to horses, cavalry, chariots and conquering armies, all of which hint to the deeper meaning of this prophecy."[2]

With this approach, the connection between the two halves of the Book of Joel becomes clear. The first two chapters prophesy the history of Israel in exile, describing the four kingdoms that will oppress Israel - Babylonia, Persia, Greece, and, most terrible of all, the final kingdom of Edom and Ishmael. During this painful time, the people of Israel will miraculously survive, even as other nations rise, fall and disappear into the dustbin of history. "And the Lord was zealous for His land, and He pitied His people" (Joel 2:18). God will not allow His people to be destroyed, even if they sin terribly. "And you shall praise the Name of the Lord your God, Who has performed wonders with you, and My people shall never be ashamed. And you shall know that I am in the midst of Israel, and I am the Lord your God, there is no other; and My people shall never be ashamed" (Joel 2:26-27). God will always dwell among the people of Israel, even in their degradation and exile. The natural life cycle of nations does not apply to the people of Israel; they will survive against all odds, despite the best efforts of their enemies.

But then, after 2,000 years of desolation, God will miraculously bring the land and people of Israel back to life. "Have no fear, O land; rejoice and jubilate, for the Lord has performed great things. Fear not, O beasts of the field, for the dwelling places of the wilderness have become covered with grass, for the trees have borne their fruit, the fig tree and the vine have given forth their strength. And the children of Zion, rejoice and jubilate with the Lord your God" (Joel 2:21-23).

In the final two chapters, Joel elaborates on the end of days, when the nations who oppress Israel - particularly Edom and Ishmael - will be judged and punished. The time will come when God will make clear to these arrogant nations that He, and only He, is running the show. "And I will perform signs in the heavens and on the earth: Blood, fire, and pillars of smoke… And the Lord shall roar from Zion, and from Jerusalem He shall give forth His voice, and the heavens and earth shall quake" (Joel 3:3, 4:16).

Dividing God's Land

The first two chapters of the Book of Joel describe the nations' oppression of Israel, and how God will not allow His people to be destroyed. But it is the final chapter that speaks to our present moment, after the people of Israel have miraculously returned to their land. Even after the prophecies of return are fulfilled and Israel is once again an independent nation, the nations of the world will be unable to stop themselves from arrogantly meddling in the affairs of the Jewish state.

"I will gather all the nations and I will take them down to the Valley of Jehoshaphat, and I will contend with them there concerning My people and My heritage, Israel, which they scattered among the nations, and My land they divided" (Joel 4:2).

During the end times, the nations of the world will gather together to malign and attack Israel - a coalition of evil we are witnessing today before our very eyes. Edomite and Ishmaelite nations that should naturally be at odds with one another, including secular European countries and jihad-supporting Muslim nations, have joined together at the United Nations and the International Court of Justice to defame and slander Israel and support Hamas. There is nothing natural about this strange alliance. "I will gather all the nations" - all of this is part of God's plan, so that these nations may all be punished together at the end of days.

The verse speaks of two different sins that the nations will perpetrate against Israel and for which they will be held accountable. "My people... they scattered among the nations." This refers to the acts of antisemitism perpetrated against the vulnerable Jews who live in exile, scattered among the nations. Think of the thousands of Jews who are threatened each day throughout the world, afraid to walk the streets of New York, London and Paris while wearing a star of David necklace. Think of Jewish college students who have been attacked on university campuses across the United States, and the morally vacuous presidents of Ivy League universities who refuse to condemn threats of genocide against God's people. God will neither forget nor forgive this evil.

But the nations are also guilty of a second sin. "My land they divided." With extraordinary self-righteousness, the Western nations demand that Israel, a tiny nation the size of New Jersey, abandon Judea and Samaria and agree to the creation of an Arab terror state at the very center of the country.

The land of Israel - Judea, Samaria and Gaza included - is the biblical and historical homeland of the Jewish people, who have maintained a continuous presence in the land since ancient times. No other nation has ever governed the land of Israel as a local sovereign entity. No other people, including the Arabs currently living in these areas, have any historical claim to the land of Israel. There has never been a "Palestinian" national entity in the land. While Arabs who are loyal to the State of Israel may be granted full individual rights, there is no legitimate Arab national claim to any part of the holy land. Yet pompous western leaders like Joe Biden and Emmanuel Macron insist that Israel must divide its already small land and create yet another Arab terror state in its midst.

Conveniently, western leaders neglect to mention that the establishment of an Arab state in Judea and Samaria would lead to the expulsion of Jews from their ancient biblical homeland. Mahmoud Abbas, the terror-supporting chairman of the Palestinian Authority, has clearly and repeatedly stated that "in a final resolution, we would not see the presence of a single Israeli - civilian or soldier - on our lands."[3] Though over two million Arabs live as citizens with equal rights in Israel, a future Palestinian state in Israel's ancient heartland would be completely *judenrein*, or "cleansed" of Jews - a result that surely would have pleased Adolph Hitler.

For thousands of years, Jews have made enormous spiritual, economic and technological contributions to the world, even as they suffered endless discrimination and persecution. But instead of thanking the Jewish people, the nations will not rest until they succeed in taking away Israel's rightful inheritance. "The people of Israel have given much to humanity... It was we who saved humanity from dark and slavish idolatry, on the one hand, and weak, bloodless forgetfulness of God on the other... In return, the nations rewarded us handsomely: by robbing us of our land."[4]

"'And I will return the captivity of My people Israel, and they shall rebuild desolate cities and inhabit [them], and they shall plant vineyards and drink their wine, and they shall make gardens and eat their produce. And I will plant them on their land, and they shall no longer be uprooted from upon their land, that I have given them,' said the Lord your God" (Amos 9:14-15).

In these verses and dozens of others, God has made it abundantly clear: the land of Israel belongs to the people of Israel alone. Those who ignore God's will and try to divide His land will be brought "down to the Valley of Jehoshaphat" where God will "contend with them." But where is the Valley of Jehoshaphat, and why will the offending nations be brought there?

Many commentators explain that the Valley of Jehoshaphat is not an actual place, but rather a symbolic name representing the future judgment of the nations.[5] "Jehoshaphat" derives from the Hebrew word "*shaphat*," meaning judgment. Later in the chapter, this valley is referred to by a different name, the "Valley of *Charutz*," meaning the "Valley of Decision" (Joel 4:14), for it is there that "multitudes upon multitudes" of the nations who joined together in trying to divide God's land will be judged and their fate decided.

What will be America's fate? Will the United States continue pressuring Israel to divide its land in violation of God's will? Or will Americans reverse the follies of its conceited leadership and stand with Israel through the tumultuous events of the end of days? America's future hangs in the balance.

The Bill Comes Due

The punishment coming for the nations that betray the people of Israel will not be pretty. "Stretch out a sickle, for the harvest is ripe; come, press, for the winepress is full; the vats roar, for their evil is great... For the day of the Lord is near" (Joel 4:13-14). The enemies of Israel are compared to ripe crops that are ready to be harvested with a sickle. Just as the crops are ready to be cut, the time will soon arrive for Israel's enemies to be cut off and destroyed.

"And Egypt shall become desolate, and Edom shall be a desert waste" (Joel 4:19). "Egypt" represents the Arab nations of Ishmael, for Ishmael was both the son of an Egyptian woman[6] and took an Egyptian woman as his wife.[7] "Edom" refers to the Western nations that support the Muslim nations in their attacks on Israel. All of these nations will be punished for their sins in the Valley of Jehoshaphat.

"Because of the violence (*Hamas*) done to the children of Judah, because they shed innocent blood in their land" (Joel 4:19). Incredibly, Joel prophesies about the "*Hamas,*" the Hebrew word for violence, that the nations will commit against God's people. Could there be a clearer reference to the evil terror group Hamas, which committed unspeakable atrocities against Israel on October 7? For this evil, Iran and its allies - the peoples of Ishmael who fund and protect Hamas - will be made desolate. But so will the nations of Edom, the morally bankrupt Western nations that support Hamas' terror and enable the murder of even more Jews.

"Judah shall remain forever, and Jerusalem throughout all generations. Now should I cleanse? Their blood I will not cleanse, when the Lord dwells in Zion" (Joel 4:20-21). Though there can be atonement for the suffering, sorrow and harm that the nations caused Israel, God emphasizes that He will never forgive the nations for the Jewish blood they have spilled. For the sin of murder, there will only be revenge. "Let it be known among the nations before our eyes the revenge of the spilt blood of Your servants" (Psalm 79:10).

Every week, on the Sabbath morning, Jews pray: "May God avenge the spilt blood of His servants, as is written in the Torah of Moses, the man of God: 'O nations, gladden His people, for He will avenge the blood of His servants; vengeance will be repaid upon His enemies, and reconcile His land to His nation' (Deuteronomy 32:43). And in the words of His prophets it is written: 'Their blood I will not cleanse.'"[8] The division of God's land leads, inevitably, to the murder of Jews. Neither Israel nor God Himself will forgive the nations who gave funding to terrorists to murder Jews and create a Muslim terror state in Israel's biblical heartland. The blood of thousands of Jewish terror victims cries out for revenge.

"And I shall lay My revenge upon Edom by the hand of My people Israel, and they will do to Edom according to My wrath and according to My fury, and they will know my vengeance, says the Lord God" (Ezekiel 25:14).

Return of Israel and Prophecy

After the nations pay for their sins, the millions of Jews who still remain in exile will finally come home. "Behold I arouse them from the place where you sold them, and I will return your recompense upon your head" (Joel 4:7). Even those secular Jews distant from their heritage - the great majority of American Jews today - will spiritually awaken and return to God and their homeland.

"And it shall come to pass afterwards that I will pour out My spirit upon all flesh, and your sons and daughters shall prophesy; your elders shall dream dreams, your young men shall see visions" (Joel 3:1). Once they are back in their land, God will pour out His spirit upon His children, and prophecy will return to the people of Israel. For it is only in God's land that widespread prophecy is possible.[9]

The day is coming, sooner than later, when the peoples of the world will understand that Israel is not like other nations. God's people are not destined to be a military superpower, nor will they ever be more populous than their neighbors. The nations soon will see that God has called this people to prophesy and dream dreams, to serve as "a light unto the nations, to open eyes that are blind, to free captives from prison, and to release from the dungeon those who sit in darkness" (Isaiah 42:6-7).

PROPHECIES OF
Israel

CHAPTER 12:

PAIN, HOPE AND PROMISE

"Be not wroth, O God, so very greatly, and remember not iniquity forever; please look, all of us are Your people" (Isaiah 64:8).

Our lives will never be the same. The horror of October 7, when Hamas terrorists slaughtered, tortured, burned and raped over 1,200 innocent Israelis as we celebrated Simchat Torah, the final day of the Sukkot holiday, was more than a horrific war crime. It was an inflection point, the inauguration of a new era in history and God's plan for the world.

As I write, Hamas is still holding 134 of our sons and daughters hostage, and the brave soldiers of the Israel Defense Forces are still heroically fighting the heartless terrorists who perpetrated the greatest massacre of Jews since the Holocaust. It is too early to fully grasp the impact of October 7. But it is clear to all that it unleashed a powerful storm of love and hate, of good and evil, that has deeply shaken the people of Israel and reverberated in every corner of the globe.

After two thousand years of exile, the people of Israel finally returned home. In fulfillment of dozens of prophecies, God's people streamed to the land from all four corners of the earth. Miraculously, a land that lay devastated for generations was nurtured back to life. Step by step, Israel's resilient people transformed this tiny nation into a "villa in the jungle,"[1] a precarious island of democracy and economic success surrounded by Islamic jihadists dedicated to its destruction.

Creating this villa came at a steep price. For the entirety of its existence, Israel has been at war with neighboring countries and terror groups. Understandably, in the years leading up to October 7, many Israelis - particularly those who know little of the Bible and God's mission for His people - were spiritually exhausted. They wanted to be normal, "like all the nations" (I Samuel 8:5). They weren't interested in the fulfillment of prophecies or redemption. Many Israelis convinced themselves that peace was on the horizon, that deep down, the Arabs surrounding Israel also wanted peace. They were "a people gathered from the nations, acquiring livestock and possessions" (Ezekiel 38:12), a nation that wanted to do business, advance their careers and enjoy the simple pleasures of life.

But this was not to be. Israel is not destined to be a "normal" nation, the "Belgium of the Middle East." Ezekiel prophesied that as Israel buries its head in the sand, Gog of Magog and his many allies and proxies would declare an existential war of annihilation against Israel, forcing Israel to confront its destiny as God's chosen people. Gog will say, "I shall ascend upon a land of open cities; I shall come upon the tranquil, who dwell securely; all of them living without a wall, and they have no bars or doors. To take spoil and to plunder loot, to return your hand upon the resettled ruins and to a people gathered from the nations" (Ezekiel 38:11-12).

Prophecies that once seemed vague and fantastical are being fulfilled before our eyes - and it is happening quickly. Each day, Israel's enemies - the people of Ishmael and Edom - find new ways to brazenly undermine and assault her, militarily and diplomatically, as the United Nations cheer them on. The pace of the assault is dizzying; it is difficult to keep up with the news. But this, too, was prophesied. Speaking of the final redemption, Isaiah said: "I am the Lord, in its time I will hasten it" (60:22). The end of days will arrive "in its time," when the world is ready, even if it takes thousands of years. But when the moment comes, "I will hasten it" - the final steps of salvation will play out quickly and there will not be a long period of time from its beginning until its end.[2]

It is comforting to know that all of this is part of God's great plan for humanity, and that our suffering has a purpose. Still, the pain is searing. Israel is a small country. Everyone here has lost a friend, neighbor or loved one. Everyone knows someone who has been taken hostage.

Islamic jihadists glorify death and are happy to sacrifice their children for their "holy war" against Israel. But Israelis, the people of the Bible, celebrate life. For us, every son and daughter who dies defending our nation is a devastating sacrifice. Since October 7, thousands of Israeli families have been emotionally shattered, and the suffering of the hostages and their families cannot be captured in words.

Redemption is coming; we believe it, we see it and we yearn for its arrival. But why must we suffer so terribly before it comes?

Darkness before Dawn

When God first sent Moses to Pharaoh, Moses' attempt to help his people was a complete failure. Pharaoh looked at Moses with arrogance and disbelief: "Who is the Lord that I should heed His voice to let Israel out? I do not know the Lord, nor will I let Israel out" (Exodus 5:2). After rejecting Moses' demands, Pharaoh punished the Israelites. From this point onwards, the Israelite slaves would have to scatter across Egypt to collect the straw they needed to produce bricks - all while producing bricks at the same pace they had before.

When the Israelites inevitably failed to produce the required number of bricks, their leaders were physically beaten by Egyptian taskmasters. Understandably, they blamed Moses and Aaron for their suffering: "May the Lord look upon you and judge, for you have brought us into foul odor in the eyes of Pharaoh and in the eyes of his servants, to place a sword into their hands to kill us" (Exodus 5:21). Overcome with grief and guilt, Moses turned to God with harsh words of his own: "O Lord! Why have You harmed this people? Why have You sent me? Since I have come to Pharaoh to speak in Your name, he has harmed this people, and You have not saved Your people" (Exodus 5:22-23).

Moses, of course, had a fair point. Hadn't the Israelites suffered enough? Why did God send Moses to Pharaoh only to make the situation even worse than it already was?

God responded to Moses by urging him to step back and see the bigger picture. "Now you will see what I will do to Pharaoh, for with a mighty hand he will send them out, and with a mighty hand he will drive them out of his land" (Exodus 6:1). In other words, God told Moses: "Do not look at this situation with only your human eyes of flesh and blood. Do not look only at this particular moment in time. Yes, My people are suffering terribly at this moment, but their suffering is necessary to bring a salvation far greater than anything you can imagine. Pharaoh's success is ephemeral, and will ultimately bring him an even more devastating punishment. The people are suffering, and so it's understandable that they demand redemption *now*, immediately. They can be forgiven. But you, Moses - you are their leader who has come to redeem them, to lift their spirits and form them into a nation. You must be able to see the bigger picture.³ You must believe that justice will be served and good will prevail!"⁴

In the painful story of Joseph and his brothers, Joseph told them that they would not be permitted to return to Egypt unless they brought their youngest brother Benjamin with them. But when Judah asked his father Jacob for permission to bring Benjamin to Egypt, Jacob initially refused and blamed Judah for the situation: "Why have you harmed me, by telling the man that you have another brother?" (Genesis 43:6). The sages explain that these were the only foolish words that Jacob ever uttered: "The Master of the Universe is orchestrating events to make Joseph king of Egypt and save Jacob's family, and he says 'Why have you harmed me'!"⁵ Though Jacob did not understand it at the time, God put him through the painful saga of Joseph and his brothers in order to save his family from starvation.

"It is a general principle: whenever God wishes to elevate a person or the world, whenever God wishes to bring good to the world, it only occurs through a deep and hidden plan. For this reason, pain inevitably precedes the good. As the sages themselves say, 'God gave three gifts to Israel, and all of them came through suffering. These are: the Torah, the land of Israel and the world to come.'"⁶

God said to Jacob: "I am the Lord, the God of Abraham your father, and the God of Isaac; the land upon which you are lying - to you I will give it and to your seed" (Genesis 28:13). The Chassidic masters explain: The land that you dig your nails into, the land you grab onto without moving from it, however painful it may be - I will give it to you and to your descendants.⁷

As it was for Moses and Jacob, so it will be in our own time, the era of redemption. "For distress shall come like a river; the spirit of the Lord is wondrous in it. And a redeemer shall come to Zion, and to those who repent of transgression in Jacob, says the Lord" (Isaiah 59:19-20). If you see a generation that experiences great suffering, it is a sign that you must look for the redeemer.⁸ "For distress shall come like a river" refers to the war of Gog of Magog, who will bring distress to the land of Israel. But then the spirit of God will arrive and erase Gog and his allies from the world, and then "a redeemer shall come to Zion."⁹

"I heard and my bowels quaked, my lips quivered at the sound; rot entered into my bone, I trembled where I stood. Yet I wait calmly for the day of distress, for a people to come to attack us" (Habakuk 3:16). The commentators explain that according to tradition, Israel can only be redeemed through great evil and suffering, the "birth pangs of redemption" that are like the suffering of a mother before she gives birth. The greater the suffering, the greater is the hope that salvation will soon arrive and the child will be born. "As a pregnant woman comes near to give birth, she shudders, she screams in her pangs, so were we because of You, O Lord" (Isaiah 26:17).[10] Along these lines, the sages predict that the son of David will not come until the wicked kingdom spreads over the entire world for nine months.[11]

The prophet Isaiah famously states that the redemption will usher in a time of peace, when "they shall beat their swords into plowshares and their spears into pruning hooks; nation shall not lift the sword against nation, neither shall they learn war anymore" (Isaiah 2:4). But the prophet Joel uses almost identical language to state the opposite: "Announce this among the nations, prepare war, arouse the mighty men; all the men of war shall approach and ascend. Beat your plowshares into swords and your pruning hooks into spears" (Joel 4:9-10). The *goal* of "Beat your swords into plowshares" can only come through the *means* of "Beat your plowshares into swords." The path to peace and redemption will be through war, as the sages say: "In the sixth year there will be thunderings, in the seventh war; at the end of the seventh the son of David will come. For war is the beginning of redemption."[12]

Rabbi Hillel Rivlin of Shklov was a disciple of the great Rabbi Elijah of Vilna who risked his life to move to Israel in 1809. He understood that redemption would not come easily. "During the height of the activities that signal the beginning of redemption - the ingathering of the exiles, the rebuilding of Jerusalem, the redemption of truth, and the sanctification of God's name - that is the time when the 'other side,' the forces of evil, will become stronger in an effort to disturb and impede the process by uprooting the truth and preventing the sanctification of God's name. About this is written: 'They have shamed the footsteps of Your anointed one' (Psalm 89:52)... We should know in advance that the more this holy enterprise grows and increases, the more the 'other side' gains strength, in order to place impediments by means of its major weapon: uprooting the truth."[13]

Over two hundred years later, an Israeli soldier who lost both of his legs in the Gaza war also understood that suffering is the price we must pay to move forward to the next step of redemption - and he was not resentful that he had to personally pay the price. When Prime Minister Netanyahu visited Elisha Meidan at the Sheba Medical Center, Elisha told the Prime Minister, "I want to tell you that I'm happy, I don't regret at all that I entered Gaza despite the fact that I'm past the draft age. I was proud to fight for my friends who fell. But it's important to me that I didn't lose my friends and suffer my injury for no reason. We have to destroy them and be victorious, we can't concede. And we can't return to October 6th from any standpoint – from a security standpoint as well as the rift in society."[14]

"Even [for] the way of Your judgments, O Lord, have we hoped for You" (Isaiah 26:8). Though God's judgments strike His people, they still hope and yearn for Him.[15] Elisha Meidan, and many others like him, are the true heroes of Israel, willingly sacrificing life and limb so that God's righteous judgment is served.

Redemption entails suffering, making it difficult to realize that we are actually progressing towards the great day when all mankind will know God. "My beloved resembles a gazelle or a fawn of the hinds; behold, he is standing behind our wall, looking from the windows, peering from the lattices" (Song of Songs 2:9). How does "My beloved" resemble a gazelle? The sages explain: "Just as a gazelle is seen but then disappears from view, so too will the redemption be revealed but then be hidden from their view."[16] In the story of Israel's return to its land, there have been many ups and downs. With every setback, the redemption "disappears from view," while every step forward that follows is a revelation of the redemption.

On August 24, 1929, Arab terrorists brutally slaughtered 69 defenseless Jews in the holy city of Hebron, raping, maiming and torturing hundreds of others. The ruling British authorities did nothing to stop the attack, which sparked several other attacks by Arabs against Jews throughout the land. Understandably, Jews in Israel and throughout the world were devastated.

In response to the massacre, Chief Rabbi Abraham Isaac Kook encouraged his fellow pioneers: "Those who have paid attention to the growth of the Jewish settlement in the land, from its first steps until now, can see with their own eyes how every setback and decline that we suffered led to greater growth and development… that out of the darkness there came a great light and the Jewish presence in the land would expand its borders… We have seen that the redemption was hidden but then revealed itself. From this we must learn to hope for better days, so that our spirits do not fall even after the horror committed today by the wicked and impure murderers who maliciously killed our lofty pious ones in Jerusalem, Hebron, Safed, and in the other holy places. This 'disappearing' of the redemption is indeed terrible and frightening, surpassing in its darkness all the setbacks we encountered when we began to rebuild the land. But it is clear that in proportion to the great hiddenness a great light will be revealed. We are certain that from this terrible blow will sprout forth a great healing."[17]

As Jews everywhere reel from the massacre of October 7, Rabbi Kook's words are needed now more than ever. We must believe that from this great darkness there will sprout forth a great healing. God has never before abandoned Israel - and He will not do so today.

"Go, My people, come into your chambers and close your door about you; hide for but a moment, until the wrath passes" (Isaiah 26:20). During the great and final war against Gog of Magog, the people of Israel will suffer but only for a short time. As the storm of war rages, the prophet encourages his people to take strength, "hide from the storm" and enclose themselves in repentance and the performing of acts of kindness for one another. Very soon, this storm will pass and better days will come.[18] From within the darkness, Israel will take strength.

"Strengthen weak hands, and make firm tottering knees... Be strong, do not fear; behold our God, [with] vengeance He shall come, the recompense of God, that shall come and save you" (Isaiah 35:3-4).

The Great Question

God has spoken. Redemption will come through suffering; there is no other way. But *why* must Israel suffer? Why must Israel endure the excruciating pain of war before she finally enjoys peace?

"I am the Lord and there is no other. Who forms light and creates darkness, Who makes peace and creates evil; I am the Lord, Who makes all these" (Isaiah 45:6-7). If God is good, why does He create evil?

In 1778, in the midst of the Revolutionary War, John Adams set off for France together with his precocious nine-year-old son, John Quincy. As they embarked on the harrowing trip across the Atlantic, Abigail Adams gave her son a farewell letter. She wrote: "These are the times in which a genius would wish to live. It is not in the still calm of life, or the repose of a pacific station, that great characters are formed. The habits of a vigorous mind are formed in contending with difficulties. Great necessities call out great virtue. When a mind is raised, and animated by scenes that engage the heart, then those qualities which would otherwise lay dormant, wake into life and form the character of the hero and the statesman."[19]

True growth requires resistance. When a business is challenged by a well-run competitor, it is forced to improve in order to compete. In sports, teams require tough competition to hone their skills and improve. Without resistance, our potential remains untapped and is never actualized.

This is the purpose of evil in the world. It attacks the good, forcing the good to use all of its strength as it rises up against the evil. This is particularly true when the forces of good are dormant or have deteriorated and fallen. When good is not progressing and fails to actualize its potential, forces of evil oppose the good and force it to awaken, move forward and develop in ways it never imagined it could.

Looking back, we can all see the way this principle has played out in our personal lives. In retrospect, we can see how the most difficult and bitter periods of our lives were crucibles of growth. Reflecting on the premature death of her parents from illness and the terrible hardships she and her brother were forced to endure throughout her childhood, Mary McCarthy writes: "If they had both lived, we would have been a united Catholic family, rather middle-class and wholesome... I can see myself married to an Irish lawyer and playing golf and bridge, making occasional retreats and subscribing to a Catholic Book Club. I suspect I would be rather stout... The fact is, Kevin and I are the only members of the present generation of our family who have done anything out of the ordinary... Was it a good thing, then, that our parents were 'taken away,' as if by some higher design?"[20]

This is the deeper and hidden purpose of evil. It is not meant, God forbid, to defeat the good, but rather to force the good to discover and develop its latent potential. God does not take joy in our pain and would prefer that we actualize our potential without any need for suffering. Nor does God Himself bring evil directly upon us. "I have created a destroyer to destroy" (Isaiah 54:16). God created a "destroyer" in the world, and when people sin, the "destroyer" attacks. There once was a king who placed a guard dog in front of a dangerous cliff to prevent people from falling. If a person came too close to the cliff, the dog would jump on him and bite him. The king himself would not bite, but rather the dog. Nevertheless, the dog was placed in this position by the king's orders for a righteous purpose - to prevent people from falling over the cliff into the abyss. It pained the king when a person was bitten by the dog, and it is certainly not the king's fault that the man is suffering. The bitten man brought the suffering upon himself.

What is true for the individual applies equally to a nation. "In days to come Jacob shall strike root, Israel shall sprout and blossom, and the face of the world shall be covered with fruit" (Isaiah 27:6). The people of Israel are like a seed that must sprout and grow into an awesome fruit-bearing tree from which all of humanity will be nourished - a tree of righteousness, beauty and life. The tree of Israel began to take root at the time of Abraham, taking root and growing slowly from then until now. When the nation lost its way and its growth stalled, evil descended upon us, awakening us to our true purpose, and forcing us to fight for God and His teachings.[21]

The suffering did not destroy us; it made us stronger. "But as much as they would afflict them, so did they multiply and so did they gain strength" (Exodus 1:12). The more the Egyptians persecuted the Israelites, the more children they had and the stronger they became! "The children of Israel sighed from the labor, and they cried out, and their cry ascended to God from the labor. God heard their cry, and God remembered His covenant with Abraham, Isaac, and Jacob." (Exodus 2:23-24). The crushing labor caused the people to cry out to God; without it, God would not have heard their cry. Israel's suffering is not a sign of disfavor. To the contrary, God brings suffering upon His people because He desperately loves them and desires that they draw closer to Him. "Only you did I love above all the families of the earth; therefore, I will visit upon you all your iniquities" (Amos 3:2).

The dramatic story of the binding of Isaac ends with some of the most banal verses in the entire Bible. "And it came to pass after these matters, that it was told to Abraham saying: "Behold Milcah, she also bore sons to Nahor your brother" (Genesis 22:20). The Bible then devotes several verses to listing the twelve forgettable sons of Nahor, Abraham's nephews, a shift purposely designed to make the reader pause and reflect. Returning from Mount Moriah and the binding that shaped the destiny of Abraham and Isaac, God wanted Abraham to know that his fate and that of his children would be different. "Abraham! You have a brother named Nahor, who did not recognize the Creator of the world, did not give the world a new Bible, and did not discover a system of ethics. Rather, he lived a comfortable, plain, egotistical life, contented with himself and his sheep. He, too, had sons, but without all the hardships, torments, waiting and growing old, without the whole zigzag of paradoxes, enigmas and disappointments. [Twelve sons], one after the other... The world has no need of them; they will not implement any ideals, will not take on any missions. A simple man of flesh and blood, an idolater who built no eternity, was given twelve sons without pain and suffering, while you, Abraham – with all your aspirations and hopes, revolutionary life's journey, and chosenness – were forced to go down the martyr's path, without any assurance that you would not have to go through a new binding the next day."[22] This was the destiny of Abraham, and this is the destiny of Israel.

"What would we be missing if David had been handed the kingship of Israel on a silver platter, without all of the suffering he endured along the way? Did Jacob not promise the royalty to Judah at the very beginning of the nation's history? Why did God first appoint Saul, a temporary king? Had Samuel not anointed David in secret while Saul still ruled; had David not been forced to play the harp for Saul; had Saul not jealously pursued David for years; had David lived a calm and quiet life without great suffering, what would we be missing? The Book of Psalms!"[23]

We have so many burning questions for God, and so much we cannot understand. God does not think or act the way we do. "You thought that I would be like you. I will contend with you and set up before your eyes" (Psalm 50:21). The time will come when we realize we only had questions because our eyes were closed.[24]

Until our redemption is complete, evil will always have a critical role to play. But its role is even greater at times of transition, when the nation of Israel must progress to a new stage of development. Change is necessary but frightening, and so we are hardwired to resist it. Building a new home requires the demolition of the imperfect house we have grown comfortable in. Left to ourselves, we might never find the courage to change even when it is obvious that we must. Evil destroys our illusions, exposing the weaknesses of the status quo and pressuring us to move forward. "It is a time of distress for Jacob, through which he will be saved" (Jeremiah 30:7).

The people of Israel stand at a crossroads. After 75 years of independence, we stand at the beginning of a new stage of redemption. Secular Zionism, which drove the heroic early pioneers to settle the land and bring it back to life, has run out of steam. A once secular and socialist nation is yearning for God. A people that longed to be normal, like all the other nations, are now ready to take the next step in fulfilling its mission as God's chosen people. "The blossoms have appeared in the land, the time of singing has arrived, and the voice of the turtledove is heard in our land" (Song of Songs 2:12).

Rabbi Abraham Isaac Kook wrote, "Redemption is part of Israel's essence, the possession of God's treasured nation. But it must develop within her… so that the thorns and thistles that sting her [and detract from its power] are removed, so that Israel can unite with her beloved and the kingdom of heaven and the kingdom of earth are brought together in unity."[25] Israel possesses the power to lead humanity back to God, but it must first be cleansed of "thorns and thistles," the spiritual flaws that are preventing Israel from fulfilling its messianic mission.

Our enemies have arrayed themselves against us, believing they will finally succeed in wiping Israel off the face of the earth. But "the Lord frustrated the counsel of nations; He put the plans of peoples to nought" (Psalm 33:10). Instead of crushing Israel's spirit, they have awakened the lion of Israel. "And the house of David shall be like God, like the angel of the Lord before them" (Zechariah 12:8). Each day of the Gaza war brought new stories of awesome Jewish heroism, of soldiers and citizens writing new chapters of the Bible before our eyes. And though the battle has just begun, multitudes of our enemies have already paid the price for their evil, for God has "returned upon them their violence" (Psalm 94:23).

I Am with You

"And their king passed before them, and the Lord was at their head" (Micah 2:13). God rules the world, and so we are assured of victory. But how will we find the strength to reach the finish line?

"In all their affliction, He does not afflict them" (Isaiah 63:9). Even as God allows us to suffer at the end of days to bring the redemption to its conclusion, He lessens our pain by saving us from our enemies. Israel's enemies inflict pain upon God's people, but the pain is lessened for God will not allow them to drive us from the land as the Babylonian and Roman empires did in earlier times. "For this is to Me [as] the waters of Noah, as I swore that the waters of Noah shall never again pass over the earth, so have I sworn neither to be wroth with you nor to rebuke you" (Isaiah 54:9). Just as God swore to never again bring the floodwaters of Noah upon the earth, so will Israel never be sent into exile again.[26]

But there is another meaning to Isaiah 63:9. Though the verse is written using the word "*lo*," meaning "does not" afflict them, our tradition is to read the word as "*loh*," meaning "to Him." Read this way, the verse has a different meaning: "In all their affliction, He was afflicted." Though He must allow us to suffer so that we reach our potential, God suffers with us. "And His soul was grieved by the toil of Israel" (Judges 10:16).

"'I loved you,' said the Lord, and you said, 'How have You loved us?'" (Malachi 1:2). We remain uncertain of God's love. Could He possibly love us, with all of our flaws? We assume He only loves us because of our holy forefathers and foremothers. And so God tells Malachi, the final prophet, to tell His people once again: I love *you*, not only your ancestors![27]

Every day, Jews pray, "With unbounded love You have loved us, Hashem our God; and with surpassing compassion have You had compassion on us."[28] God's love for His people is unbounded and surpassing. "You performed awesome deeds for which we did not hope" (Isaiah 64:2). When our forefathers cried out in pain from slavery in Egypt, they could never have hoped for the awesome deeds that God would soon perform for them. His salvation was so great, it was beyond the scope of their imagination.

As the great war of Gog of Magog descends upon Israel, as nation after nation turns its back on us, let us remember: God will bring us a salvation we cannot even dream of!

"He made an end to darkness" (Job 28:3). God determined how many years the world will dwell in darkness, but the darkness will come to an end.[29] "The people who walked in darkness, have seen a great light; those who dwell in the land of the shadow of death, light shone upon them" (Isaiah 9:1). There is a light at the end of the tunnel; we will not forever walk in darkness. "Rejoice not against me, my enemy; although I have fallen, I will rise; although I will sit in darkness, the Lord is a light to me" (Micah 7:8).

CHAPTER 13:

STEP BY STEP: A REDEMPTION THAT CANNOT BE RUSHED

Following the slaughter of October 7, Israeli forces struck back at Hamas from the air and later through a wide-scale ground invasion of Gaza. Yet even after half a year of battle in Gaza, the war goes on. Uprooting Hamas terrorists hiding behind human shields and underground in terror tunnels is a slow and dangerous business. From the start, Israeli leaders warned the public that the war against Hamas would likely continue for at least a year, and possibly much longer - a massive strain on families, the economy and society as a whole.

We believe that God will stand with Israel and that the war against Ishmael *will* be won. But how long will it take?

In many ways, the war in Gaza that began on October 7 symbolizes Israel's century-long struggle against Ishmael. Every year, Arab terrorists commit thousands of terror attacks against Israelis. Every week, we hear the same terrible story - another Jew murdered, and several others critically injured. IDF forces seek out the terrorists, eliminate them and destroy their homes. But killing Arab terrorists is like a game of Whac-A-Mole; as soon as you kill one, two more pop up. And so the process repeats itself again and again, with more lives lost and more shattered families. It is the war that never ends.

In retrospect, even the Six-Day War, which seemed to be a happy exception to this rule, fits this pattern. In the Six-Day War, Israel overran its Arab enemies, liberated Jerusalem and conquered Judea, Samaria, the Golan Heights and the Sinai Peninsula - all in under a week. But in hindsight, it's now clear that the Six-Day War was only the opening salvo of a decades-long battle for sovereignty over Judea, Samaria, and Gaza - a war that is still raging today. Israel won the opening round of fighting, but tenacious Arab terrorists have continued the fight to this day.

This is not, God forbid, to deny Israel's unbelievable growth and accomplishments since the Six-Day War. In 1967, not one Jew lived in Judea and Samaria; today, there are over half a million Jews who make Israel's biblical heartland their home. Even as the war rages on, prophecies are undoubtedly being fulfilled.

But why is the fulfillment of prophecy happening so slowly? "On that day, I will raise up the fallen Tabernacle of David, and I will close up their breaches, and I will raise up its ruins, and build it up as in the days of yore" (Amos 9:11). With all the kindness God has bestowed upon His people since the founding of the modern State of Israel, "that day" still seems like a distant dream.

Though we are deeply grateful for God's blessings - blessings our great-grandparents could only dream of - we still wonder: can this really be redemption? Why is Israel's redemption so slow, so "natural," that most of humanity does not yet see God's hand in its return to the holy land? Why doesn't God redeem His people with open miracles and wash away the Ishmaelites like He did to the Egyptians at the splitting of the sea?

The Long Sunrise

Every Passover, for seven full days, observant Jews remove all bread and leavened products from their homes and offices and replace it with *matzah*, the "bread of affliction." "For seven days you shall eat... *matzot*, the bread of affliction, for in haste (*b'chipazon*) you went out of the land of Egypt, so that you shall remember the day when you went out of the land of Egypt all the days of your life."

When the Israelites left Egypt - or, more accurately, when Pharaoh *ordered* them to leave Egypt - they did so "*b'chipazon*," in haste. They were forced to leave so quickly on their great journey into the wilderness that there was no time to let their dough rise. This haste was no accident, but a fundamental part of the

Exodus miracle, so much so that Jews must eat *matzah* every year to remember the hastiness of the redemption. "Why do we eat this *matzah*? The dough of our ancestors did not have time to rise when God, the King of Kings, appeared and redeemed them" (Exodus 12:39).

Though haste was a defining element of the Exodus, the opposite is true of the final redemption. "For not with haste (*chipazon*) shall you go forth and not in a flurry of flight shall you go, for the Lord goes before you, and your rear guard is the God of Israel" (Isaiah 52:12). Isaiah could not be more explicit: "People of Israel, I know that you long for a speedy deliverance, a second Exodus. But hear me clearly; your redemption will be slow!"

In an oft-cited passage, the sages emphasize Isaiah's point. "Rabbi Chiyah Rabah and Rabbi Shimon ben Chalafta were walking in the valley of Arbel just before dawn and they saw the first lights of the coming dawn piercing the sky. Rabbi Chiyah Rabah said to Rabbi Shimon ben Chalafta: 'Thus is the redemption of Israel – at the beginning, it comes little by little, but as it continues it will grow bigger and bigger.'"[1]

The slow pace of Israel's ingathering to the land was prophesied by Jeremiah. "I will take you, one from a city and two from a family, and I will bring you to Zion" (Jeremiah 3:14). With the advent of modern Zionism, the people of Israel did not return to the land all at once, but rather one by one, led by brave young pioneers who left most of their family behind in small Eastern European and North African villages. The joy of returning to the land would be tempered by the pain of separation. Many of the Jews who left for the holy land in the 19th and early 20th centuries never saw their loved ones again.

The same mix of emotions is found in Isaiah's description of Israel's return: "Behold, these shall come from far; and, lo, these from the north and from the west, and these from the land of Sinim. Sing, O heavens, and rejoice, O earth, and mountains burst out in song, for the Lord has consoled His people, and He shall have mercy on His poor. And Zion said, 'The Lord has forsaken me, and the Lord has forgotten me'" (Isaiah 49:12-14)

Is Isaiah describing a joyous time ("Sing O heavens, and rejoice") or a painful time ("And Zion said, 'The Lord has forsaken me'")? The answer, it seems, is both. The ingathering of the exiles will come before the building of Zion. When the exiles return to the land from the four corners of the earth, Jerusalem will still be desolate. Isaiah describes this contrast powerfully. On the one hand, the exiles will return from all over the world, and nature, the heavens and the earth, will rejoice and recount this awesome miracle. But on the other hand, he describes how Jerusalem at this time will sit as a widowed woman in her mourner's shawl, grieving because her husband left and forgot about her.[2]

This is precisely what occurred after Israel was reborn in 1948. Hundreds of thousands of Jews joyously returned to Israel after the founding of the state. But the Temple Mount in Jerusalem remained under Jordanian control for 19 years, like "a widow in her mourner's shawl," until Israel liberated the city in 1967. Redemption takes time to develop; the pain and brokenness of two millennia of exile will not be healed all at once.

The prophet Micah also spoke of redemption in stages. "And you, tower of the flock, the tower of the daughter of Zion - to you it shall come; yea, the first government shall come, a kingdom to the daughter of Jerusalem" (Micah 4:8). The commentators explain that 'the daughter of Zion' refers to the tribes of Judah and Benjamin, who were exiled from Zion after the destruction of the second Temple by the Romans. These tribes will be the first to be gathered to the land. Afterwards, there will come 'the first kingdom,' a small government that will lead Israel in the way they were ruled during the era of the Book of Judges. Finally, there will arise "a kingdom to the daughter of Jerusalem," a permanent kingdom that is the kingdom of the house of David.[3] Just like the words of Isaiah, Micah's prophecy has come true before our eyes. Today, Israel is governed by a "first government," a parliamentary democracy that will serve as a bridge to the government we are yearning for, the kingdom of the House of David.

In the early 20th century, the Zionist movement was dominated by secular and socialist Jews who had forsaken the Bible and the ways of their ancestors. Many leading rabbis of the time opposed the Zionists; though they longed for Zion, they wanted no part of a movement or a nation that refused to live according to God's will. In retrospect, their attitude was understable but mistaken.

In his famous Valley of Dry Bones prophecy, Ezekiel makes clear that Israel's physical redemption will come before its spiritual rebirth. "So I prophesied as I was commanded, and there arose a noise when I prophesied, and behold a commotion, and the bones came together, bone to bone! And I looked, and lo! sinews were upon them, and flesh came upon them, and skin covered them from above, but there was still no spirit in them. Then [God] said to me, 'Prophesy to the spirit, prophesy, O son of man, and say to the spirit, 'So says the Lord God: From four sides come, O spirit, and breathe into these slain ones that they may live'" (Ezekiel 37:7-9).

First, the bones, flesh and skin come together, representing the physical reconstitution of the people of Israel in the land of Israel. When Israel was refounded in 1948, this prophecy was fulfilled. "But there was still no spirit in them." In 1948, when the State of Israel was founded, secular Jews dominated the new country while religious Jews were a politically and culturally irrelevant minority.

For Israel's spirit to be revived, a second prophecy was required. "So says the Lord God: From four sides come, O spirit, and breathe into these slain ones that they may live." Step by step, and at first imperceptibly, Israelis drew closer to tradition. After almost thirty years of uninterrupted rule by the left-wing socialist parties Mapai and Labor, Israel's growing and religiously traditional Sephardic population elevated Menachem Begin to power in 1977. Though Begin was not an Orthodox Jew, his public embrace and obvious respect for Jewish tradition marked a sea change in Israeli politics - a change that reflected the beginning of the nation's return to God.

Since then, the shift towards traditional religious belief and observance in Israeli society has only picked up steam. Once a rare sight in the Israeli Knesset, *kippot*[4] are now commonly worn by the majority of the governing coalition, who proudly profess their religious observance. As Western nations become increasingly secular, Israel is moving in the opposite direction.

Israel's 75-year progression from a primarily secular and socialist nation to a religiously traditional and conservative society increasingly aware of its redemptive mission is nothing short of astounding. The shift has come about slowly over decades and it is by no means complete. But it is happening. "In the end, the community of Israel will awaken… to seek the soul of the rebirth of the nation, its redemptive secret, which is hidden in the depths of the present but which is the driving spirit of our people's urge to welcome the renewal of our glorious future."[5]

The long and slow path to redemption will often be painful and difficult. "A song of ascents. When the Lord returns the returnees to Zion, we shall be like dreamers" (Psalm 126:1). These ascents, or steps, "hint to the levels and stages of Israel's redemption and return. Not in one generation or even one era… but the combination of all the events in Israel's history can be seen as chapters in the treatise of redemption. 'He will go along weeping, carrying the valuable seeds; he will come back with song, carrying his sheaves' (Psalm 126:6)." There are chapters of crying and tears, and chapters of joy and celebration. But all of them are necessary to bring redemption.[6]

"Be exceedingly happy, O daughter of Zion; Shout, O daughter of Jerusalem. Behold! Your king shall come to you. He is just and victorious; humble, and riding a donkey" (Zechariah 9:9). The redeemer is described as riding on a donkey, a parable laden with meaning. As Bilaam the prophet could attest, donkeys have a mind of their own. Not only does the donkey move slowly, but he is also stubborn and will sometimes refuse to move forward or kneel under his master. Sometimes you have to hit the donkey, while other times he moves forward as directed.[7] Can there be a better symbol of our long and rocky path to redemption?

Redemption will not suddenly arrive after generations of stagnation or cyclical patterns of advancement and regression lacking direction or purpose. In each generation there is another ascent, from level to level, even when it seems that the world is declining and moving further away from God. At times, the progress is evident to all. But in many generations, advancement is only possible through destruction and suffering. Sometimes progress follows a straight line, while other times it unfolds along a broken and twisty path. But the direction is unmistakable. Step by step, everything is rising upwards, towards a fixing of the world and the future redemption.[8]

A Miraculous but Costly Redemption

If the final redemption is destined to be slow, why did God redeem Israel from Egypt in haste?

Typically, the process of national liberation unfolds gradually; people establish institutions, infrastructure, and a system of governance. Nations evolve organically, drawing from diverse cultural influences. India, once part of the British Empire, was profoundly influenced by its former colonial masters. India adopted Western ideas of liberty, equality, and human rights, and its legal system and educational culture were shaped by the British. Newly emerging nations inherit and assimilate the accomplishments of their predecessors.

When God redeemed the people of Israel from Egypt, His goal was to create an entirely new kind of nation - "a kingdom of priests and a holy nation" (Exodus 19:6). To accomplish this goal, it was crucial for the nation of Israel to be conceived and nurtured in an environment free from the contamination of Egyptian values and culture. Israel needed to establish itself on completely holy, divine foundations, independent of any external cultural influence.[9]

But how could this be achieved? The only way to save the Israelites from being influenced by their Egyptian masters was through a hasty and sudden redemption - an unnatural national birth. If they had left Egypt more naturally and slowly, the people would have inevitably assimilated Egyptian values and culture. And so the nation was literally forced to flee, with no time for their dough to rise.[10]

Like helpless babies, the Israelites lacked the ability to fight back against Pharaoh and liberate themselves. The entire Exodus, from the Ten Plagues to the splitting of the sea, was orchestrated by God alone; the people were passive observers. "And the Lord brought us out from Egypt with a strong hand and with an outstretched arm, with great awe, and with signs and wonders" (Deuteronomy 26:8).

Though the hasty redemption was necessary, it also came at a cost. The shift from slavery to freedom was both sudden and drastic, and the people of Israel were simply not ready for what came next.

After God split the sea and wiped out the entire Egyptian army in one fell swoop, "Moses led Israel away from the Red Sea" (Exodus 15:22). The sages explain that Moses had to force the people, against their will, to move forward in their journey to Sinai. The Egyptians had adorned their steeds with ornaments of gold, silver, and precious stones, and after they drowned, their valuables washed up on the shores of the sea. Instead of excitedly continuing the journey to Sinai, the Israelites obsessively scoured the shores of the sea, looking for treasure.[11] After witnessing an open miracle that would reverberate across the entire world, all they could think about was gold! The nation was "young" and spiritually immature.

Throughout their wanderings in the desert, the Israelites frequently complained and struggled to live up to the holy mission assigned to them at Mount Sinai. God took them out of Egypt, but like immature adolescents, it would take time for them to mature and learn to live as a free, healthy and independent nation.

Forty years later, when the next generation of Israelites was about to enter the holy land, Moses promised them, "For the Lord, your God, is the One Who goes with you, to fight for you against your enemies, to save you" (Deuteronomy 20:4). Though they were better prepared than their parents' generation, the Israelites remained unsure of themselves and their abilities. "Don't worry," said God, "you won't have to do much. I'll take care of your enemies for you." Just as God saved them in Egypt, so would He destroy their enemies in the land of Israel. "And He brought us to this place, and He gave us this land, a land flowing with milk and honey" (Deuteronomy 26:9). Once again, God was the primary actor, while the people were relatively passive. As the painful stories of the Book of Judges make clear, it would take hundreds of years for the nation of Israel to mature and reach its potential.

A Partnership with God

Why must redemption come slowly? Why can't redemption arrive all at once, so that all of humanity will recognize it and turn their eyes to God? Is our slow redemption a sign that we do not deserve a greater and more miraculous redemption?

"On that day, says the Lord, you shall call Me 'my husband' (*ish*), and you shall no longer call Me 'my master' (*ba'al*)" (Hosea 2:18). In the end times, God's relationship with Israel will change. "[Israel will be] like a bride in her father-in-law's house, and not like a bride in her father's house."[12] What is the meaning of this change?

In Hebrew, two different words are used for "husband" - "*ba'al*" and "*ish*," each with different connotations.

A "*ba'al*" can also mean "master," and it implies an imbalanced form of marriage. A *ba'al* actively "acquires" his wife; all she needs to do is extend her finger so he can place a ring upon it. This was a common form of marriage in ancient times, when a man could buy himself a wife for six camels - whether she liked him or not. "They broke My covenant, although I was a master (*ba'al*) over them" (Jeremiah 31:31). Israel broke its covenant with God and no longer wishes to be His people? Too bad. Israel's *ba'al*, her "master - husband," will enforce the covenant, whether Israel wants it or not.

A marriage of this sort, common in earlier generations, might be deemed successful or even happy. But in one way, it is fundamentally lacking. When there is an imbalance in power, when one spouse is more dominant, husband and wife cannot fully and completely unite as one. True unity requires each spouse to freely choose and actively move towards the other. And so the sages describe this sort of relationship as a "bride in her father's house." Though the bride may love her husband, she remains in her parents' home, separated from her husband. There is a distance between them; the marriage has not yet been consummated.

Complete attachment to one another is only possible when each spouse equally desires the other, when both husband and wife turn to and choose one another of their own free will. This is the marriage of *ish* (husband) and *isha* (wife). The very name "*ish*" implies a marriage of equality. *Ish* (husband) and *isha* (wife) are essentially the same word in masculine and feminine forms. Such a marriage is compared to "a bride in her father-in-law's house," in which the marriage is complete and husband and wife live together in unity. This is the unity that Israel, the "bride," will achieve with her beloved, God, at the end of times. "On that day, says the Lord, you shall call Me 'my husband' (*ish*), and you shall no longer call Me 'my master' (*ba'al*)."

How will the imbalance in Israel's relationship with God be corrected? "For the Lord has created something new on the earth, a woman shall go after a man" (Jeremiah 31:21). In the end days, the dynamic in the relationship will shift. Israel, the "woman," will no longer be passive, but rather rise up and actively pursue God, her "husband." "Afterwards shall the children of Israel return, and seek the Lord their God and David their king, and they shall come trembling to the Lord and to His goodness at the end of days" (Hosea 3:5). At the end of days, the tables will turn; it will no longer be God who seeks out His people, but rather His people who seek out God.

Herein lies the difference between the redemption from Egypt and the final redemption. The Exodus was a one-sided redemption, through which God became Israel's *ba'al*, her "master-husband." It took place on God's timeline, in haste, "but it did not last, for nothing that happens quickly is lasting… for when something happens with haste it is because there is a fear that a window of time will pass and the opportunity will be lost."[13] The Exodus had to happen quickly, but because it happened that way it was imperfect and could not be an everlasting redemption.

The final and eternal redemption, however, in which Israel asserts its proper place in its marriage with God, will happen little by little, along a human timeline. Unlike the Exodus, which was conducted entirely by an infallible God, the final redemption involves the efforts of flawed and fallible human beings. Inevitably, there will be failures and delays, deviations from God's will, for human beings are slow learners. Real and lasting change in the hearts of man cannot happen quickly. "That guiding principle of the redemptive process as one of 'little by little,' which determines the process of Israel's redemption in all its practical and spiritual aspects, also comprises within it all the interruptions and delays, and the retreats and failures, and all the entanglements of this entire process and the chain of events in this gradual course."[14] "For not with haste shall you go forth and not in a flurry of flight shall you go" (Isaiah 52:12).

When God redeemed Israel from Egypt, the Israelites were like a helpless baby who can do nothing for itself. In such a redemption, when all of the effort is expended by God and Israel is purely a recipient of God's charity and kindness, there is an element of embarrassment. Any spiritually healthy person who is forced by difficult circumstances to accept charity feels, deeply and painfully, that charity is the "bread of shame."[15] In the millennia since the Exodus, the people of Israel matured in their relationship with God and began to rectify the imbalance in their relationship with Him. Through the step-by-step process of the final redemption - in which Israel must make great sacrifices to return to the holy land, build it up, and fight its enemies - Israel will become true partners with God and earn a redemption without shame.[16] "It is not a weakness but rather a strength that the redemption of Israel comes little by little."[17]

"Therefore, so has the Lord God said: 'Behold, I have laid as a foundation a stone in Zion, a fortress stone, a precious cornerstone, a foundation well founded; the believer shall not hasten'" (Isaiah 28:16). The building of Jerusalem begins with only one stone, as it says, "I have laid as a foundation a stone in Zion," for God desires to test us. But this stone will be "a precious cornerstone, a foundation well founded." Israel's mission is to fulfill the command of broadening: "Widen the place of your tent, and let them stretch forth the curtains of your habitations and do not spare!" (Isaiah 54:2). Israel must not be passive nor turn back because of any obstacle.[18]

"And it came to pass after these things, that God tested Abraham" (Genesis 22:1). When God tests us, He is not giving us a difficult exam to see if we will pass it. God's tests are meant to reveal a person's inherent qualities and transform their latent potential into tangible reality, so these qualities are openly expressed. Abraham was blessed with awesome potential, but it needed to be actualized.[19] Similarly, the potential for "redemption is embedded in the nature of Israel."[20] The long and difficult process of redemption, the many tests that Israel is forced to confront at the end of days, are meant to reveal the greatness that lies within God's people and the other nations, so that they may assume their place as God's partners in redeeming the world. This is why God sends enemy nations to attack Israel. "These are the nations which the Lord left through whom to test Israel" (Judges 3:1).

Though the process is painful, the final redemption will ultimately be greater than the redemption from Egypt. "Days are coming, says the Lord, when they shall no longer say, 'As the Lord lives, Who brought up the children of Israel from the land of Egypt,' But, 'As the Lord lives, Who brought up and Who brought the seed of the house of Israel from the northland and from all the lands where I have driven them, and they shall dwell on their land' (Jeremiah 23:7-8).

Though a step-by-step redemption is clearly God's plan, many religious Jews cling to a belief in "magical messianism,"[21] wherein the Messiah will reveal himself on a magic carpet and fly all the Jews from America and the rest of the exile to Israel, where a nice-sized home, a big backyard and two cars will be waiting for every family. They believe redemption will arrive suddenly; that after two thousand years of exile, a great light will shine from above and God will redeem us all.[22] They want redemption to come down to them "fully prepared by God, with the gates of the land opened for them through miracles, so that all the Israelites scattered across the globe will be brought to Zion, their holy city, on wings of eagles."[23] They refuse to accept that God wants Israel to take the initiative, to make a leap of faith by returning to the land, and to build a strong, vibrant nation with the courage and willpower to overcome its enemies.

"Who is blind but My servant, and deaf as My messenger whom I will send?... There is much to see but you do not observe, to open the ears but no one listens" (Isaiah 42:19-20). Who are the people who are blind to the miraculous events of the last 150 years? Who are the people who do not hear the sounds of redemption? These are God's servants, religious Jews who continue to serve Him and fulfill His commandments! "You have to be blind not to see the revolutions in the world and among the people of Israel over the last fifty years, all of which were brought about by God to bring redemption to Israel."[24]

"Who is blind but My servant?" It is one of the great tragedies of modern Jewish history that so many religious Jews choose to remain in exile even as ancient prophecies are fulfilled in the holy land. These Jews remain in exile, blind to God's movements in history, because they are waiting for a second miraculous Exodus from Egypt. In doing so, they are missing the actual redemption taking place before their eyes.[25] As one of Israel's leading rabbis wrote following the miracle of the Six-Day War, "It is a great sin to pretend that nothing has happened and to ignore the great acts of God."[26]

By ignoring the awesome events of our time and insisting that God wants them to remain in exile, Jews today repeat the sin of the Jews of Babylonia who chose to remain in exile even after King Cyrus decreed that they could return home to Jerusalem and rebuild the Temple. "Had Israel ascended from Babylon [united] like a wall, the Temple would not have been destroyed a second time."[27] They also repeat the sin of the ten spies, who preferred to stay in the wilderness - where they enjoyed open miracles, like manna falling from heaven - than to enter the land of Israel and engage in the long, painstaking process of building up the land. By rejecting the land of Israel, they also rejected God's chosen plan for redemption.

The great Jewish thinker Maimonides states: "In the future, the Messianic king will arise and renew the Davidic dynasty, restoring it to its initial sovereignty... The Bible testified to his coming, as Deuteronomy 30:3-5 states: 'God will bring back your captivity and have mercy upon you. He will again gather you from among the nations... Even if your Diaspora is at the ends of the heavens, God will gather you up from there... and bring you to the land.'"[28] In other words, the Bible gives us a sign by which we will know when redemption is on its way: when the people of Israel return to the land, it is proof that redemption is here.[29]

"I will bring your descendants from the east, and gather you from the west; I will say to the north, 'Give them up!' And to the south, 'Do not keep them back!' Bring My sons from afar, and My daughters from the ends of the earth" (Isaiah 43:5-6). Soviet Jews from the north, Ethiopian Jews from the south, American Jews from the west, and the *Bnei Menashe*[30] from the east - the great ingathering prophesied thousands of years ago is being fulfilled today.

In 1948, there were 600,000 Jews in Israel. By 2023, 75 years after the founding of the State, there were over 7 *million* Jews in Israel - an astounding elevenfold increase in Jewish population. Even with Israel's high birth rate, growth of this magnitude is only possible because of the ingathering of Jews from all over the world. Since 1948, about 3.5 million Jews have made *Aliyah* to Israel - an indisputable fulfillment of biblical prophecy and proof that we are living in a time of redemption. In time, we pray, the remaining Jews of exile will understand that the final redemption requires our own initiative and that we must partner with God to hasten its coming.

"The smallest shall become a thousand and the least a mighty nation; I am the Lord, in its time I will hasten it." (Isaiah 60:22). This verse, perhaps more than any other, is central to Jewish eschatology.

"Rabbi Joshua the son of Levi pointed out a contradiction. It is written concerning the redemption: 'In its time [the redemption will come],' while it is also written, 'I [the Lord] will hasten it!'" Which one is it? Will redemption arrive at a designated time at the end of history, or will God hasten to bring it sooner? If they are worthy, I will hasten it. if not, redemption will come at the due time."[31]

The sages interpret this verse as presenting two mutually exclusive ways for redemption to arrive. Either redemption will arrive "in its time," or God "will hasten it." But the simple reading of the verse, that when the time for redemption arrives God will hasten it, should not be ignored.[32] Simply understood, the phrase "in its time" does not refer to a particular point in time, but rather to a *process* of redemption - a process that will occur step by step, through a partnership of God and man. This process of redemption, this "time," has a certain flexibility. For God will "hasten it" if we intensify our own efforts to bring it about. It is as if God is saying, "Please, do your part to bring redemption, for the time has already come. Push, hurry, and I will shorten the duration of the redemptive process.[33] "I am the Lord, in its time I will hasten it."

The renewal of Jewish life in Hebron after the Six-Day War began on the first night of Passover in 1968. A group of sixty idealistic pioneers, including several young men who would later become Israel's leading rabbis,[34] rented the Park Hotel and celebrated the first Passover Seder in Hebron since 1929, when Arab rioters massacred 67 Hebron Jews and the British ordered all Jews to leave the city. Also in attendance was Moshe Shamir, a secular left-wing author who stuck out like a sore thumb among the group of right-wing, religious activists. Nevertheless, Rabbi Haim Druckman asked Shamir to share some thoughts appropriate to the festival. The others in attendance braced themselves; who knew what this man might say!

Shamir spoke about one of the highlights of the Passover Seder, the song "*Dayenu*," "It would have been enough." In each stanza of the song, we recall another kindness that God performed for the people of Israel and proclaim "It would have been enough" - that this kindness alone would have been reason enough for celebration.

Shamir asked a classic question about the *Dayenu* song. "The fourteen verses of *Dayenu* have drawn the attention of the commentators throughout the ages. Why should we imply that we could forgo even one of the gifts given to us by God? How would we have gotten along at all without every one of them?" As an example, we sing "If God had given us the Bible, and had not brought us into the land of Israel - it would have been enough!" But is that really true? Would receiving the Bible, but not the land of Israel, really have been enough?

The author continued, "The truth is that this song has only one aim: to teach us how each and every generation of Jews tends to settle for the achievements of the past, to settle for what its forefathers had accomplished — and to rest on its laurels, with no aspiration for anything not achieved thus far. Even today, in our time, right here in Israel - we have that same tendency to say *Dayenu*, 'it would have been enough for us.' The State of Israel? *Dayenu*. A unified Jerusalem and liberated Hebron? *Dayenu*. Wasn't it just last year at the Passover Seder, only a month before the Six-Day War, that we said, 'If God had given us Israel but had not given us Jerusalem and Hebron — *Dayenu*, it would have been enough'? We must know that there will be many more "*Dayenus*" before we reach the final and complete redemption." Deeply moved, Rabbi Druckman stood up and kissed Shamir on his forehead. [35]

In every generation, it's up to us to take another step forward. Redemption is in our hands.

Do Not Fear the Long Road

G.K. Chesterton once wrote that "An optimist is a man who looks after your eyes, and a pessimist is a man who looks after your feet... For there might, perhaps, be a profitable distinction drawn between that more dreary thinker who thinks merely of our contact with the earth from moment to moment, and that happier thinker who considers rather our primary power of vision."[36]

When we view the events of our time "from moment to moment," the situation appears bleak. The Jewish state is diplomatically isolated, global antisemitism is growing exponentially, and Israel is surrounded by millions of radical Islamists committed to its destruction. But the "realistic" pessimists are missing vision. When we step back and reflect on the larger arc of history, on the undeterred progression of the redemptive process, we find reservoirs of strength we never knew we possessed.

People with vision, who understand that redemption is a long and complicated process, are people of *patience*. Giants of the spirit embody this patience; they remain focused and committed to their goals over years and decades. But those who demand things 'now' are small people who worship at the altar of immediacy. "'Peace now,' 'Redemption now,' 'Security now' everything now, now, now. We must strengthen our patience! Patience does not mean giving up. Patience is tied to the desire that everything should be fixed, but with the understanding that it will happen step by step. [A redemption that is] step by step is not weakness. To the contrary, it is the highest form of strength."[37]

We cannot know how the redemption will unfold, but one thing we know for certain is that it will continue along its slow and natural course so that we may have the opportunity to partner with God in bringing it. We should not expect a ball of fire to descend from the heavens and consume Ayatollah Khamenei in Iran or a mysterious plague that will harm only Hamas terrorists but leave the people of Israel unscathed. Israel will continue to battle its enemies over time and, God willing, grow stronger and stronger with each passing year. The step-by-step process of redemption demands sacrifice, courage, spiritual growth and most of all, patience and faith. But make no mistake - it is happening.

It is easy to lose heart, to despair over the long road that still lies ahead. It may very well be that our generation will not live to see the complete and final redemption that we long for. It is possible that the Temple will not be rebuilt in our generation, and that we are destined to live the rest of our days in a seemingly endless war with the people of Ishmael. But this is no reason to lose heart.

"And it was in the heart of David my father to build a house for the name of the Lord, the God of Israel. And the Lord said to David my father, 'Since it was in your heart to build a house unto My name, you did well that it was in your heart. Nevertheless, you shall not build the house; but your son that shall come forth out of your loins, he shall build the house for My name'" (I Kings 8:17-19). David yearned to build the Temple with his own hands - but it was not to be.

How did David go on with his life, knowing he would not live to see what most desired? He prayed: "Concerning Solomon. O God, give Your judgments to a king and Your righteousness to a king's son" (Psalm 72:1). The sages explain David's prayer: "Said David before the Holy One, Blessed is He, 'I accept the afflictions for myself, but as for Solomon, give Your kindness to the son of the king.'"[38] David understood that it was his destiny to endure the suffering and struggles necessary to elevate Israel and prepare them for the building of the Temple. Though David himself did not live to see the Temple, he was ready to "accept the afflictions" so that his son, Solomon, could enjoy peace and blessing.

We are the "David generation." It is our destiny to fight so that our children and grandchildren can live in peace and build the Temple we dream of. Painful as it may be, we take strength in knowing that redemption is assured - that better days await the people we love.

Though the war against Hamas, Hezbollah and Iran drags on with no end in sight, the people of Israel remain strong. Throughout the country there are signs hanging out of windows and taped to fences that share the same profound message: "*Am Yisrael lo mefached miderech arucha,*" "The people of Israel are not afraid of a long road."

CHAPTER 14:

JEWS AND ISRAELIS: LABOR PAINS ON THE WAY TO REDEMPTION

When Benjamin Netanyahu first became prime minister in 1996, he won with a simple slogan coined by some of his Habad supporters: "*Netanyahu: Good for the Jews.*" The morning after Netanyahu's surprising victory, Shimon Peres, the outgoing prime minister, summarized his defeat with one terse statement: "The Jews defeated the Israelis."

Peres understood that the Oslo Accords and the wave of Arab suicide bombings, the hot-button issues of the time, were disguising the true battle for power in Israeli society. As Yair Lapid would later write about the Gaza Disengagement, "It was not despite the settlers but because of them. It was never about the Palestinians… There was a completely different motive: over the past twenty years, the Religious Zionists made extensive use of the secular nation to fulfill a series of political and mostly religious aims… but Israelis don't like being anyone's mules, no matter who's riding them."

In 1977, when a reporter asked Menachem Begin what kind of prime minister he intended to be, he said: "The good Jewish kind." It was an identity that Begin carried with him to the end of his life. Tellingly, he chose to be buried in a simple grave on the Mount of Olives, the traditional cemetery of the

"Jews," instead of Mount Herzl, alongside modern Israel's other great leaders.[1]

The tension between the two halves of modern Israeli society, between the largely traditional and right-wing "Jews" and mostly secular and left-wing "Israelis," bubbled over in the spring of 2023 during the mass left-wing protests against judicial reform. Most of those protesting judicial reform were not particularly conversant with the details of the proposed reforms, but they made up for their lack of knowledge with extraordinary passion. With sincere conviction and genuine fear, they shouted "Save our country!" What they really meant, however, was "Save the secular Israel we and our parents grew up with!"

Since its founding as a primarily secular state in 1948, Israel's population has dramatically changed. Unlike the United States, which grows increasingly secular with each passing year, Israel's younger generation is *more* religious than its parents' generation. Politically, the power dynamics have shifted dramatically since the left-wing Labor Party dominated Israel during the first thirty years of statehood. Secular Israelis, who have fewer children than religious Jews, are now unable to form a governing coalition without the help of Arab parties or right-wing voters disaffected with their own leaders. Understandably, secular Israelis feel they are losing control of "their" country - and they are afraid of the consequences.

Redemption in Stages

Dr. Pinchas Polonsky, a Russian-Israeli Jewish philosopher, argues that the first three biblical kings - Saul, David and Solomon - represent a three-part messianic process, in which each phase embodies the core values and aspirations of successive generations within the people of Israel.[2] According to this framework, the Book of Samuel, which tells the story of Kings Saul and David, is uniquely significant for our time. It is the blueprint for redemption, a book that can guide the people of Israel through the labor pains of redemption.

Though Saul, David and Solomon were individuals, the parallel stages of the final redemption will not necessarily be led by an individual. Instead, there will be whole generations that correspond to each of these unique leaders. "A star has gone forth from Jacob, and a *tribe* will arise from Israel which will crush the princes of Moab and uproot all the sons of Seth" (Numbers 24:17). In his interpretation of Bilaam's prophecy, Rabbi Haim ibn Attar explains that the redemption will not arrive through an obvious sign from Heaven nor through one particular individual, but rather "a tribe will arise from Israel" - large segments of the nation itself will bring redemption through its combined efforts.[3]

The vast majority of Israelis today descend from the tribes of Judah, Benjamin and Levi, though fragments of some of the ten lost tribes have been found and returned to Israel.[4] Nevertheless, even among the descendants of Judah, Benjamin and Levi, there are different "tribes" of modern Israelis that express similar inclinations to all twelve biblical tribes of Israel. Secular Israelis possess the characteristics of Joseph and the ten northern tribes, while religious Jews possess the characteristics of Judah.[5]

Saul, the first king of Israel, pursued security and stability, successfully achieving these objectives by uniting the nation and fortifying their control over the land of Israel. Spiritual aspirations, however, were not at the forefront of his agenda, and so he made no effort to restore the Tabernacle to its prior glory.

In Dr. Polonsky's framework, King Saul represents the first stage of the final redemption, the secular pioneers who led the Jewish people's herculean efforts to return to their homeland, settle the land and establish the modern State of Israel. Like Saul, the secular pioneers - the "Israelis" - showed little interest in religion. Their goal, like the people of Saul's time, was to establish a state so "That we also may be like all the nations; and that our king may judge us, and go out before us, and fight our battles" (I Samuel 8:20). Their priorities were sovereignty and security.

Saul, of course, was not the only Israelite king to prioritize physically building up the land over spiritual concerns. The sages ask: "Why did King Omri [the father of Ahab] merit sovereignty [over the ten northern tribes of Israel]? Because he added a city to the land of Israel, as it is written, 'And he bought the mountain of Samaria from Shemer for two talents of silver; he built up the mountain and called the name of the city which he built, after the name of Shemer, the lord of the mountain - Samaria'" (I Kings 16:24). Though "Omri did what was bad in the eyes of the Lord, and he was more wicked than all those that preceded him" (I Kings 16:25), he succeeded in building up the land and strengthening the people of Israel, which was no small achievement. Most of modern Israel's early leaders followed in the footsteps of Omri; though they were not religious believers, they dedicated their lives to the success and security of Israel as part of the first stage of the final redemption.

Despite its great accomplishments, the secular Zionism that drove Israel's pioneers to settle the land under extremely difficult circumstances has lost its energy and drive. The very same secular Israelis who fulfilled Jeremiah's prophecy "and the children shall return to their own border" (Jeremiah 31:16) were also responsible for uprooting God's children from the holy land through the 1993 Oslo Accords and the 2005 Disengagement from Gaza. Prime Minister Ariel Sharon, who encouraged and supported the establishment of Jewish settlements in Judea, Samaria and Gaza in the 1980s, forcibly removed all Jews from Gaza and northern Samaria in 2005. Lacking a strong belief in God and the Bible, Sharon's commitment to building up the land was tenuous and crumbled under international pressure, and so the builder became a destroyer.[6] Like Saul, Sharon's failures made clear that the people of Israel require a different kind of leader.

King David was an altogether different sort of king. More than any other ruler in Israel's history, David was uniquely sensitive to God's will, prioritizing God's honor above his own. Facing Goliath, he said "Who is this uncircumcised Philistine that he should defy the armies of the living God?" (I Samuel 17:26). By the end of his long reign, he not only brought security and stability to Israel, but also a religious renaissance.

David represents the second stage of redemption, when the people of Israel will experience a religious revival and rediscover their unique purpose and national mission as God's chosen nation. This second phase - the rise of the "Jews" - has already begun. The current generation is open to the teachings of Judaism in a way its parents' generation was not. Even before October 7, thousands of "secular" Israelis would attend the concerts of religious Israeli superstar Ishay Ribo, clearly inspired by his proudly biblical songs and teachings, and groups of idealistic Orthodox Jews launched religious revivals in what were once militantly secular Israeli cities.[7]

David's extraordinary successes paved the way for his son, Solomon, to initiate the third phase of redemption: building the Temple in Jerusalem and spreading belief in God and the Bible to other nations. We have not yet reached this final Solomonic stage of the redemption, but these lofty goals no longer appear as fantastical as they once did. Little by little, we are drawing closer.

A Painful Transition

Our current moment mirrors the conclusion of the initial redemption phase - the reign of Saul - and the commencement of the second phase, marked by the religious revival under King David. Just as Saul feared David's growing popularity and sought to eliminate him, today's leading "Israelis," the established secular Zionist leadership, are doing everything they can to hold onto power and to discredit the burgeoning religious community's political goals. For years, the IDF has refused to promote many highly qualified religious officers who refuse to toe the leadership's leftist line.[8] Meanwhile, Israel's Supreme Court uses a self-perpetuating selection process to ensure the court remains ideologically rigid and left-wing, giving secular justices the power to reverse the policies of conservative governments to the detriment of Israel's religious population.[9]

How can Israel's religious community, the "Jews" who personify the reign of David, navigate this painful transition from the first to the second stage of redemption? How can they lead Israel into a new era of religious identity and revival, without descending into a devastating conflict with the "Israelis," the people of Saul?

Thankfully, the Book of Samuel charts a path forward. Whereas most of David's military battles against foreign foes are summarized in one short chapter (II Samuel 8), *twenty* chapters are dedicated to the dramatic story of the painful transition from the reign of Saul to the moment when David is finally accepted as king over all of Israel.

If the playbook for defeating Israel's external enemies is, at least in theory, relatively simple,[10] the internal struggle between Saul and David was emotionally charged, extraordinarily complex, and a process that played out over many years. Our generation must study these chapters with great care, for David's response to Saul's persecution is meant to guide us today to ensure Israel does not descend, God forbid, into civil war.

Humility, Empathy and Strength

In Jewish consciousness, King Saul will always be the king who failed. The glorious beginning of his reign, his anointing at the hands of Samuel and his early military victories contrast sharply with the darkness that typified the end of his reign: his lack of trust in God during the war against Amalek, his persecution of David and his horrific slaughter of the priests of Nov.

However, an honest assessment of Saul demands that we also appreciate his successes - accomplishments that played a critical role in the destiny of Israel. By uniting the nation and bravely defending it in battle against its enemies, Saul laid the foundation for David's future accomplishments. A king who truly loved his people, Saul fought and ultimately died to defend them, setting a powerful example of bravery and self-sacrifice.

Though Saul's dramatic downfall damaged his reputation, one man never lost sight of Saul's greatness. Even as Saul repeatedly attempted to kill him, David maintained a deep respect for Israel's first king. As a young man in Saul's royal household, David considered himself unworthy of marrying the king's daughter. "Who am I, and what is my life, or my father's family in Israel, that I should be son-in-law to the king?" (I Samuel, 18:18). And though Saul and his army pursued David through the wilderness of Ein Gedi with the clear goal of murdering David, David refused to harm the king, crying out, "I will not put forth my hand against my lord; for he is God's anointed... After whom will the king of Israel come out? After whom will you pursue? After a dead dog, after a flea!" (I Samuel 24:10,14).

David was a greater man than Saul; he, not Saul, was destined to lead the people of Israel. But he nevertheless appreciated and valued Saul's critical contributions to the nation, and refused to engage him in combat.

Israel's ascendant religious community finds itself in a similar situation to that of David. After decades of taking the back seat to larger and more influential constituencies, the growing religious community now wields significant cultural and political power. But as soon as the "Jews" prevailed at the ballot box, the "Israelis" responded with jealousy and fear, blocking highways with burning tires and staging weeks-long protests. Like King Saul, they sense their power is slipping away, and they are afraid of what will happen to the secular Israel they have always known. They believe that safeguarding their own, secular vision of Israel necessitates preventing their religious brethren who adhere to "outdated principles" from acquiring political power and imposing their religious way of life on the secular people of Tel Aviv.

None of this is fair or even logical. The "radical religious settlers" - a group to which I personally belong - have no interest in imposing Iranian-style theocracy. Nevertheless, we must do everything in our power to empathize with the "Israelis" and appreciate their fears, as David did for Saul.

First, we must not forget the awesome accomplishments of Israel's secular community, just as David never lost sight of Saul's greatness. To a great extent, it was the parents and grandparents of secular Tel Avivians who drained the swamps and built up the holy land after millennia of neglect, and for that, we must be forever grateful. There would be no Israel to fight over if not for them. Religious Jews must acknowledge that the great physical contributions of secular "Israelis" are the foundation upon which they hope to build a nation dedicated to God.

Second, we must try to put ourselves in their shoes. Tragically, too many secular Israelis were raised without an appreciation for the holiness and beauty of Judaism and the Bible. From their perspective, Judaism threatens their freedom and their way of life. It's not shocking that a secular community accustomed to controlling the media and the levers of power will find the prospect of a Knesset full of beards, sidelocks and yarmulkes to be truly frightening. That said, if we make the effort to empathize with and understand their fears, we can begin to allay them and ultimately overcome their misperceptions.

Third, like David, we must strike a delicate balance between empathy and standing up for ourselves. David did not meekly allow Saul to kill him, and religious Jews must not cave to the demands of the secular minority. We must find a way to stand up for ourselves and our principles without, God forbid, fighting back with anger.

Most importantly, we must remember that we will reach the final phase of our redemption only by bringing the tribes of Benjamin and Judah together in unity. When David first fled the house of Saul, he met secretly in the middle of the night with Samuel the prophet. According to the sages, David and Samuel studied the Bible together, analyzing its verses to determine the precise location in the territory of Benjamin where the future Temple would be built.[11] As Moses prophesied: "And of Benjamin he said, 'The Lord's beloved one shall dwell securely beside Him; He protects him all day long, and He dwells between his shoulders'" (Deuteronomy 33:12). It was Saul's tribe, the tribe of Benjamin, that would one day host God's Temple. David did not yearn to defeat Saul, but rather to partner with him in building a home for God on earth.

Who will Walk in Front?

Jews and Israelis must unite, but who will lead?

"*Tzibbur*," the Hebrew word for "community," consists of three letters - *tzadi, bet, reish* - which can also be understood as an acronym. *Tzadi* stands for "*tzaddik*," a righteous person. *Bet* stands for "*beinoni*," an average person. And *reish* stands for "*rasha*," an evil person. A community, a "*tzibbur*," consists of all three kinds of people. Even evil sinners have a place in the community, and there are times when their contributions are critically important for the broader welfare of society. But a society can only function if it follows its proper order and the righteous assume leadership. The letters of "*tzibbur*" are spelled in the proper order - the righteous first, then the average people, and lastly, the sinners. If the order is reversed and the sinners assume leadership, the word "*tzibbur*" is reversed and becomes "*rovetz*," meaning "crouching." When sinners assume leadership, "Sin is crouching (*rovetz*) at the door" (Genesis 4:7).[12]

As Jacob made clear before his death, the tribe of Judah is destined to lead the people of Israel. "The scepter shall not depart from Judah" (Genesis 49:10). Initially, all of Israel accepted David and Solomon as their kings. Tragically, this national consensus fell apart when Jeroboam became king of the ten northern tribes, turned away from God and refused to allow the northern tribes to worship at the Temple in Jerusalem. Still, the sages explain that God did not give up on Jeroboam: "After the Holy One, blessed be He, had seized Jeroboam by his garment and urged him, 'Repent, and then I, you, and David the son of Jesse will walk in the Garden of Eden.' Jeroboam asked: 'And who shall be at the head?' God replied: 'The son of Jesse shall be at the head.' 'If so,' [said Jeroboam,] 'I do not desire it.'"[13]

God offered Jeroboam the chance to "walk in the Garden of Eden with David," to work together with the tribe of Judah to bring the people of Israel to redemption and the glory of God to the entire world. But to the question, "And who shall be at the head?", there could only be one answer: David and the tribe of Judah! Only David, the "Jewish" king, can lead the nation. Jeroboam was "a mighty man of valor" and a "diligent worker" (I Kings 11:28), but only David, who yearned to "dwell in the house of the Lord all the days of my life" (Psalm 27:4), is capable of leading God's people so they may fulfill their mission as God's chosen nation. As Ezekiel writes when describing the future unity of the tribes of Israel, "And My servant David shall be king over them, and one shepherd shall be for them all" (Ezekiel 37:24).

But Jeroboam would not yield. His jealousy overwhelmed him, and with him, the ten northern tribes, the "Israelis," fell into a terrible spiritual decline that ultimately led to their exile from the land. Without Judah's leadership, the leadership of the "Jews," the "Israelis" lose direction, forgetting their greater mission and national destiny.

To heal this pain, we await an "Israeli" leader like Jonathan, son of Saul, who was humble enough to accept that David must lead. Jonathan should have feared and resented David, for he was Saul's eldest son and next in line to be king of Israel. Yet Jonathan acknowledged with a full heart that David was meant to be king, symbolically giving his own royal garments to his beloved: "Then Jonathan made a covenant with David, because he loved him as his own soul. And Jonathan stripped himself of the robe that was upon him, and gave it to David, and his apparel, even to his sword, and to his bow, and to his girdle" (I Samuel 18:3-4).

Jonathan was not consumed with jealousy, for he understood that while David was destined to be king, he, too, had a significant role to play. "And you shall reign over Israel, and may I be to you as a viceroy" (I Samuel 23:17). With incredible humility and understanding, he formed a friendship with David that surpassed all others and became the Jewish model of selfless friendship. "A love that is not dependent on anything never ceases. Which is a love that is... not dependent on anything? The love of David and Jonathan."[14]

When Jonathan was tragically killed in battle alongside his father and brothers, David eulogized him by comparing his love to that of women: "I am distressed for you, my brother Jonathan, you were very pleasant to me. Your love was more wonderful to me than the love of women!" (II Samuel 1:26). David favorably compared Jonathan's love to "the love of women" because, like a marriage, their friendship represented the secret of unity - unity that will bring Israel to the final redemption, joined together as one under the banner of King David.[15]

"And the envy of Ephraim shall cease, and the adversaries of Judah shall be cut off; Ephraim shall not envy Judah, nor shall Judah vex Ephraim" (Isaiah 11:13).

Labor Pain

In recent years, many experts have warned that Israel is at the precipice of civil war. They believe we are reliving the final decades of the second Temple era, when factionalism and infighting among the Jewish people led to devastation and destruction at the hands of the Roman Empire.

I disagree. The inspiring unity of the people of Israel in response to the attacks of October 7 demonstrates that while divisions in Israeli society run deep, love and brotherhood run deeper. After months of bitter infighting, Israelis of every background prayed together and fought together, side by side. Everyone recognized their shared identity as one united family.

Israel is not approaching the bitter end of a devastating cycle of baseless hatred and infighting. It is experiencing the labor pains of redemption, a suffering that is unavoidable as God's people move forward in the redemptive process. This is not the end; this is the beginning. As our prophets promised, Israel will ultimately be transformed from a secular nation of socialist kibbutzim into the vibrant religious center of the world - though we must not expect it to happen quickly or easily.

Israel is experiencing a painful labor, and we do not know how long it will last. But one thing we know for certain: the unity we long for will certainly come, for God has promised it. "Who has heard such a thing? Who has seen such things? Is a land born in one day? Is a nation born at once, that Zion both experienced birth pangs and bore her children? 'Will I bring to the birth stool and not cause to give birth?' says God. 'Shall I Who causes birth now shut the womb?' says your God" (Isaiah 66:8-9). As Israel lurches from one internal crisis to another, the situation often appears grim - superficially. But in reality, this is the only path to redemption. Redemption must begin with Saul, continue with David, and culminate with the birth of Solomon. There can be no other way.

Rabbi Abraham Isaac Kook once said to an American tourist: "You must make *Aliyah* to Israel! Do you not see the many crises that are plaguing the Jews of the United States?" The American replied: "Are there no crises in Israel?" Rabbi Kook explained: "Here in Israel there are 'crises of birth,' but in exile our people experience 'crises of death.'"

Israel's social friction is painful. But God has promised that the day will come when a descendant of David will again be king and unite the tribes of Israel, when the synagogues of Tel Aviv are as full as those of Jerusalem, when the entire nation, both "Jews" and "Israelis," will serve God together, as one.

CHAPTER 15:

FIGHT LIKE DAVID: THE BIBLICAL RESPONSE TO TERROR

Terror attacks are not new to Israel. Even before the horrors of October 7, Arab terrorists attacked Israelis on a daily basis - murdering, maiming and terrifying the people of Israel.

After every attack, the Jewish community springs into action, countering devastation with comfort and hatred with love. When terrorists murdered our neighbors, Lucy, Rina and Maia Dee, Israelis of all walks of life from all over the country sent food, candy and love, while Jews all over the world reached out to the family and committed themselves to increasing their Bible study in their memory. This is Israel's true "cycle of violence"; Arab terrorists murder Jewish children, and kindhearted Jews respond by showering the victims with love.

But inevitably, when the *shiva*[1] ends, the government officials and Jewish celebrities who visited the bereaved family turn their attention elsewhere. The rest of us go back to our carpools and commutes, praying to never experience this cycle again – but knowing in our hearts that we almost certainly will. We know we must soldier on; what else can we do until redemption arrives?

Actually, there is much we *can* do, if only we have the will.

Yes, we are broken, and yes, our hearts are filled with love and pain for all of Israel's bereaved families and those whose loved ones are still missing. But we are also angry. No, it's beyond anger; we are *furious*.

God said to Moses: "Take revenge for the children of Israel against the Midianites" (Numbers 31:2). *This* is the Bible's teaching on war.

It must be said, proudly and repeatedly: we want every vile jihadist who participated in the murder of 1,200 innocent Israelis on October 7 to *die* – and quickly. The people who aided and abetted the terrorists, who gave them support and shelter? We want them to feel the iron fist of the people of Israel. And the millions of Ishmaelites and Edomites who applauded this sick and evil slaughter? We yearn for the day when their joy turns to tears, when they will tremble before us and beg for mercy. And we pray this day comes soon, that *our* generation will partner with God to "avenge the blood of His servants, wreak vengeance upon His foes, and make clean His people's land" (Deuteronomy 32:43). "Our Father, our King, avenge *before our eyes* the spilt blood of Your servants."[2]

I can already hear the alarmed protests from those who find talk of revenge uncomfortable. As one rabbi wrote to me after the murder of the Dees, "Are we no better than our enemies? Either we are a bunch of animals who are no better than our tormentors or we are not." It seems to be an article of faith among many Jewish leaders that forceful action against our enemies – the kind of action that will make terrorists think twice before attacking us again – is somehow immoral or unJewish.

In his classic article, *Kol Dodi Dofek*, Rabbi Joseph B. Soloveitchik directly addressed these concerns. "Pay no attention to the saccharine suggestions of known assimilationists who... think they are still living in Bialystok, Brest-Litovsk, and Minsk of the year 1905, and openly declare that revenge is forbidden to the Jewish people in any place, at any time, and under all circumstances. 'Vanity of vanities!' (Ecclesiastes 1:2). Revenge is forbidden when it is pointless, but if one is aroused thereby to self-defense, it is the most elementary right of man to take his revenge."[3]

Yes, we must be better than our Arab enemies. We must be better at ferociously defending our children than they are, for the murder of one Jew is one murder too many. We must value the lives of our people more than they value their own. And we must be better than our enemies at uprooting and destroying the evil that infests our homeland.

Tragically, our government has too often forgotten the fundamental teachings of the Bible, and innocent families are paying the price. By responding weakly to terror in the past, we have sent our enemies an unacceptable message: that we are willing to tolerate a certain level of terror and that we will juggle the value of Jewish lives with other political, military and economic considerations.

There was a time when Israel's leaders understood the danger of a moderate response to terror. In 1959, Moshe Dayan said "it was not in our power to secure every water pipe from explosion and every tree from being uprooted. It was not in our power to prevent the murder of workers in the orchards and families in their sleep. But it was in our power to set a high price for our blood, a price higher than what the Arab population, the Arab army, and the Arab governments were willing to pay."[4]

Merely catching terrorists and bringing them to "justice" does not prevent future attacks. Over and over again, in the years leading up to October 7, the IDF eliminated the individual terrorists who committed these atrocities, but future terrorists were not deterred. Arab terrorists consciously chose to sacrifice their own lives to murder Jews for the rewards that awaited them in heaven and the financial benefit their families would receive because of their sacrifice. Through the Palestinian Authority's infamous Pay for Slay program, the PA makes monthly payments to the family members of terrorists who die while murdering Jews.

Israel's long standing restraint in the war against Arab terror reflects a fundamentally flawed understanding of the enemy. Because Israeli leaders falsely assumed the majority of Arabs in Judea, Samaria and Gaza wanted peace and did not support the terrorists, they limited the IDF's military response, so as not to anger the broader Arab population and cause more "grievances." But this approach only encouraged more terror.

Neville Chamberlain's humiliating overtures to Hitler in the late 1930s gave the dictator the confidence he needed to launch World War Two. Instead of condemning Hitler for his aggressions, Chamberlain bent over backward to appease him. He was willing to personally meet with Hitler, whenever and wherever Hitler wished, with no concern for protocol. The "peace" he achieved at the Munich Conference in September 1938, in which he averted war by agreeing to Germany's occupation of the Sudetenland (the German-speaking part of Czechoslovakia), merely bought Hitler more time to build up the German army. "It was 'peace' on the house, with a side order of Czechoslovakia."[5] A year later, as his army swept across Poland, Hitler would laugh at Chamberlain.

Like Chamberlain's appeasement of Germany, Israel's weak response to terror leads our Arab enemies to believe we do not have the will to fight. Every "targeted response" is perceived as a weakness that only encourages more attacks that lead to more dead Jews.

How can Israel stop Arab terror and protect its people? By learning from the example of King David, who avenged the murder of his family and brought peace to Israel.

When David became a fugitive from the jealous King Saul, he brought his parents and brothers to the king of Moab to protect them from the wrath of Saul (I Samuel 22). Tragically, the sages explain that David should not have trusted the Moabites, the relatives of his great-grandmother Ruth.[6] "The king of Moab killed [David's family], and nobody escaped except for one brother of David."[7]

David's mother, father and brothers were mercilessly murdered in cold blood. How did David respond? Was he measured in his response? Did he carefully distinguish between the great majority of "innocent" Moabites and the few bad actors who had murdered his family?

Not exactly. "And he smote Moab, and measured them with a line, making them lie down on the ground; he measured out two lengths of cord for those who were to be put to death, and one length for those to be spared. And the Moabites became servants to David, bringing tribute" (II Samuel 8:2). In one short verse, we learn matter of factly that David humiliated and slaughtered two-thirds of the Moabite army, ensuring the Moabites would never again perpetrate terror against the people of Israel. David made the price of terror untenable – and so the terror ceased.

Did God approve of David's harsh retribution against the Moabites? Not only did God approve of David's actions, but He also ensured David's victory: "And God saved David wherever he went. And David reigned over all Israel; and David administered justice and charity for all his people" (II Samuel 8:14-15).

Every morning, traditional Jews remember that God desires the destruction of evil. In David's words: "Let the faithful exult… with high praises of God in their throats and two-edged swords in their hands, to execute vengeance upon the nations and punishments upon the peoples… to execute the doom decreed against them. This is the glory of all His faithful. Hallelujah!" (149:6-7,9).

For 3,000 years, our people have prayed like David, whispering the beautiful words of Psalms through the darkest days of our exile. It is high time we learn to fight like him as well.

David was not passive. David did not sit back and wait for God to act, for an earthquake to swallow up his enemies. David did not wait for a future messianic era, when God would miraculously destroy Israel's enemies. David understood that the people of Israel must partner with God in carrying out His will, that we must be the sharp edge of God's sword.

David did not fight the terrorists that plagued his people with half measures, nor was he afraid to punish the "innocent civilians" who supported the terrorists who murdered his family. "I have pursued my enemies and overtaken them, never turning back until they were consumed. I have crushed them so that they cannot rise; yea, they are fallen under my feet" (Psalm 18:38-39). David did not "contain" evil; he destroyed it.

David was unconcerned with world opinion or with self-righteous condemnations of other countries. He was not ashamed to seek revenge. "Oh God, smash their teeth in their mouth; shatter the fangs of lions, God... The righteous man will rejoice when he sees revenge; he will bathe his feet in the blood of the wicked. Men will say, 'There is, then, a reward for the righteous; there is, indeed, divine justice on earth.'" (Psalm 58:7,11-12).

David's actions were harsh – but they were both moral and effective. By responding forcefully to those who murdered his family, David ushered in an unprecedented era of peace, enabling his son, Solomon, to build God's Temple in Jerusalem. Most important of all, David gave us the playbook for redemption – if only we are willing to use it.

If the disaster of October 7 and the war against Hamas, Hezbollah and Iran has proven anything, it's that Israel's defensive approach to terror has failed. The IDF knew all about Hamas' weapons, its terror tunnels, its genocidal ideology and its obsessive goal of slaughtering as many Jews as possible and destroying the State of Israel. But instead of proactively destroying this evil, Israel installed security cameras, built fences and barriers, and perfected the Iron Dome air defense system.

In the early years of the state, when Israel proactively attacked its enemies, as it did in the Sinai Campaign of 1956 and the Six-Day War of 1967, it achieved spectacular military victories. But since then, Israel has shifted to a policy of fortification, defense and containment - a policy that, in the jungle of the Middle East, sends a message of weakness to Israel's many enemies.

Jewish morality and justice demand that we be constantly on the offensive. It is time to proudly and proactively conquer and settle the land for the simple reason that God gave it to us. We must destroy our enemies - not only because they are dangerous, but because they are evil.

The time has come to change the name of Israel's army from the "Israel Defense Forces" to the "Israel Victory Forces." Now is the time for Israel's military to stop defending, and to begin attacking, to conquer the land of Israel and destroy its enemies.[8]

War is not pleasant; in this imperfect world, innocent people inevitably suffer. But a government's responsibility, first and foremost, is to defend its own people. Between October 2001 and June 2003, the United States unintentionally killed about 3,500 Afghan civilians through aerial bombings during Operation Enduring Freedom. Civilian deaths are tragic, but the free world understood that after the murder of American citizens on 9/11, the United States had to do everything in its power to defend its people. Yes, we must hold ourselves to a higher standard than terrorists – but not to impossibly high standards that restrict our ability to defend our people.

"But wait," I can already hear my fellow Jews saying, "the sages say that Jews are 'merciful, capable of shame and people who bestow kindness upon others.'"[9] That is certainly true. But as my friend Rabbi Pesach Wolicki often says, these are national traits of the Jewish people, traits that are neither inherently good nor evil. If we are merciful to the wicked, if we are ashamed before The New York Times, and if we bestow acts of kindness upon those who seek to harm us, these traits will enable evil and lead to untold harm. Kindness to our enemies is a form of cruelty to our own people. As Menachem Begin said, "The world does not pity the slaughtered. It only respects those who fight. For better or for worse, that is the truth. All the people of the world knew this grim truth except the Jews. That is why our enemies were able to trap us and shed our blood at will."[10] It's time we learned this lesson.

The self-righteous Edomites in Europe and America will surely condemn us for defending ourselves, as they always do. But it's time we stop trying to please the nations of the world; it never helped and it never will.

"May it be good in Your eyes to bless Your people Israel at every time, in every hour, with Your peace."[11] For thousands of years, our people have yearned for peace, and we will not stop praying for peace until the Messiah comes. But love alone will not stop the terrorists. The path to peace will not be strewn with roses; it will be achieved through faith in God and the fortitude to make our enemies pay for their sins. Like David, we must not forget – and we dare not forgive.

CHAPTER 16:

JEWS WHO REFUSE TO SEE: FROM NAZI GERMANY TO GAZA

In retrospect, it seems absurd. In the early years of the Nazi regime, well-meaning Christians and even some Jews still believed that Adolf Hitler could be reasoned with and even domesticated. Even Karl Barth, the great Christian thinker who would later strongly oppose Hitler and Nazism, made several attempts to meet with Hitler in 1934. The Holocaust was still several years in the future, even if, in retrospect, all the warning signs were already there.

But at least one German pastor already understood the danger. In a letter to his friend, Erwin Sutz, Dietrich Bonhoeffer wrote: "I believe any discussion between Hitler and Barth would be quite pointless - indeed, no longer to be sanctioned. Hitler has shown himself quite plainly for what he is, and the church ought to know with whom it has to reckon… The Oxford movement was naive enough to try and convert Hitler - a ridiculous failure to recognize what is going on."[1]

Hitler and the Nazi regime would go on to murder more than six million Jews and millions of other innocent people across the world. And they would do so with the help of the vast majority of ordinary Germans, a people steeped in a virulent culture of eliminationist antisemitism, whom Daniel Goldhagen famously described as "Hitler's willing executioners."[2]

Throughout the 1930s, as the Nazi regime moved inexorably toward war and genocide, Bonhoeffer could not understand the blindness of his fellow pastors. Why couldn't they see that in order to defeat evil, it must first be identified and condemned? How could they, and so much of the civilized world, fail to see what was so obvious to him?

It is no overreaction to say that our generation is as blind today as Karl Barth and the German pastors were in the 1930s.

A few weeks before October 7, a well-meaning Jewish friend of mine who lives in New York - let's call him Daniel - wrote to me by WhatsApp: "I don't blame the Palestinians generally, it's more their leadership and other 'allies' that have left them in a position where there isn't much else to root for beyond terrorism... What is the average Palestinian's alternative to believe in for their kids?... The leaders are garbage and the terrorists are garbage but there are plenty of people who just want a better life for their kids, and the only option they see as possible is armed resistance. Not that different from how we saw it not so long ago. That doesn't make it right, but it's just normal, and we should try to provide a better alternative because no one else is..."

Even after the horrors of October 7, Daniel doubled down on his view that most Arabs in Gaza, Judea, and Samaria are good people who just want a better life for their families. As terrorist rockets launched by Hamas rained down on my Israeli community and my family regularly ran to our bomb shelter, I read more texts from Daniel asserting that only Hamas and other terrorist groups were to blame.

I understand Daniel's desire to believe in the basic goodness of Ishmael, the Arabs of Gaza, Judea and Samaria. I've employed Arab construction workers in my home, and at least a few of them seemed friendly. We all *want* to believe, and I am no exception, that these Arabs are a good people ruled by evil terrorists - that if only we could free them from their evil leadership, we would have peace.

To consider the alternative - that the approximately three million Arabs living in Gaza, Judea and Samaria actively support the murder of Jews - is both terrifying and difficult for many people to absorb. Jews and Christians are raised to be kind and merciful; it's hard for us to believe that average Arab mothers and fathers raise their children to hate and murder Jews, simply because they are Jews. We are accustomed to looking inward, to blaming ourselves for the evil perpetrated against us. And so Daniel convinced himself of a comforting narrative, that most Arabs in Gaza, Judea and Samaria are innocent.

But this is not a time for wishful thinking. Like the Jews of Europe in the 1930s, our very lives depend on seeing the world clearly and looking evil in the eye. When you live in Judea as I do, surrounded by hundreds of thousands of Arabs who want to slaughter my family, this is no exaggeration. And these days, as massive crowds of Palestinians and their supporters call for Jewish genocide all over America, delusional perspectives like Daniel's are putting the lives of Americans at risk as well.

Who are these "innocent Palestinians," *really*?

Hamas terrorists don't fall from the sky. Hamas terrorists - and there were over 40,000 of them in Gaza at the start of the war on October 7 - were raised and educated in a society of men, women and children that is obsessively focused on murdering Jews and erasing Israel from the map.

What kind of culture produces thousands of men who proudly video themselves raping teen girls before executing them? What kind of society glorifies baby killers who burn the bodies of their infant victims as heroes? Terrorists are not a guilty minority terrorizing an innocent majority. They are not "lone actors," but rather the messengers and representatives of their people - just as I am a representative and messenger of the Jewish people.

In 2006, in a democratic election, Hamas - a terrorist group whose charter openly calls for the genocide of Jews and the eradication of Israel - won a majority 74 of 132 seats in the Palestinian Legislative Council. A December 2023 poll showed that 72% of Arabs in Gaza, Judea and Samaria believed that the Hamas slaughter, torture and rape of over 1,200 innocent Jewish men, women and children on October was "correct," with support for Hamas rising after the brutal attack - despite the destruction they have brought upon the Gaza Strip.[3] Hamas is unquestionably the chosen and preferred leadership of the people of Gaza.

A large majority of Arabs in Gaza, Judea and Samaria support terrorism and the murder of Jews, a fact repeatedly proven through surveys. After the murder of Jewish brothers Hallel and Yagel Yaniv in Huwara this year, a survey[4] by the Palestinian Center for Research on Policy and Investigations (PCPSR) showed that 71% of Arabs said they supported the murders. "From the River to the Sea" is not a Hamas slogan. It is an *Arab* slogan. These are the "innocent Palestinians" we constantly hear about in the media.

After October 7, Israeli authorities detained and interrogated over 4,000 Gazan Arabs who had work visas in Israel and were employed in the communities where Hamas terrorists committed their inhuman atrocities. These "average Palestinians" are the people who provided the necessary intelligence to Hamas. There are many reports of former workers mapping out the communities that they raided, identifying homes of security personnel, which families had dogs and even how many children lived in each home.

Average Gazan Arabs did not simply support the atrocities of October 7; great numbers of them spontaneously joined in the murder, rape and kidnapping of innocent Jews on that terrible day. Thousands of Gazan civilians rushed into Israeli towns to assist Hamas, decapitating Jewish children and raping Jewish women.[5]

Gadi Yarkoni, elected mayor of the Eshkol Regional Council under the center-left Blue and White party, lost his legs in a mortar attack during the 2014 Gaza war. After October 7, his idealism was shattered: "The second wave of Arabs who came into the country were just as cruel as the terrorists of the first wave. We saw that it was not only Hamas who came to slaughter us. It was all the residents of Gaza, including people who worked in our kibbutzim."[6]

On Israel's Channel 12 news, Yarkoni responded to the TV anchor's claim that most Palestinians are innocent, saying: "I have changed. I don't talk like you. I don't know what's going on with our hostages and missing people. Their families are crying out, and the people of Gaza, who we once thought were good, are responsible. It's not just Hamas and Islamic Jihad. Ordinary people from Gaza took [our citizens]."

The "poor mothers" of Gaza are not innocent. Journalist Jotam Confino reported on a Hamas terrorist who called his mother on the day of the attack. "I killed 10 Jews with my own hands. I'm using the dead Jewish woman's phone to call you now." His mother replied, "May God protect you."[7]

Dr. Einat Wilf, a former member of the Labor party and a self-described feminist and atheist, called out the world's blindness: "We are told that most Palestinians do not support Hamas. Very well. Where then are the large-scale Palestinian protests demanding Hamas release the abducted hostages - children, toddlers, grandparents, civilians - immediately and unconditionally? Where then is the sole Palestinian protester standing in Times or Trafalgar Square with a sign that says "Not in My Name"? Where is the one Palestinian intellectual who will write an op-ed expressing deep shame that acts of the greatest cruelty in human history were carried out in the name of "Free Palestine" and "From the River to the Sea"? If the PLO, Fatah and Palestinian Authority represent moderate Palestinians, where is the outcry? The horror? The heartfelt denunciations? Why must international pressure be fruitlessly brought to bear to try to elicit even a pale shadow of them? If Hamas is not supported in Gaza, where then is the Palestinian in Gaza who will come forth with information about the hostages? Even in Nazi Germany, when some Germans understood that Hitler was bringing disaster upon their country, there were those who attempted to assassinate him. Where are the Palestinians in Gaza who will take action against Hamas? And why is it that the instinctive response of so many to these questions is to make excuses as to why not even one of these things should be expected of any Palestinian anywhere?"[8]

"When Palestinians write poems, they write poems of murder. When they sing songs, they sing songs of death. When they give birth to children, it is to raise them up to kill and die. Old and young, men and women, they live for no other purpose than to murder Jews in the name of Allah.

Given a piece of land, they set up rockets on it. Given a house they dig tunnels under it. Given a tool, they turn it into a blade. Given a child, they turn him into a weapon. And as the worshipers of Moloch had done in ages gone, they pass even their own sons and daughters through the flame."[9]

Yet millions of good people around the world continue to delude themselves and buy into the lie that the average Arab in Gaza, Judea and Samaria wants peace.

The great Zionist leader Vladimir Jabotinsky once described a conversation he had with Dr. Max Nordau, Theodor Herzl's partner in launching the Zionist movement. Frustrated by the passivity of the Jewish people at a time when action was desperately needed, he asked Nordau how it was possible for the Jews to do nothing. Nordau explained: "The Jew learns not by way of reason but from catastrophes. He won't buy an umbrella merely because he sees clouds in the sky; he waits until he is drenched and catches pneumonia - then he makes up his mind."

The great tragedy of the Oslo Agreements was built upon this delusion of "innocent Palestinians who want peace." Thousands of Jews have died over the last 30 years because we refused to accept the truth. *We cannot defeat an enemy we refuse to see.* "Who is blind but My servant, and deaf as My messenger whom I will send?" (Isaiah 42:19).

Shortly after the people of Israel left Egypt, the Amalekite warrior tribe attacked the weakest members of Israel without warning. "You shall remember what Amalek did to you on the way, when you went out of Egypt, how he happened upon you on the way and cut off all the stragglers at your rear, when you were faint and weary" (Deuteronomy 25:17). Like modern Arab terrorists, the Amalekites murdered the elderly, women and children.

God's response was extreme: "Inscribe this [as] a memorial in the book, and recite it into Joshua's ears, that I will surely obliterate the remembrance of Amalek from beneath the heavens" (Exodus 17:14). As the people prepared to enter the land of Israel, Moses reminded them of God's eternal war with Amalek: "[Therefore,] it will be, when the Lord your God grants you respite from all your enemies around [you] in the land which the Lord, your God, gives to you as an inheritance to possess, that you shall obliterate the remembrance of Amalek from beneath the heavens. You shall not forget!" (Deuteronomy 25:19).

To this day, Jews annually fulfill the commandment to remember what Amalek did each year on the Shabbat before the holiday of Purim, known as *"Shabbat Zachor,"* the "Shabbat of Remembering." Each year, we recall the ancient attack of the Amalekites against our forefathers.

When the Israelites first entered the land of Israel and the Amalekite hordes remained an active threat to their safety, the purpose of this annual "remembering" was clear. "Do not be passive! Destroy the Amalekites before they destroy you!" But in modern times, the purpose of this "remembering" is less obvious. The nation of Amalek ceased to exist as a recognizable or independent nation thousands of years ago. There are no people alive today who identify as Amalekites or claim Amalekite ancestry. Why is it necessary to continue remembering what Amalekites did to Israel thousands of years ago? Why would God issue an eternal command to remember the evil deeds of a nation that no longer exists?

In 1956, Rabbi Joseph B. Soloveitchik, one of American Jewry's greatest thinkers, published a small book entitled *Kol Dodi Dofek, The Voice of My Beloved Knocks.* Reflecting on the Holocaust that ended only eleven years earlier, he wrote: "The evil intentions of the Arabs are not only directed against our national independence but against the continued existence of the Jewish presence in Israel... the notion of "the Lord will have war against Amalek from generation to generation" (Exodus 17:16) is not confined to a certain race, but includes a necessary attack against any nation or group infused with mad hatred that directs its enmity against the community of Israel. When a nation emblazons on its standard, "Come, let us cut them off from being a nation so that the name of Israel shall no longer be remembered" (Psalms 83:5), it becomes Amalek. In the 1930's and 1940's the Nazis, with Hitler at their helm, filled this role. In this most recent period, they were the Amalekites, the representatives of insane hate. Today, the throngs of Nasser and the Mufti have taken their place. If we are again silent, I do not know how we will be judged before God. Do not rely on the justice of the 'liberal world.' Those pious liberals were alive fifteen years ago and witnessed the destruction of millions of people with equanimity and did not lift a finger. They are liable to observe, God forbid, the repetition of the bloodbath and not lose a night's sleep."[10]

Amalek is more than a particular nation descended from Esau.[11] It is a biblical prototype, a model of genocidal hatred that would continue to inspire like-minded antisemites through the rest of history, and which continues today in the form of Islamic jihadism. Today, the children of Ishmael have taken on the mantle of "Amalek," calling openly and repeatedly for the wholesale slaughter of the Jewish people.

But the question remains. Why must the people of Israel set aside one Sabbath each year to remember what Amalek did to our ancestors? If the genocidal intent of the Amalekites and their spiritual descendants is so obvious, why must God command us to remember it?

Even after October 7 revealed the sickening evil of our enemies and their genocide-loving supporters throughout the world, millions of people refuse to acknowledge the obvious: that the Arabs of Gaza, Judea and Samaria are hate-filled modern-day Amalekites. Somehow, there are still many Jews who are deeply concerned for the welfare of the "innocent Palestinians" suffering under Hamas rule. They simply cannot accept the truth - that the vast majority of Muslims do not want peace with Israel.

God foresaw that His people would struggle to confront the painful truth of evil. It is difficult for decent and civilized people to comprehend the evil motivations of nations like Amalek. We assume that our enemies are like us - basically good people who want a good life for themselves and for their children. By projecting our own basic goodness upon others, we unconsciously delude ourselves into believing that our enemies share our basic assumptions and motivations.

To remedy this dangerous intellectual error, it is absolutely critical to remember, every year, that pure evil, the evil of Amalek, still exists - and that it must be utterly destroyed.

To be clear, this does not mean that Israel can or should kill the three million Arabs of Gaza, Judea and Samaria. Absent a clear and direct command from God Himself, like that given to King Saul in the Book of Samuel, it is forbidden to annihilate an entire population - though Israel can and must kill every Arab terrorist who dares to threaten the lives of the people of Israel. Rather, the lesson of Amalek is that a society can become so corrupt, so sick and evil, that it is *worthy* of destruction.

Practically, the Arabs of Gaza, Judea and Samaria must emigrate. There are 22 Arab nations that could easily absorb them. In the meantime, we in Israel must stop employing these people in our homes and businesses. We must give these evil people no incentive to stay. It won't happen overnight, but we must begin the process of removing them from the land. It is us or them; our lives depend on it. "But if you do not drive out the inhabitants of the Land from before you, then those whom you leave over will be as spikes in your eyes and thorns in your sides, and they will harass you in the land in which you settle" (Bamidbar 33:55).

Remembering the evil of Amalek is no mere intellectual exercise. The failure to remember and hate evil inevitably leads to tragedy. After the slaughter of October 7, the Chief Rabbi of Safed, Rabbi Shmuel Eliyahu, wrote "We believed that if we stroked the snake softly and kindly enough, the snake would transform into a lamb. But when you pet a snake, it bites you. How many more Jews must die before we realize that a snake is truly a snake?"

In the Book of Samuel, King Saul destroyed the Amalekite tribe led by King Agag. Though he violated God's command by keeping King Agag alive, the prophet Samuel soon remedied the situation. "And Samuel said, 'As your sword bereaved women, so will your mother be bereaved among women.' And Samuel hewed Agag into pieces before the Lord in Gilgal" (I Samuel 15:33). King Agag and his Amalekite line were destroyed on that day - or so it seems. Hundreds of years later an infamous descendant of King Agag appeared on the scene to once again threaten God's people. "King Ahasuerus promoted Haman the son of Hammedatha *the Agagite* and advanced him, and placed his seat above all the princes who were with him" (Esther 3:1). If King Agag and his family were killed by Samuel and Saul, how could Haman the Agagite appear generations later in the Book of Esther?

The sages explain that because Saul initially spared King Agag in violation of God's command, Agag had a window of opportunity before he was killed by Samuel. In that short time, Agag engaged in relations with a random woman, who conceived a child during the encounter. This child would continue King Agag's line, ultimately resulting in the evil Haman, who would try his hardest to destroy the Jewish people.[12] The message is clear: if we fail to recognize the evil of Amalek, we will fail to destroy it - and evil that is not utterly destroyed will come back to haunt us.

We ignored the Amalekite evil in our midst for far too long, and paid an unbelievably painful price. It is time to repent - for God's sake, and for our own.

"And on that day the deaf shall hear the words of the book, and out of the obscurity and out of darkness shall the eyes of the blind see" (Isaiah 29:18).

CHAPTER 17:

SAUL'S FAILURE AND BIBI'S DECISION: THE FUTURE OF GAZA

In November 2022, soon after Benjamin "Bibi" Netanyahu was elected to his fifth term as Prime Minister, journalist Bari Weiss asked him to name his favorite biblical character. Netanyahu replied with a fascinating answer: "King Saul. He was tragic."[1] Left-wingers who spent decades trying unsuccessfully to defeat Bibi laughed at his response,[2] predicting he would end up just like King Saul, who tragically died in battle. But the truth is that Bibi's kinship with King Saul runs far deeper than they realize.

Only a few weeks after the horror of October 7, as the IDF prepared to launch its ground invasion of Gaza, the Prime Minister invoked God's command in Deuteronomy 25:17 to wipe out Amalek: "You must remember what Amalek has done to you." "Our soldiers will bravely and powerfully fight an enemy more ferocious than any other… Remember what the Amalekites have done to you! We remember, and fight Amalek now. Our armed forces are determined to eliminate this evil from the world, for the benefit of our existence and for the benefit of humanity. Israel's soldiers are part of a 3,000-year legacy. We will defeat the murderous enemy and secure our place in our land. We always said: Never again! And never again is now."[3]

Bibi appropriately compared today's murderous Hamas terrorists, who revel in the torture and murder of Jews, to the ancient tribe that heartlessly attacked the women, children and elderly of Israel in the wilderness.[4] But as Saul would later learn, fulfilling God's commandment to wipe out Amalek is easier said than done. Saul's failure to fulfill God's will led to his downfall as king and his replacement by King David, his "fellow who was better than him" (I Samuel 15:28). Today, the most pressing question for the Prime Minister is whether he truly understands the tragedy of Saul and the lesson of Saul's failure, for his own future depends on it.

The Sin of Saul

When God commanded Saul to destroy Amalek, He left no room for doubt; Amalek must be utterly destroyed. "You shall not have pity on him: and you shall slay both man and woman, infant and suckling, ox and sheep, camel and ass" (I Samuel 15:3). Saul dutifully gathered the people of Israel for war and destroyed the Amalekites. But as he neared the completion of his mission, he stumbled: "And Saul and the people had pity on [King] Agag, and on the best of the sheep and the cattle, and the fatlings, and on the fattened sheep... and they did not want to destroy them" (I Samuel 15:9).

Saul's failure to kill Agag and all of Amalek's cattle was his undoing. God regretted anointing Saul as king of Israel and dispatched the prophet Samuel to inform Saul of his fate. "Since you rejected the word of the Lord, He has rejected you from being king" (I Samuel 15:23).

As Saul himself admitted to Samuel, he had sinned against God. But God's anger and Saul's severe punishment do not appear to fit the crime. Saul largely fulfilled God's command to wipe out the Amalekites; his only sin was misguided mercy upon the Amalekite king and the best of the livestock. Why does this seemingly minor sin make him unfit to remain the king of Israel?

A careful reading of the verses reveals the true nature of Saul's sin. The Hebrew language possesses several words that mean "having mercy." Interestingly, when God commanded Saul to "not have mercy" on Amalek, God did not use the common Hebrew word for mercy, "*rachamim*," but rather the less common word, "*chemlah*." When describing Saul's misplaced mercy, "*chemlah*" is used again: "But Saul and the people had mercy (*chemlah*) on Agag..." What is the difference between "*chemlah*" and "*rachamim*"?

Rachamim is used to describe the difficulty one man has in seeing the death or suffering of another man. In other words, "*rachamim*" refers to the *emotional* reaction of mercy that we experience when seeing other people who are suffering. By contrast, the word "*chemlah*" is used when describing a man's difficulty in seeing the destruction of someone else's possessions and "he decides, using his own judgment, that it would be unfortunate if these items were destroyed and that it would be better for them to be preserved." Unlike "*rachamim*," a word that captures emotional pity, "*chemlah*" refers to an intellectual reaction in which one protests the destruction of property.[5]

Tellingly, God did *not* warn Saul that he should avoid "*rachamim*," emotional mercy, for the people and animals of Amalek. Saul was a human being, and it was only natural for him to react emotionally to the slaughter of Amalek, even if destroying them was God's will. On the contrary - any healthy human being *should* become deeply emotional and feel "*rachamim*" when tasked with such a difficult mission.

When God warned Saul, He warned him not to have "*chemlah*" on Amalek. In other words, God explicitly warned Saul of intellectual arrogance. "Be warned, Saul! Do not think that you, with your human reason, know how to handle the Amalekites better than I do!" But this is precisely what Saul did. He intellectually rejected God's command in favor of his own "superior" thinking. Under pressure from the people, Saul decided that it was wrong to kill the Amalekite king and foolish to destroy the best of Amalek's sheep and the oxen. What a waste of good cattle!

This was a grave sin and an unforgivable offense. If a king acts as a messenger of God, as God's representative here on earth, then "he will sit on the throne of God as king" (I Chronicles 29:23). But if he takes authority for himself, it is as if he has wrested the throne away from his Creator. And so a leader of Israel who rejects the word of God in favor of his own ideas is destined to suffer the fate of Saul. "The Lord has torn the kingdom of Israel from you... and has given it to your fellow who is better than you" (I Samuel 15:28).

The Faith of Abraham

Saul was hardly the first man of the Bible to grapple with a difficult command from God. After decades of infertility, God miraculously blessed Abraham and Sarah with a son in their old age. Isaac was the answer to years of heartfelt prayers and tears. But then, inexplicably, God commanded Abraham to offer Isaac as a sacrifice. "Please take your son, your only one, whom you love, Isaac, and go away to the land of Moriah and bring him up there for a burnt offering" (Genesis 22:2).

Given His earlier promises to Abraham, God's command could only have seemed illogical and cruel. What benefit could come from sacrificing his son in the wilderness? Isaac was the only possible heir to continue Abraham's legacy; slaughtering him would bring an end to Abraham's great project of teaching humanity to serve God. By any reasonable consideration it was pointless.

This, of course, was Abraham's great test. Would he humbly place his own intellect aside and unquestioningly follow God's will? Would he remember, as Isaiah said, that "My thoughts are not your thoughts" (55:8), that God's wisdom is far greater than that of man?

Where Saul failed, Abraham rose to the challenge. He proved himself to be God's greatest servant, "for now I know that you are a God-fearing man." And unlike Saul, destined to die in battle for his sins, God assured Abraham of victory: "and your descendants will inherit the cities of their enemies" (Genesis 22:17).

Amos' Warning

God understands that we are human and that even the greatest leaders inevitably stumble. David, the greatest of Israel's kings, was overwhelmed by desire and sinned by taking Bathsheba. Solomon, too, was led astray by his foreign wives. But as Saul discovered, not all sins are created equal.

"So said the Lord: For three transgressions of Judah, yea for four, I will not return them; for they rejected the law of the Lord, and they did not keep His statutes, and their lies misled them…" (Amos 2:4). In calling out the sins of Israel, the prophet Amos did not spare any punches. But what were the sins that led him to lash out in this way on God's behalf?

"They rejected the law of the Lord," and for that reason "they did not keep His statutes." The reason they sinned was not because of their evil inclinations and desires but rather because of their intellectual heresy. This heresy, in turn, was caused by the "lies that misled them," the popular but false ideologies of their time.

Amos' prophecy was not meant only for the Israelites of his time. With the Jewish people's prophetic return to Israel after thousands of years in exile, Amos' message has taken on renewed relevance. Why do Israel's enemies refuse to make peace? Why have all of Israel's concessions to the Arabs only led to more terror and pain? Why must the people of Israel suffer so terribly?

The answer is simple if difficult to absorb. Over the last thirty years, Israeli leadership has repeatedly ignored God's will, making national decisions that directly violate His law as outlined in the Bible. Predictably, God has made His displeasure clear.

Hagi Ben Artzi, Prime Minister Netanyahu's brother-in-law and one of Israel's greatest Bible scholars, outlines three national sins - *intellectual* sins - that he believes are the cause of Israel's suffering at the hands of its enemies.[6]

The first sin was the signing of the Oslo Accords of 1993, which gave the murderous Palestinian Authority control over much of Judea and Samaria, Israel's biblical heartland. This "covenant" with terrorists, granting power and land to people who seek Israel's destruction, was a repetition of Israel's sin during the era of the judges. "And you shall not make a covenant with the inhabitants of this land… but you have not obeyed Me" (Judges 2:2-3). Israeli leaders ignored God's command, believing that they knew better than God - that they could achieve peace by retreating from parts of the holy land. But all they achieved was suffering, as God said would happen: "If you do not drive out the inhabitants of the land from before you, then those whom you leave over will be as spikes in your eyes and thorns in your sides, and they will harass you in the land in which you settle" (Numbers 33:55).

The second sin was Israel's abandonment of the Gaza Strip in 2005, which allowed Hamas terrorists to take control of the region. "Following the Oslo Accords, the Second Intifada broke out, which led to thousands of deaths, exploding buses, and more. But instead of dealing a crushing blow to our enemies, throwing out the murderers, and ridding the country of them, we gave them the Gaza Strip as a reward. We destroyed 22 Jewish settlements, a flourishing region, which we gave them as a gift. Here, too, the rabbis were opposed to the government's abandonment of Gaza. This was the second time that the State of Israel rejected God and said to all the rabbis, 'You are of no interest to us - we will carry out this plan and we don't care how angry you are.'"

The third sin was committed in 2011, when Prime Minister Netanyahu, supported by 26 government ministers, freed thousands of murderous Hamas terrorists in exchange for Gilad Shalit, an Israeli soldier abducted by Hamas. Israel released 1,207 terrorists in exchange for Shalit, an exorbitant price that only encouraged Hamas to kidnap more Israelis. For this reason, the sages rule that we "must not ransom captives for more than their value, for the good order of the world."[7] Today, we are paying the price for this mistake; Yahya Sinwar, the mastermind behind the October 7 slaughter, was one of the prisoners released in that deal.

When the leaders of Israel believe they know better than God and lack the courage to call out and destroy our enemies, it is a sign that Israel is once again reliving the reign of Saul.[8] Tragically, it is the people of Israel who pay the price.

The Future of Gaza

Step by step, Israel's heroic soldiers are winning the war against Hamas in Gaza. Though the war may drag on for many more months, Israel can and must uproot Hamas from the region. But what will happen next? What will Israel do with Gaza?

Once again, the Bible is clear. Israel must resettle the Gaza Strip, for it is part of God's promised land as delineated in the Book of Joshua: "Gaza with her towns and her villages, to the river of Egypt" (Joshua 15:47). In 2005, the Israeli government ignored God's command, arrogantly uprooting all of the Jewish settlements in Gaza. The result - 18 years of non-stop terrorism and rocket attacks, followed by the horrific slaughter of October 7 - was disastrous. Will Israel make the same mistake again today?

On January 10th, 2024, Prime Minister Netanyahu said: "I want to make a few points absolutely clear. Israel has no intention of permanently occupying Gaza or displacing its civilian population…" A few weeks earlier, when asked about the possibility of reestablishing Jewish settlements in the Gaza Strip, he said "it's not a realistic goal."[9]

From his public statements, it seems that Bibi has every intention of repeating the sin of the Gaza Disengagement. In the name of "realism," he is dismissing the will of God. But is anything too difficult for God? "Behold, the hand of the Lord is not too short to save, neither is His ear too heavy to hear" (Isaiah 59:1).

Netanyahu, however, only sees the hard facts on the ground. He knows that there are close to two million Arabs living in Gaza that no other country wishes to accept, and that Israel's most important ally, the United States, is adamantly opposed to Jews resettling the Gaza Strip.

He's right, of course; returning to Gaza isn't "realistic." But Netanayahu would do well to remember the words of Israel's founding Prime Minister, David Ben Gurion, who said that "any Jew that does not believe in miracles is not realistic." Though not a religiously observant Jew, Ben Gurion understood what Netanyahu does not: that the normal rules of geopolitics do not apply to Israel!

Jacob, the forefather of modern Israel, was a dreamer. "And he dreamed, and behold! a ladder set up on the ground and its top reached to heaven…" (Genesis 28:12). Dreamers are not deterred by the reality of what *is* but are driven by what *should be*. Jacob fathered a nation of dreamers, a nation of optimists who would not be disheartened by seemingly insurmountable obstacles or international pressure. The people of Israel plant their feet on the ground, but never stop yearning for the heavens.

To believe that God's promises are "unrealistic," after so many of God's other "unrealistic" prophecies have been miraculously fulfilled, is a failure of leadership. A little more than 100 years ago, the land of Israel was a largely desolate collection of barren deserts and swampland, with a tiny Jewish population of a few thousand Jewish pioneers. Today, the land is astoundingly beautiful and fertile, and over seven million Jews live in Israel, with many more returning home each year. In 1947, 1956, 1967 and 1973, Israel was attacked by multiple Arab nations that sought to destroy the Jewish state and push its people into the Mediterranean Sea. Not only didn't they succeed, but Israel turned the tables on its enemies and reclaimed its ancient lands, including Judea, Samaria, the Golan Heights and Gaza. The rebirth of the land, the ingathering of Israel, and Israel's military victories - were any of these "realistic"? Clearly, when it comes to the people of Israel, we must redefine the meaning of the term!

God understood how difficult it would be for the leaders of Israel to remain faithful to His commands, and so He commanded every king of Israel to write two Torah scrolls for himself. Wherever he travels, an Israelite king must carry a Torah scroll with him, to remember that his mission is to fulfill God's will and not his own. "And it shall be with him, and he shall read it all the days of his life, so that he may learn to fear the Lord, his God, to keep all the words of this Torah and these statutes, to perform them… so that he will not turn away from the commandment, either to the right or to the left, in order that he may prolong [his] days in his kingdom, he and his sons, among Israel" (Deuteronomy 17:18-20). Only a king who is willing to subordinate his own will to that of God will retain the right to rule God's people.

This is Prime Minister Netanyahu's great test. Despite heavy pressure from the United States and the international community, he must stand strong and reject their demands for Israel to once again abandon the Gaza Strip. This is no simple task. All those who care for Israel must ask God to give the Prime Minister and his cabinet the wisdom, faith and strength to stay true to God's will. Our Father our King, bless the nation of Israel, its leaders and ministers, and guide them in the ways of wisdom, valor and faith.

"And He saw that there was no man, and He was astounded for there was no intercessor, and His arm saved for Him, and His righteousness, that supported Him" (Isaiah 59:16). Even if "there is no man" worthy of leading His people, God has promised that He will redeem us. We believe, with complete faith, that the people of Israel will return to Gaza. God's nation will be sovereign over all of Judea and Samaria and every inch of the promised land. The only question is when - and *who* will merit to lead them.

CHAPTER 18:

ZEPHANIAH'S CRY: DON'T RELY ON AMERICA!

On March 25, 1955, a joyous wedding took place in Patish, a Jewish community in southern Israel near the Gaza border. The community members donned their finest attire as they gathered for the festivities. The celebration, however, didn't last long. A group of fedayeen Arab terrorists from Gaza stormed the wedding, hurling grenades and opening fire on the guests. The attack left 19 people wounded, and 22-year-old Varda Friedman, who had come to Patish to help as a social worker, was killed.

Upon arriving two days later to express support for the community, David Ben-Gurion, then serving as Defense Minister after a year-long retirement from politics, was dismayed to see residents preparing to abandon their homes due to safety concerns. Though no longer Prime Minister, Ben-Gurion still held a revered position in Israeli society, and he felt a profound sense of responsibility for the tragedy that struck Patish. He understood Israel's obligation to protect its citizens, and the weight of safeguarding the nation rested heavily on his shoulders.

In an interview with journalist Moshe Zak, Ben Gurion said: "Look at these Jews. They've come from Iraq, Kurdistan, North Africa… they've come from countries where their blood is worthless, where it's permissible to abuse them, torture them, beat them, to be cruel towards them. They've gotten used to being helpless victims of the gentiles. Here is where we must prove to them that their blood is no longer worthless; that the Jewish people have a state and an army that won't allow them to be slaughtered again; that their lives and property are worth something. We need to make them stand upright, instill in them the feelings of sovereignty and pride. We need to show them that those who rise up against them will not escape punishment, because they are citizens of a sovereign country that is responsible for their lives and their safety."[1]

Several days later, in Jerusalem, he forcefully advocated for a plan he deemed the most logical solution: Israeli occupation of the Gaza Strip, disregarding potential reactions from superpowers and the United Nations. IDF Chief of Staff Moshe Dayan and numerous members of the Mapai political party rallied behind him.

Prime Minister Moshe Sharett vehemently opposed the plan, fearing it would provoke severe international backlash. Sharett, along with most of the government, dreaded economic sanctions, diplomatic delegitimization, and isolation for Israel. They argued that without UN Resolution 181, the establishment of the State of Israel would not have been possible.

Ben Gurion disagreed. A month later, at an IDF parade, he gave a speech that is remembered in Israel to this day. "It is not in the global arena but rather from within that Israel will be strengthened and stand... these are the things that will determine our destiny more than any external factors in the world. Our future is not dependent on what the gentiles will say but rather what the Jews will do! Only the daring of the Jews established the state, not some decision by that *'Um-shmum.'*"

In Hebrew, "*Um*" is an acronym for the United Nations. When Ben Gurion said "*Um-shmum*," it was akin to saying "United Nations-shmoonited nations!" in English.

Ben Gurion continued: "As a member of the Jewish people I say: With all due respect to the institutions of the United Nations and its members, until Isaiah's prophecy that 'nation shall not lift up sword against nation' is fulfilled, and as long as our neighbors plot to destroy us, we won't have security unless it's through our own strength... The Security Council acts out of bias and glaring discrimination... In our region, acts of murder, sabotage, robbery and trespassing by our neighbors are becoming more and more frequent, and we must put an end to it – even if no one else wants to or is able to do so."[2]

Sixty years later, Israelis are still debating whether they should rely on other nations in their battle against Islamic terror. Should Israel put its faith in

America and defer to its wishes? Or must God's people "go it alone" and defy the powerful nations of the West at the risk of losing their support?

Like Zechariah, the prophet Zephaniah describes the events that will occur at the end of days and the upheaval and suffering that will overtake the world. "The great day of the Lord is near; it is near and hastens greatly, the sound of the day of the Lord, wherein the mighty man cries bitterly. That day is a day of wrath; a day of trouble and distress; a day of ruin (*shoah*) and desolation (*m'shoah*); a day of darkness and gloom; a day of clouds and thick darkness" (Zephaniah 1:14-15). Tellingly, Zephaniah is one of only a few prophets to speak of "*shoah*," the Hebrew word for ruin and desolation which would later be used in modern times to refer to the Holocaust. When using this painful word, it's possible he was also referring to events of our own generation - to the horrors of October 7, when more Jews were murdered in a single day than on any day since the Holocaust.

How could God allow this horror to happen? What sin would Israel commit to bring this evil upon themselves?

"And it shall come to pass on that day, that I will search Jerusalem with candles, and I will visit upon the men who are settled on their lees, who say in their heart, 'The Lord shall do neither good nor harm'" (Zephaniah 1:12). One who believes that God "does neither good nor harm," that God does not have a central role to play in the events of our time, denies the foundational doctrine of divine providence. A true believer does not merely believe in the God of Genesis, the God who created the world. A person of genuine faith must also believe in the God of Exodus, the God who conducts the world He created and rewards and punishes mankind, measure for measure.

Divine providence guides events at all times and in all places. But God's providence is particularly evident regarding the people and land of Israel. God made clear in the Bible that the destiny of Israel will be different from that of normal nations. The dry bones of Israel will come to life, and against all odds, the scattered exiles will return home. As Zephaniah, Zechariah, Amos and others prophesied, the people of Israel will return to Gaza and once again take possession of all of its land.

Yet Israeli leaders of almost all political parties, both left and right, suffer from the same devastating flaw. As they manage Israel's complex relations with allied and enemy nations, they ignore the most influential "superpower" of all: God Himself. Oblivious to God's role in Israel's destiny, Israeli leaders placed their trust in the United States, a disastrous decision that has caused untold harm to the people of Israel.

In my past life as a synagogue rabbi, I was fascinated by the power and influence that certain wealthy congregants held over the synagogue and the rest of the community. CEOs and owners of companies, these wealthy people employed several members of the community. And of course, the synagogue depended on their large contributions to pay its bills.

Their generosity was admirable, but it was often a double-edged sword. Due to their largesse, these congregants wielded enormous influence in ways that could be quite destructive to the very community they so generously supported. The synagogue made questionable decisions intended to please these donors, who also held sway over their social circles. Money brings influence, in more ways than one. There is no such thing as a free lunch.

The same dynamic plagues Israel's relationship with the United States. Ever since Hamas terrorists invaded Israel on October 7, Israel's complex relationship with the United States has impeded the course of its righteous war against Hamas. It's true that America supplies Israel with much of the weaponry and ammunition it needs to eradicate Hamas. But like the contributions of wealthy congregants, this largesse - which America frequently threatens to cut off - comes at a very steep cost.

In the final chapter of the Book of Zephaniah, the prophet describes a fundamental change that will take place in Israel at the end of days - a shift that must occur for Israel to achieve its mission. "On that day you shall not be ashamed of all your deeds [with] which you rebelled against Me... And I will leave over in your midst a humble and poor people, and they shall take shelter in the name of the Lord. The remnant of Israel shall neither commit injustice nor speak lies; neither shall deceitful speech be found in their mouth, for they shall graze and lie down, with no one to cause them to shudder" (Zephaniah 3: 11-13).

Zephaniah prophesies that Israel will learn true humility, and because of that, she will no longer have to be afraid. No one will "cause them to shudder" any longer. But how, exactly, will this change come about?

Rabbi Meir Wisser explains: "In earlier times... Israel established alliances with other powerful nations, asking them for military assistance. And because they relied on these powerful nations, they learned from their evil ways. But at the end of days, when all of the nations recognize God and serve Him, Israel will no longer sin, because 'no one will cause them to shudder,' and they will no longer learn from those nations' [false] ideologies and [evil] deeds."[3]

What is the sin at the root of Israel's suffering? Zephaniah places the blame for Israel's suffering squarely on its dependence on powerful nations like the

United States. By placing its trust in America, Israel is physically and spiritually damaged in several ways that are not immediately apparent.

Though the US gives over $3.3 billion in foreign aid to Israel each year, the long-term impact of this support is deeply damaging to the nation it is meant to help. It has a suffocating effect on the development of domestic Israeli defense companies because the terms of the aid package require Israel to purchase the vast majority of its arms and ammunition from American companies. The result is that Israel has ceded its arms manufacturing to the United States, placing all of its eggs in the American basket. Given the tenuousness of America's support for Israel, this approach leaves the Jewish state alarmingly susceptible to American pressure, in more ways than one.

Over the years, American leaders have shown that US support for Israel comes "with strings attached." At any moment, the United States can withhold military aid from Israel, leaving Israel in a dangerously vulnerable position. In May 2024, as Israel began a complex invasion of Hamas' stronghold in Rafah, the Biden administration stopped the delivery of thousands of critically important precision weapons to Israel due to pressure from anti-Israel Democrats trying to force Israel to end its war against Hamas - a decision that would allow the terror organization to survive, rearm and murder Israelis again in the future.[4] Israel's reliance on American largesse makes it almost impossible for Israel's leaders to withstand American pressure, even when that pressure puts Israeli lives at risk.

The Biden administration's decision to withhold badly needed arms from Israel in 2024 is reminiscent of another time President Biden undercut the Jewish state. In 1982, during a closed-door meeting of the Senate Foreign Relations Committee, Biden reportedly warned Prime Minister Begin that military aid to Israel could be halted due to Israel's offensive campaign in Lebanon. Begin responded with outrage, saying "Don't threaten us with cutting off aid to give up our principles. I'm not a Jew with trembling knees. I am a proud Jew with 3,700 years of civilized history. Nobody came to our aid when we were dying in the gas chambers and ovens. Nobody came to our aid when we were striving to create our country. We paid for it. We fought for it. We died for it. We will stand by our principles. We will defend them. And, when necessary, we will die for them again, with or without your aid."[5] Where have you gone, Menachem Begin? Our nation turns its lonely eyes to you.

After October 7, the United States pressured Israel to provide enormous shipments of humanitarian aid to the people of Gaza. Though this sounds like a reasonable and even moral request, it was, in fact, immoral and deeply damaging to Israel's war effort, as this "humanitarian aid" was immediately commandeered by Hamas and used to resupply its army of terrorists. This prolonged the war, for the only way to force Hamas terrorists out of their terror tunnels is to cut off their supply chain. Can you imagine President Franklin Roosevelt supplying humanitarian aid to German civilians during World War II? Neither can I.

In the name of protecting non-combatants, the US also pressured Israel into fighting dangerous battles in the streets of Gaza, instead of simply destroying these targets from the air. Tragically, this led to the unnecessary deaths of many Israeli soldiers - husbands, fathers and sons who will never come home to their loved ones.

American pressure not only increases the costs of Israel's victory, but also places that victory in doubt. How can Israel possibly destroy Hamas in the southern Gaza Strip if America demands that Israel prevent harm to every last non-combatant? No military - the US military included - can achieve victory under such constraints.

The Biden administration consistently pressured Israel to finish the war against Hamas as quickly as possible and to reinstate the corrupt Palestinian Authority as the governing body in Gaza, despite the PA's well-deserved reputation for widespread corruption, its complete lack of standing among the Arabs of Judea and Samaria, and its long term goal of wiping Israel off the map. At the same time, the Biden administration inexplicably granted Iran $10 billion in sanctions relief *after* Iran's proxy Hamas committed horrific atrocities against Israel on October 7. In other words, the administration has helped Israel with one hand while supporting Israel's enemies with the other. It's fair to wonder whether Israel would be better off if America stayed out of the Middle East altogether.

American aid is damaging in other ways as well. The Israeli security establishment was lulled into a false sense of security, believing that its alliance with America would dissuade Hamas from launching a major attack on Israel. Too many of Israel's leaders were blinded by their trust in America, assuming the backing of the world's greatest superpower would remain ironclad in any future war. All of these illusions were tragically dispelled on October 7, when Israel's alliance with America did nothing to prevent the wholesale slaughter of over 1,200 innocent Israelis. It wasn't American firepower that prevented another Holocaust on October 7, but the bravery of ordinary Israelis who, armed only with their personal handguns, ran to battle and stopped Hamas from penetrating further into Israel, preventing an even greater massacre of civilians.

These criticisms should not be seen as a condemnation of the United States. Throughout its history, the US has been a nation of extraordinary kindness, rebuilding Europe after World War II and intervening in humanitarian crises around the world. For hundreds of years, it offered a safe haven to persecuted Jews all over the world, though it is sadly less safe for Jews today. The problem is not that Israel considers America its greatest ally, but that the relationship is unbalanced - that Israel's alliance with America is like that of a slave and his master. From the lofty heights of Washington, D.C., American leaders look down upon their Israelite servants. If an American leader deigns to meet with the Israelis, that alone obligates Israel's leaders to give thanks for the rest of his days.[6]

Israel's unhealthy reliance on the United States means that it is uniquely vulnerable to damaging cultural influences currently emanating from America. Far too many Israelis place the United States on a pedestal, hungrily absorbing American movies, music and ideologies. America's role as Israel's influential "big brother" means that its woke culture and moral confusion have an outsized influence on Israel's own culture. "The voice is the voice of Jacob, but the hands are the hands of Esau" (Genesis 27:22). Jacob is distinguished by his voice, his words and ideas, while Esau is distinguished by his hands, his physical power. But today, because Jacob's descendants rely upon Esau for physical support, they also revere the "voice of Esau," which corrupts and cheapens Israeli culture.[7]

Alongside American weapons, Israel imports the very worst of American culture. During the months leading up to October 7, Israeli society was torn apart due to non-stop protests over the prospect of judicial reform - protests eerily reminiscent of the Black Lives Matter riots of 2020 and which were encouraged and actively supported by the Biden administration[8] and American progressives. Israeli leftists were only too eager to learn from their "big brothers" in the US.

Israel is a small nation, and it has never aspired to be a superpower like the US. Israel's strength is meant to come in another form - as a moral and religious superpower. "I will make you a light of nations, so that My salvation shall be until the end of the earth" (Isaiah 49:6). The people of Israel are meant to influence the cultures of the rest of the world, not vice versa.

In the era just before the destruction of the first Temple, the Assyrian Empire threatened the far smaller kingdoms of Israel and Judah. When Assyria began to conquer the region and swallow up the smaller nations and city-states of the Middle East, the kingdom of Judah hoped that Egypt, a regional superpower, would step in to protect them. They would be sorely disappointed. As Assyria conquered the northern tribes of Israel and exiled its people, Egypt did nothing. Ultimately, Jerusalem, the capital of Judah, was saved through Divine intervention, not through any help from the Egyptians.

Ezekiel prophesied that the day will come when the people of Israel will finally learn their lesson and no longer place their trust in foreign superpowers like ancient Egypt or the United States: "And it [Egypt] will no longer be the confidence of the House of Israel, bringing iniquity into remembrance when they turn after them, and they shall know that I am the Lord God" (Ezekiel 29:16). Israel will no longer rely on superpowers or learn from their pagan cultures, turning their hearts instead to the God of Israel.

"We must free ourselves of those chains; we must stand on our own feet in the holy land... Even our master, our first father Abraham, when he traveled to our land, was told: 'Go forth from your land and from your birthplace and from your father's house, to the land that I will show you. And I will make you into a great nation, and I will bless you, and I will aggrandize your name, and you shall be a blessing (Genesis 12:1-2).' Meaning, it is impossible to merit the land of Israel without abandoning the culture of the other lands. So long as you are attached to customs that are foreign to our spirit you will remain, essentially, in exile [even if you are physically in the land of Israel]. For physically leaving the lands of the nations is not enough to achieve freedom and redemption, rather, even more essential is abandoning the worldview of the nations and knowing that God, and God alone, is master over the entire world. 'For He is your Lord, and prostrate yourself to Him (Psalm 45:12).'"[9]

Israel will only fulfill its divine mission when its leaders give God His proper seat at the head of the table. Until then, Israel will remain captive to the whims of earthly superpowers like the United States. Israel must place its confidence in God, and overcome its fearful habit of trying to please America. In the words of Rabbi Abraham Isaac Kook, "Fear is one of the forbidden traits, and is the result of [national] depression and exhaustion that we must avoid like poison. We must be armed with courage and the knowledge that our goals are pure, just and a fulfillment of God's will. We must remove from ourselves the desire to please all people and nations, even the kindest and best among them. Instead, we must place our hope for success in God... and seek to please our Creator, the Creator of all."[10]

"It is a nation that will dwell alone, and will not be reckoned among the nations" (Numbers 23:9). When Israel recognizes that it is a unique nation destined to be alone and places its trust in God, she will "dwell" in safety and honor, and no other nation will dare to challenge her. But when Israel places her trust in the nations, she "will not be reckoned" - the nations will lose respect for Israel and denigrate and attack her. By placing her trust in America, Israel loses America's respect.

Though most Americans are not yet conscious of this, America itself desperately needs Israel to be strong and independent. The United States is the most powerful nation on Earth, but it has lost its way. Millions of young people continue to drift away from the religious beliefs of their parents, resulting in a young generation that supports terrorist groups like Hamas and rejects Judeo-Christian values. America has raised a generation of young pagans, a generation that worships man and its own desires. Unsurprisingly, the results are disastrous. With the decline of traditional Judaism and Christianity in America, spiritual energies have not vanished but have reverted to the uninstructed, natural, pagan ways which our ancestors once proudly rejected. As sexual licentiousness increases, so does loneliness, and as the pursuit of individual freedom intensifies, families and communities grow weaker.[11] Younger Americans are lost, aimless and unhappy.[12] Suffering from family breakdown, declining birth rates and record levels of depression, America has lost its way - and it has much to learn from Israel.

Despite having so many reasons to be miserable, Israelis are among the happiest people in the world.[13] Israel has the highest birth rate in the developed world[14] and has raised a generation of young people who are more religiously traditional than their parents[15] and who rushed to volunteer for the army after October 7.[16] Now more than ever, a declining America needs Israel to assume its proper role and become a light unto the nations, to help the United States rediscover its biblical heritage. The fate of the West depends on it.

On February 18, 2024, Israel's cabinet unanimously opposed the unilateral recognition of a Palestinian state.[17] The decision came amidst increasing international pressure, particularly from the United States, with reports revealing the Biden administration's collaboration with Arab partners on a detailed plan for the establishment of a Palestinian state within a defined timeframe. Israel's leadership publicly rejected American policy despite Secretary of State Antony Blinken's repeated assertions of America's commitment to Palestinian statehood.

While a public disagreement with the United States is always concerning in the short term, Israel's defiance is encouraging. The sages state that "The sole difference between this world and the days of the Messiah is subjugation to foreign kings."[18] As Rabbi Pesach Wolicki argues, the distinction between Jewish exile and redemption transcends mere physical location. The Jewish people may be living in their land, but if they are dominated or controlled by other nations, they are not truly free and remain in "exile." By this measure, yielding to US pressure and altering the course of the conflict in a manner favorable to Israel's enemies would prolong the Jewish people's exile, perpetuate their subjugation to foreign powers and delay the arrival of the Messiah. But if Israel can stand strong and continue to defy the United States, this moment of defiance will mark a new stage in the redemption of the world.[19]

Israel can defend itself and destroy its enemies without an unhealthy reliance on America. Like a son-in-law who tells his controlling father-in-law, "Keep your money, I'll make my own decisions," it's time for Israel to liberate itself and declare true independence. Along these lines, Yoram Ettinger, one of Israel's top security experts, argues that in the long term, it is essential that Israel wean itself from American foreign aid, which will boost Israel's local defense industry and strengthen its standing with America and the rest of the world.[20]

In 1948, when Harry Truman imposed an arms embargo on Israel as she fought for her life against seven Arab armies, Israel was far weaker than she is today. Salvation came from unexpected places. Poland, despite its long history of antisemitism, provided training and arms to Jewish underground groups like the Irgun, the Lechi, and the Haganah. Czechoslovakia supplied weapons. Incredibly, Italian mafiosi and Irish dockworkers in New York worked with Jewish teens to illegally transport weapons to Israel. God will never abandon the Jewish people, and He will never run out of messengers to bring salvation.[21]

When Israel finally learns to place its trust in God and no longer relies upon America, the European Union or the corrupt United Nations, God's people will become the light unto the nations they are destined to be. "From Zion will come forth Torah, and the word of God from Jerusalem" (Isaiah 2:2). The peoples of the world will be drawn to Israel and emulate her ways, which will lead them to abandon their idols and "call in the name of the Lord." "For then I will convert the peoples to a pure language that all of them call in the name of the Lord, to worship Him of one accord" (Zephaniah 3:9).

"And they shall come and they shall see My glory. And I will place a sign upon them, and I will send from them refugees to the nations, Tarshish, Pul, and Lud, who draw the bow, to Tubal and Javan, the distant islands, who did not hear of My fame and did not see My glory, and they shall recount My glory among the nations" (Isaiah 66:18-19). "And the Lord shall become King over all the earth; on that day shall the Lord be one, and His name one" (Zechariah 14:9).

CHAPTER 19

A RELIGIOUS REVIVAL? MORDECAI, ESTHER AND THE LION WITHIN

> *Wake, Israel, wake! Recall to-day*
> *The glorious Maccabean rage…*
> *Oh deem not dead that martial fire,*
> *Say not the mystic flame is spent!*
> *With Moses' law and David's lyre,*
> *Your ancient strength remains unbent.*
> *Let but an Ezra rise anew,*
> *To lift the banner of the Jew!*[1]

Over the last century, the vast majority of American Jewry became progressively and seemingly inevitably more secular. With an intermarriage rate of 72%, all signs have pointed to the imminent end of the largest and most important Jewish community outside of Israel. Until now.

In late January 2024, conservative New York radio talk show host Sid Rosenberg visited Israel for the first time, broadcasting his popular show from Jerusalem. "I say all the time, if Hamas wanted to try and ruin the spirit of the Jewish people and break us - the exact opposite has happened, you've brought the Jew out in me… I've always been a proud Jew, but I've skipped going to synagogue and over the past few years, even the High Holidays. But two weeks after October 7, my wife joined a temple, I've started to go to Friday night Shabbat dinners… and I've even sat and learned Torah with a rabbi."[2]

Meanwhile, Matisyahu - the superstar reggae musician who in recent years distanced himself from Judaism - reacted similarly to the massacre of October 7. On the Ami's House podcast, he explained that his "*pintele Yid*," his "Jewish spark," was awakened. "Over the years, [being Jewish] became less central to me. And right now it's come back, full force."[3]

Israel's religious revival, particularly among IDF soldiers, is well documented. High demand for *tzitzit*[4] and phylacteries and moving scenes of religious and secular soldiers praying together have become tangible signs of a widespread spiritual awakening. "Days are coming, says Hashem, and I will send famine into the land, not a famine for bread nor a thirst for water, but to hear the word of God" (Amos 8:11). Israeli soldiers and much of the nation are thirsty for God's word. "This tangible living thirst, which fills the practical lives [of the people of Israel] with its light… calls out to the nation to wake up, rise up and shake off the dust of humiliation."[5]

The impact among diaspora Jews, though less obvious, is just as real. Talya Paskin, a jewelry designer from the UK, saw a 600% surge in the sales of her Star of David necklace, a trend also seen by other designers who sell jewelry with Jewish themes.[6] According to a survey of diaspora Jews taken in the wake of October 7, 86% of respondents said that community members were experiencing a "deeper connection to their own Jewish identity."[7]

The sleepy and assimilated Jewish communities across the world are awakening and beginning to discover who they truly are.

Israel's Inner Lion

Have you ever seen the kids' movie *Madagascar*? The movie tells the story of a group of "wild" animals at the Central Park Zoo in New York City. The crowds are in awe of these exotic beasts. Everyone's favorite is Alex the lion, the "King of New York"; the children cheer every time he roars.

But it's all a show. In reality, these animals are anything but ferocious. Pampered by trainers who wait on them hand and foot, their habitats, carefully designed to look like the wild, are safe and comfortable. The animals are living the good life.

Still, Marty the zebra finds himself dreaming about the wild. He can't shake the feeling that he wasn't made to live in a zoo, that he was born to roam free in the grasslands of Africa. On Marty's tenth birthday, the other animals try to cheer him up, to no avail. His restlessness ultimately leads him to escape the zoo, with his friends – the lion, hippo and giraffe - in tow. They soon find themselves in the jungle of Madagascar.

These zoo animals were born to live free, possessing the jungle instincts of the wild. But being raised in a zoo, away from their natural habitat, left them unprepared for the wild. This is the movie's primary joke; see what happens when you drop a bunch of domesticated New York City animals into the wilds of Madagascar!

But little by little, the animals discover their natural instincts. Alex the lion realizes that he is the king of the jungle, finding strength he never knew he had. By the end of the movie, the lion, zebra and others have become the wild and powerful animals they were born to be.

Madagascar is more than an entertaining kids' movie. It is the story of American Jewry.

For generations, American Jews have lived in a "golden cage." The United States was far more than a safe haven for Jews - it was the single greatest exile the Jewish people ever experienced. American Jews reached heights of wealth and success unmatched by any other diaspora Jewish community in history.

This success led to self-delusion. American Jews convinced themselves that the United States was their new Jerusalem - that America was truly their home. Though they generally supported the State of Israel, Israel was not for *them*, not personally. Israel was for those unfortunate "other Jews" who tragically were not blessed to live in the United States, the *goldene medina*, the "golden land."

Like Alex, Marty, and the other animals of *Madagascar*, American Jews forgot that the "exile zoo," even a beautiful zoo like America, is not a Jew's natural habitat. They enjoyed the zoo so much that they decided to make it their permanent home, abandoning the ancient Jewish dream of returning to the holy land. They lost touch with their "inner lion"; they forgot that they were God's chosen people, tasked with a unique mission to become a light unto the world. They abandoned the Bible, and in doing so, they ignored their Jewish souls. Like Alex the lion, eating sushi in the Central Park Zoo instead of hunting his prey in the plains of Africa, they lost touch with their true selves.

To fulfill their purpose, Jews must be in their natural habitat, attached to the inheritance God set aside for them in the land of Israel. Israel is not merely a "Jewish center," where Jews can live openly and comfortably among a Jewish majority. The soul of the people of Israel is bound up with the land of Israel; detached from it, they cannot be whole. "Holy children, you will be a blessing to the land, in the precious land you will be blessed, and on holy ground you will spread forth your branches."[8] When a Jew returns to the land, it's like connecting a plug to an electrical outlet. The lights go on, and the soul begins to shine.

American Jews were blind to all of this. They believed they were already home - until October 7. Like a ton of bricks smashing the windshield of a car, October 7 shattered their illusions. As Rabbi Yaakov Moshe Charlop perceptively said, "When the holy nation of Israel loses sight of the strength of its soul and the people forget... how blessed they are to be Jews, 'Because the Lord's portion is His people Jacob, the lot of His inheritance,' (Deuteronomy 32:9), the nations of the world will come and smack them in the face and stomp on them with feet of arrogance."[9]

When thousands of hateful people marched for Hamas in the streets of New York City, American Jews began to realize that they were living among far more antisemites than they ever imagined. When polls showed that over 50% of young people in America think Israel should be wiped off the map and replaced with a Palestinian state,[10] Jews began to question whether they have a future in America. After October 7, Jews throughout the United States began to understand, deeply and profoundly, that they are *Jews* – whether they like it or not. They began to understand that Israel is more than just a Jewish country. It is their *destiny*.

Little by little, American Jews are discovering the lion that dwells within them. After decades of sticking their heads in the sand and ignoring the growing cancer of antisemitism, they have begun to fight back. "Behold, they are a people that rises like a lioness and raises itself like a lion" (Numbers 23:24). When Bilaam looked down upon the Israelites from the mountains of Moab, he saw a nation of lions - holy and powerful warriors ready to fight for God.

This is the DNA of the people of Israel. A zebra cannot cannot change its stripes, and even a lion that has spent its entire life in captivity remains, at heart, a lion. So too, a Jew in exile remains God's child, even if he has wandered far from home. The only question is when he will return.

A Glorious Salvation and Lost Opportunity

Though today's spiritual revival may seem unprecedented, the Jewish people have been here before. During the time of the Book of Esther, the great majority of Jews in the Persian Empire were assimilated. The sages ask, "For what reason were the Jews of that generation deserving of destruction?... Because they participated in the banquet of the evil [Ahasuerus]."[11] Distant from God and their heritage, Jews shamefully participated in a party that celebrated the rejection of biblical values. Most Jews of that era identified as Persians first and Jews second, if they identified as Jews at all.

We tend to view Mordecai and Esther as righteous Jews who, from the very start of the Book of Esther, rejected the assimilation of their brothers and sisters. The sages portray Mordecai as a rabbi, a member of the Great Assembly[12] and one of the nation's great spiritual leaders, while Esther is described as a deeply religious woman who secretly maintained her Torah observance in Ahaseurus' palace. But there is another, more historical approach offered by many commentators, which views Mordecai and Esther very differently.[13]

"Mordecai" and "Esther" are Persian names. Mordecai is named for the Babylonian god Mordoch, while Esther is named for a Persian goddess. The contrast to their fathers' Hebrew names, "Yair (Jair)" and "Avichayil (Abihail)," is stark. The implication is that their parents, Jewish exiles from Jerusalem, established themselves in Persian society and hoped their children would become full-fledged Persians, unencumbered by Hebrew Jewish names. We see the same phenomenon today among American Jews who give their children non-Jewish names like Brittany, Oliver and Emma, hoping to mask, or at least deemphasize, their children's Jewish identity.

Mordecai, a successful politician who "sat at the gate of the king" (Esther 2:19), was likely educated in Persian schools and entirely comfortable navigating its halls of power. When Mordecai informed Ahaseurus' administration of Bigtan and Teresh's plot to assassinate the king (Esther 2:21), his warnings were taken seriously and acted upon, for he was a respected member of the empire's political class. But like many successful American Jews in politics today, Mordecai's Jewish heritage initially had no impact on his political views or his career.

How did Esther manage to conceal her Jewish heritage from King Ahaseurus? How is it that no one within the Jewish community revealed her identity? A straightforward interpretation suggests that Esther, much like Mordecai, was a fully assimilated Jew who had distanced herself from the Jewish community of Shushan, the Persian capital. By hiding her Jewish identity, she was able to ascend to the highest levels of influence and power.

Like the other assimilated Jews of their time, neither Mordecai nor Esther heeded the call of a previous emperor, Cyrus the Great, allowing the people of Israel to return to their land. In other words, they were very similar to most American Jews of our own time, who show little interest in fulfilling biblical prophecy and returning to God's land.

"And Haman said to King Ahasuerus, 'There is a certain people scattered and separate among the peoples throughout all the provinces of your kingdom, and their laws differ from those of every people, and they do not keep the king's laws; it is therefore of no use for the king to let them be. If it pleases the king, let it be written to destroy them...'" (Esther 3:8-9).

The sages explain that when Haman first brought up the possibility of destroying the Jews, Ahasuerus replied that he was afraid of the God of the Jews. Haman reassured the king by saying "*Yeshno am echad*," "There is a certain people." The word "*yeshno*," meaning "there is," is related to the word "*yashen*," meaning "asleep." The verse can therefore be read as "There is a sleeping people." In effect, Haman reassured Ahasuerus that they could succeed in destroying the Jewish people because the Jews were "asleep and negligent of the commandments" and could not count on God's protection.[14]

The sages describe Israel's seventy-year exile in Babylonia and Persia following the destruction of the first Temple as a time of "deep sleep."[15] Though many Jews still personally observed the Bible's commandments, they "fell asleep" as a *nation*. They neglected the *national* commandments of the Bible - the sacrifices, the agricultural laws and, worst of all, the obligation to live as a sovereign people in their own land.[16]

Before Ahasuerus assumed the throne, King Cyrus proclaimed that the Jewish people were welcome to return to Jerusalem and rebuild the Temple: "All the kingdoms of the Earth the Lord God of the heavens delivered to me, and He commanded me to build Him a House in Jerusalem, which is in Judea. Who is among you of all His people, may his God be with him, and he may ascend to Jerusalem, which is in Judea, and let him build the House of the Lord, God of Israel; He is the God Who is in Jerusalem" (Ezra 1:2-3). Yet the Jews of Persia slept through the "alarm clock" of Cyrus' decree. They were comfortable in Persian society, content to be "Persians of Jewish faith" and to remain a religious minority scattered throughout the Persian Empire. Return to Israel? No, thank you.

After Ahasuerus sealed the decree authorizing the genocide of the Jews, "the couriers went forth in haste by the king's order, and the edict was given in Shushan the capital, and the king and Haman sat down to drink, and the city of Shushan was *perplexed*" (Esther 4:15). Perplexed? The Jews of Shushan heard that a holocaust was decreed upon them by the most powerful man on earth, and they were *perplexed*? "Shocked," "terrified," "panicked" - any of these terms would describe an appropriate to such a horrible decree. But why were the Jews of Shushan "perplexed"? What was confusing? The decree was as clear as could be!

The Jew's confusion reflects the psychology of the Jewish community at that time. Shushan was a cosmopolitan metropolis, the cultural, financial and political center of the ancient world. The Jews of Shushan were successful and assimilated and identified fully as Persians. They possessed the same rights as any other Persian citizen, and only a few months earlier had participated in the King's magnificent feast. An antisemitic decree like this was simply unthinkable.

But then the impossible happened. Letters were "sent by the hand of the couriers to all the king's provinces, to destroy, kill, and cause to perish all the Jews, both young and old, little children and women, on one day" (Esther 4:13). This is why the Jews of Shushan were "perplexed." They could not comprehend why their beloved empire, to which they dedicated their entire lives, was now planning their destruction. Yes, they were certainly terrified, but their more revealing reaction was perplexity. As it is for most American Jews today, Judaism was a minor element of their identity; they were "Persians of the Mosaic persuasion." But all at once, their illusions were cruelly shattered.[17]

This was not the last time assimilated Jews living in exile would be "perplexed." In the 1930s, the assimilated Jews of Germany, who identified fully as patriotic Germans, were deeply perplexed when the Nazi horror descended upon them. And today, millions of American Jews are also perplexed, shocked by the massive outburst of antisemitism across the country in the wake of October 7.

As the horrors of October 7 have done for so many Jews today, the rise to power of the notorious antisemite Haman triggered a spiritual crisis for Mordecai and the other assimilated Jews of Shushan. People they thought were friends and allies remained silent in the face of Haman's decree, just as so many liberal and progressive "friends" of American Jews have remained silent today after Hamas brazenly raped, tortured and massacred over 1,200 Jews.[18]

Ahasuerus' genocidal decree shook them from their stupor. As the sages said, "The removal of Ahasuerus' ring [for the sealing of Haman's decree] was more effective [at encouraging the Jews to repent] than the forty-eight prophets and the seven prophetesses who prophesied on behalf of the Jewish people."[19]

For the first time, Mordecai understood that he was part of the nation of Israel, discovering a Jewish pride he never knew he had. He refused to bow to Haman, risking his life and reclaiming his Jewish identity. He rediscovered his roots as a son of the tribe of Benjamin, the only son of Jacob who had never bowed to Esau, the forefather of Amalek and Haman.

When Haman's decree calling for the genocide of the Jewish people became known, Mordecai dressed in sackcloth and ashes and "cried with a loud and bitter cry" (Esther 4:1). No longer would Jews remain silent as antisemites ran rampant through the streets! The time had come to act. The only question was whether Esther, the assimilated Jewish queen, would join Mordecai and rise up to defend her people.

Hearing about Mordecai's public mourning and identification as a Jew, Esther was terrified. After all she and Mordecai had accomplished, after all their efforts to hide their Jewish identities, why was Mordecai risking everything and associating with openly Orthodox Jews?

But this was not the same Mordecai that Esther had known before. While Esther enjoyed her life in the king's palace, Mordecai made the fateful decision to return to his roots and align himself with the nation of Israel. He informed Esther of the decree and commanded her to approach the king on behalf of her people. Understandably, Esther hesitated. Approaching the king was dangerous - and why should she do so on behalf of a nation she hardly knew and didn't understand?

At this fateful moment, Mordecai challenged Esther with a manifesto of Jewish peoplehood: "Do not imagine to yourself that you will escape in the king's house from among all the Jews. For if you remain silent at this time, relief and rescue will arise for the Jews from elsewhere, and you and your father's household will perish; and who knows but that you have come to your royal position for such a time as this?" (Esther 4:13-14).

It was clear to Mordecai that Esther must choose, just as every American Jew must ultimately choose. Would she play a role in Israel's destiny and stand up for her people, or would she commit spiritual suicide and permanently erase her Jewish identity? Esther made the noble choice. She reclaimed her Jewish identity and risked her life to defend the brothers and sisters she hardly knew. She became the heroine of the Purim story, manipulating both Haman and Ahasuerus to gain salvation for her people and, ultimately, herself.

As Mordecai and Esther went, so did the Jews of their time. The terror of Haman and the heroism of Esther sparked a religious revival unlike anything the nation had experienced before. "They confirmed what they had accepted earlier,"[20] rededicating themselves to observing the Bible in the wake of the miracle of Purim.

Nevertheless, despite the religious revival, only a small percentage of Jews in the Persian Empire returned to Israel to rebuild the Temple and reestablish Jewish independence and nationhood. When the immediate threat of Haman passed, the people once again fell asleep. Only 42,360 Jews returned to Israel with Ezra (Ezra 2:64), while the vast majority, including the wealthiest and most influential Jews, remained in the diaspora. The great medieval thinker and poet, Rabbi Judah Halevi, laments: "Divine Providence was ready to restore everything as it had been at first, if they had all willingly consented to return. But only a part was ready to do so, while the majority and the aristocracy remained in Babylon, preferring dependence and slavery, and unwilling to leave their houses and their affairs… In accordance with their mean mind they did not receive full measure. Divine Providence only gives man as much as he is prepared to receive."[21] Tragically, an incredible opportunity - to return to the land and usher in the final redemption - was lost.

"Go Home Jacob, Go Home!"

In June 2020, at the height of the George Floyd riots, thousands of protestors in Minneapolis demanded that the city defund, downsize or completely abolish the police department. A large group of demonstrators marched to the home of Jacob Frey, the ultra-liberal Jewish mayor of the city, and demanded that Frey share his opinion on the matter. Would he commit to defunding the Minneapolis Police Department? Quietly, meekly, Jacob Frey said "no." The speaker promptly grabbed the microphone and said, "Get the f— out of here." The crowd began to scream at the mayor, again and again: "Go home Jacob, go home!" Defeated, Jacob Frey slowly walked away with his head down. "Go home Jacob, go home!"[22]

There are times when God speaks through prophets, but there are also times when the words of those prophets are written on subway walls and tenement halls, when God's messages reach us from the most unlikely places. Watching this scene unfold in Minneapolis, hearing hundreds of people scream "Go home Jacob, go home!," I heard an echo of similar words uttered thousands of years ago, to a different Jacob.

After living in exile for 20 years in Laban's house, Jacob was confronted by an angel of God: "I am the God of Beth-El, where you anointed a monument, where you vowed to Me a vow. Now arise, leave this land and return to the land of your birthplace" (Genesis 31:13). In other words, "Go home Jacob, go home!"

Over and over again, God is calling out to American Jewry. "Go home Jacob, go home!" With each passing year, God's call is getting louder. It can be heard in the streets of New York, where Jews are cursed and attacked. It can be heard in the halls of power in Washington DC, where presidents are no longer afraid to turn their backs on the Jewish people. And you can hear it loud and clear on the campuses of Columbia University, UCLA and hundreds of other universities of hate.

In the wake of the Kishinev Pogrom of 1903, the great Zionist leader Vladimir Jabotinsky penned a short poem:

> *"Once, in that town, under a heap of garbage*
> *I noticed a piece of parchment -*
> *A fragment of the Torah*
> *I picked it up and carefully removed the dirt*
>
> *Two words stood out: 'b'eretz nochriya' – in an alien land.*
>
> *This scrap of parchment*
> *I nailed above the door to my own home.*
> *For in these two words out of the Book of Genesis*
> *Is told the entire story of the pogrom.*"[23]

Throughout the 1930s, Jabotinsky traveled across Europe, urging Jews to emigrate and move to the holy land before it was too late. In August 1938, on the 9th of *Av*, the day of mourning for the Temples destroyed in Jerusalem and the saddest day of the Jewish calendar, he spoke to the Jewish community of Warsaw. "It is already three years that I am calling upon you, Polish Jewry, who are the crown of world Jewry. I continue to warn you incessantly that a catastrophe is coming closer. I became gray and old in these years. My heart bleeds, that you, dear brothers and sisters, do not see the volcano which will soon begin to spit its all-consuming lava. I see that you are not seeing this because you are immersed and sunk in your daily worries... Listen to me in this 12th hour: In the name of God! Let any one of you save himself as long as there is still time. And time there is very little... and what else I would like to say to you in this day of the 9th of *Av*: whoever of you will escape from the catastrophe, he or she will live to see the exalted moment of a great Jewish wedding: the rebirth and the rise of a Jewish state. I don't know if I will be privileged to see it; my son will! I believe in this as I am sure that tomorrow morning the sun will rise."[24]

Jabotinsky heard God's call in an "alien land." But how many American Jews of our own time are listening? American Jews have awakened, but will they fall back asleep? How many will acknowledge that the rising antisemitism in America today is a clear sign from God urging them to return to the holy land and unite with their brethren in Israel? How many will rise up and reclaim the inheritance of their forefathers? Will any American Jewish leaders stand up and lead their people back to Israel?

In the late 19th century, George Eliot wrote of the Jews of her time, "Among its finer specimens there may arise some men of instruction and ardent public spirit, some new Ezras, some modern Maccabees, who will know how to use all favoring outward conditions, how to triumph by heroic example, over the indifference of their fellows and the scorn of their foes, and will steadfastly set their faces towards making their people once more one among the nations."[25] But where will we find these heroic Maccabees?

True leadership will not come from wealthy or prestigious Jewish leaders and organizations who fear that moving to Israel would risk their positions and status. Nor will most rabbis stand up and lead their people home, for "the shepherds of our people are in a deep sleep, not because of any evil of the heart but because of the weakness of their souls."[26] The "elders" are not equipped for the work of redemption.[27] Most rabbis are too timid to publicly challenge the status quo and acknowledge that American Jewry is in great danger. The great majority are afraid to unequivocally call for mass *Aliyah* to Israel. At the very least, I pray that American Jewish leaders will not try to prevent the emigration of American Jewry to Israel, "for one who slows the ingathering of Jews to the land delays the redemption... and prevents great light [from entering the world], and there is no limit to the damage he may cause."[28] If American Jews return to Israel, it will be in spite of, not because of, their leaders.

Who, then, will lead God's people home? The modern Maccabees George Eliot sought will be found among the "Jews in the pews" - the dentists, administrative assistants and stay-at-home moms who leapt into action after October 7 to stand up for Israel, even as many "official" leaders of the Jewish community did not.[29] We will find them among the Jewish college students who found the strength of will to push back against pro-Hamas campus rioters, even as the Jewish community did not show up to support them. It will be the simple Jews, the grassroots activists without prestige or name recognition, who will lead the return.

Aliyah, moving to Israel, is not easy. Uprooting one's life, learning a new language, restarting one's career - each of these challenges are daunting on their own, and they can be overwhelming all at once. But as Hillel Halkin wrote, "When has Jewish life not been hard? In the days of the Bible? Under the Romans? During the Middle Ages?... When... Jews in the Diaspora teach their child the story of Hanukkah they praise the Maccabees and blame the hellenizers who did not wish to go to war with the might and culture of Greece; when they read about the Inquisition, they disapprove of the tens of thousands of Jews who became Christians to escape it and they applaud the tens of thousands of others who braved penury and exile in order to remain Jews; when they think of the Holocaust they feel ashamed of those Jews who collaborated with the Nazis and did not go decently to their deaths with their brothers instead. And yet each of these groups that they condemn acted as they they did to escape death, torture, or degredation; each was being asked to pay a far higher price, to do something much harder... than to have to live in a free and independent Jewish state."[30]

Yes, making *Aliyah* is difficult, but some things are worth the price. "So said the Lord: I remember to you the lovingkindness of your youth, the love of your nuptials, your following Me in the desert, in a land not sown" (Jeremiah 2:2). If our forefathers could follow God into the desert with little more than the shirts on their backs, I have no doubt that Jews today can find the strength to follow God once again. "Be strong and have courage" (Joshua 1:6), for God and the people of Israel will be there for each other as Jews make the journey home.

The sages teach: "When Rabbi Zeira ascended to the land of Israel, he could not find a ferry to cross the Jordan River. He took hold of a rope that was strung across as a makeshift bridge and crossed the Jordan. A certain Sadducee said to him: 'Hasty people who put your mouths before your ears! When God gave the Torah to the people of Israel, you said "We will do" before "We will hear" (Exodus 24:7), [accepting the commandments of the Bible before you knew what the commandments were]. You remain hasty [to this day. Why couldn't you wait a little longer to cross the river on a ferry, like a normal person?] Rabbi Zeira said to him: Moses and Aaron did not merit entering this land; who is to say that I will merit seeing this land? [And so I hurried across before anything might occur to prevent my entrance into the holy land]."[31]

Rabbi Zeira understood that the opportunity to move to Israel may not always be available. When the door is open, a Jew must run to the land, without waiting for perfect conditions. The chance may not come again.

This is a moment of prophetic opportunity. "Oh, let Your dead revive! Let corpses arise! Awake and shout for joy, You who dwell in the dust!"

(Isaiah 26:19). A new spirit of hope and faith has revived a community that was for too long a lifeless corpse. American Jews are awakening, and now have the chance to complete the salvation begun by Mordecai and Esther. Perhaps the Jews who still remain in the diaspora, the exiled "sheep" of Israel, are finally ready to become the "lions" they are meant to be. "And the remnant of Jacob shall be among the nations, in the midst of many peoples, as a lion among the beasts of the forest, like a young lion among the flocks of sheep. Your hand shall be raised above your oppressors, and all your enemies shall be destroyed" (Micah 5:7-8).

This time, we pray the script will change. 2,500 years after Mordecai and Esther, the people of Israel have awakened - and the land of Israel is beckoning. "Sound the great shofar for our freedom, raise the banner to gather our exiles and gather us together from the four corners of the earth."[32]

Go
To The Land
That will make everything sweeter
And harder
And deeper
And right…

Go
To The Land they wanted to get back to
All those years
And years
But couldn't.[33]

Return to who you are
Return to what you are,
Return to where you were
Born and reborn again.
Return again, return again
Return to the land of your soul.[34]

"Let but an Ezra rise anew, To lift the banner of the Jew!"

PART IV:
CONCLUSION

CHAPTER 20:

SOON, SOON, SOON: FROM WAR TO REDEMPTION

In 1913, a young Jew named David Cohen was traveling from Russia to Germany. Along the way, he stopped in Radin, a small town in what is today Belarus, to visit his teacher, Rabbi Israel Meir Kagan, one of the great rabbis of the generation.

As they sat together in the evening, Rabbi Kagan said to the young man: "It used to be, when I recited our daily prayers and would reach the words 'To Jerusalem Your Holy City, bring us back in mercy,' I would think to myself - 'This is prayer, prayer, prayer.' And when I would say the words 'May the offshoot, the descendant of Your servant King David, soon flower,' I thought to myself - 'This is prayer, prayer, prayer.' But now, when I say 'To Jerusalem Your Holy City, bring us back in mercy' and 'May the offshoot, the descendant of Your servant King David, soon flower,' I think to myself: 'slowly, slowly, it is happening; now, now, soon, soon, soon! Whether this will happen in my lifetime, I do not know; for I am already old. But in *your* days, David, it is certain, it is certain, it is certain.'"[1]

And so it was. Rabbi Kagan died in 1933, but Rabbi David Cohen, who later became one of Israel's leading thinkers and rabbis, would merit to see the liberation of Jerusalem in 1967, when prayer - "To Jerusalem Your Holy City, bring us back in mercy" - became reality.

Events are moving quickly, as God's redemptive plans move forward at ever quickening speed. The horrific evil perpetrated against Israel on October 7 and the war that inevitably followed marked the beginning of a new chapter in redemption, unleashing a demonic hatred that has shaken the civilized world to its core. Painful as it may be, we have merited to live at the time of the final redemption, the redemption our ancestors prayed and yearned for. It is coming, "Now, now, soon, soon, soon!"

A Revealing War: Ishmael, Edom and America

War is terrible, but it is also revealing.

Pressured situations reveal an individual's true character. When a young couple is preparing for their wedding, spending their days choosing tablecloth colors and flower arrangements, they may love each other, but they can't truly *know* each other. Only after they marry, when they are under stress, struggling to pay the rent and shouldering the burden of raising children - only then will they reveal their true natures.

The same is true of nations. War is terrible, but it plays a critical role in the development of nations, revealing fissures that were previously obscure and clarifying worldviews and ideologies.[2] When a nation is under the pressure of war, when barbarians overrun the gates and threaten to destroy everything its people hold dear - these are the moments when a nation discovers what it is made of. Will its people stand up for good against evil? Or will they fearfully remain on the sidelines or, worse yet, join the forces of evil?

The people of Ishmael, the many nations that have embraced radical Islam, have always been clear about their goals - to establish Islamic rule in Israel, the Middle East and ultimately the entire world. For a time, most Muslim leaders were careful not to speak of their true intentions to the West, but in the wake of October 7, the days of obfuscation are over.

Only a few weeks after October 7, Ghazi Hamad, a senior member of Hamas' political bureau, did not mince words. "Israel is a country that has no place on our land. We must remove it because it constitutes a security, military and political catastrophe to the Arab and Islamic nation. We are not ashamed to say this." When asked whether this meant the complete annihilation of Israel,

Hamad replied: "Yes, of course… We must teach Israel a lesson, and we will do it twice and three times. The Al-Aqsa Flood is just the first time, and there will be a second, a third, a fourth. Will we have to pay a price? Yes, and we are ready to pay it. We are called a nation of martyrs, and we are proud to sacrifice martyrs."[3] Could Hamas be any clearer about its goals?

Hamas' supporters are equally clear about their goals. On April 22, 2024, Essa Al-Nassr, a member of the Qatari legislative Shura council, spoke at an Arab League session. He said "There will be no peace nor negotiations with the Zionist entity… they are killers of prophets." He went on to commend the "Al-Aqsa Flood, Hamas' October 7th massacre, claiming that this was only a "prelude to the annihilation of the corruption of the 'second Zionist entity' upon earth."[4]

Meanwhile, the Edomites, the secular woke progressives of America and Europe, have also shown their hand. David called out to God to save him from "all nations who forget God" (Psalm 9:18), but our challenge is even greater. For we are fighting enemies who not only forget God, but declare open war against Him, people who work day and night to undermine the Judeo-Christian biblical values that made the West great in the first place.

On May 10, 2024, the General Assembly of the United Nations voted overwhelmingly, by a vote of 143 to 9, to treat the fictional "State of Palestine" as an observer state, urging the Security Council to favorably consider its full membership. Many supposed "friends" of Israel joined together to undermine the Jewish state, including European nations like France, Denmark, Greece and Belgium. Like their spiritual forefather Esau, the Europeans speak words of friendship even as their actions betray their true goals: the destruction of Israel.[5]

The American Left's war against the Bible has birthed a morally rudderless generation that supports rapists and baby killers. Pro-Hamas protests across the United States are only growing in intensity and numbers, and particularly among America's "best and brightest." In April 2024, thousands of protesters at Columbia University could be heard screaming "We are Hamas!" "Hamas make us proud, kill another soldier now!" "We are all Hamas, pig!" One Jewish Columbia University student was repeatedly kicked in the stomach during the protests as a pro-Hamas agitator told her to go "kill yourself."[6] Every day brings more outrageous news of antisemitism, US sanctions against Israelis and American pressure designed to make Israel lose its war against Hamas.

Though most Americans are good people who reject the evils of Islam, few are willing to stand up for biblical values. When students at NYU set up a pro-Hamas encampment on school grounds, NYU faculty members formed a human chain around the students following threats of mass arrests. Yet the Jewish students on campus brave enough to push back stood alone. Where was the "silent majority" of decent Americans? Why were they nowhere to be found?

The hatred spread even to the sleepy town of Woodstock, New York, where half a million young people once sang together with a message of peace and love. In May 2024, pro-Hamas demonstrators gathered outside of the local public elementary school, where they blocked the road and prevented parents from picking up their kids. They screamed at young Jewish children on their way to school, shouting that their parents are baby killers and complicit in genocide. Bryce Gruber, a Jewish mother with two young children, enrolled at the school, reported that the demonstrators yelled "Zionists and Jews are the problem" and "America must fall." A protester even took photos of Gruber and her young children, threatening to put their images on a public "Zionist watch list." Gruber was shocked that local police did nothing to stop the harassment, saying "This is New York. We're an inch from full pogroms." Most disturbing of all, Gruber describes how the neighborhood came out to cheer for the pro-Hamas rioters.[7] Like everyday Germans cheering for Hitler, the people of Woodstock appear ready to become Hamas' willing executioners.

The unabashed antisemitism now common on American city streets is a sign that America itself is in mortal danger. As Dennis Prager often says, "Non-Jews who think antisemitism is only the Jews' problem need to read about miners' canaries - about miners who think that when canaries die of noxious fumes those fumes won't kill them. Nothing better identifies incipient evil than antisemitism."[8] "Decent non-Jews who don't fight antisemitism don't understand that antisemitism represents a mortal threat to them. Tens of millions of non-Jews were killed because decent non-Jews ignored Hitler early on, dismissing him and Nazism as a Jewish problem."[9]

The Ishmaelites and Edomites of America are committed to destroying America as we know it. On April 5, 2024, the last Friday of Ramadan, Tarek Bazzi, a Michigan-based activist, declared at a rally in Dearborn, Michigan: "Imam Khomeini, who declared the International Al-Quds Day, this is why he would say to pour all of your chants and all of your shouts upon the head of America." He then led the crowd in chants of "Death to America" and "Death to Israel."[10] The jihad supporters shout their hatred from the rooftops. But where are the counter-protests? Why are good people silent? Where are the self-proclaimed "friends" of American Jewry, the liberals who mouthed platitudes at pro-Israel events in years gone by?

"She has no comforter among all her lovers; all her friends have betrayed her; they have become her enemies" (Lamentations 1:2). When President Biden blocked arms shipments to Israel in the midst of a war and pro-Hamas rioters took over Columbia University, where was Senate Majority Leader Chuck Schumer, the man who repeatedly and arrogantly calls himself *"Shomer Yisrael,"* the "Guardian of Israel?"[11] The moment it became politically inconvenient, he "betrayed her" and became Israel's enemy.

Not all the news is bad. In the wake of October 7, traditional Jews and Christians are taking steps towards forming an alliance. Jews and Christians appalled by the US administration's abandonment of Israel launched Keep God's Land, a movement promoting Israeli sovereignty over the entirety of the land of Israel. At the same time, Christians appalled by growing antisemitism in America founded the October 7th Coalition, a growing movement dedicated to fighting Jew-hatred in the United States. Little by little, many Jews and Christians are beginning to realize that our shared belief in the Hebrew Bible matters more than our differences.

"The Lord frustrated the counsel of nations; He put the plans of peoples to nought" (Psalm 33:10). The people of Israel will prevail; God will not abandon His people. But which way will America go? Will the Jews and Christians who still believe in the Bible rise up and steer the nation back from the abyss? Or will they passively allow the Edomites to take control of the nation and support Ishmael's assault on Israel and America itself?

The stakes are higher than many realize. History demonstrates that a nation's fate is closely linked to its treatment of the people of Israel. Ancient Egypt only became a world power and enjoyed its golden age during the time of the "New Kingdom," when Joseph unified the nation and the Israelites settled in Goshen. Following the slavery of the Israelites and the Exodus, during the era of the Tanites, Egypt was plagued by political division and economic crisis, and lost its status as the dominant superpower of the Middle East.

For generations, the status of Spanish Jewry fluctuated with each ruler. However, in the early 15th century, their position stabilized, allowing the Jewish community to thrive and achieve significant political and economic influence. Don Isaac Abarbanel, the most famous Jew of this era, served as treasurer to both King Alfonso V of Portugal and King Ferdinand II and Queen Isabella of Castile-Aragon. During this time of Jewish flourishing, the kingdoms of Aragon and Castile united to form Spain, which emerged as Europe's leading power. However, at the end of the 15th century, Spain's forced conversions and expulsion of hundreds of thousands of Jews marked the beginning of its decline. France and England soon surpassed Spain as dominant European powers, and Spain's territories and international status diminished. Today, Spain is among the poorest countries in Europe.

More recently, Turkey's transformation into the powerful Ottoman Empire coincided with the arrival of many Jewish exiles from Spain. Following this influx, the Ottomans conquered the land of Israel. However, as blood libels against Jews spread across the empire in the late 19th century, the empire experienced a swift decline, culminating in its complete collapse at the end of World War I, leaving Turkey as one of the poorest nations in the region.

A similar pattern can be observed in England. In 1656, Oliver Cromwell readmitted Jews to England, marking the beginning of Great Britain's rise to become the world's largest empire, ultimately governing territories that today correspond to 56 sovereign nations - including the land of Israel, which it conquered from the Ottomans. However, when Great Britain began to favor the Arabs and restricted Jewish immigration to Israel in the 1930s - at a time when Nazi Germany threatened the entire Jewish population of Europe - its power and influence waned. By the end of World War II, Britain had lost its superpower status and most of its territories. Today, Britain's future looks even darker as its radical Muslim population grows rapidly.

A similar fate befell Russia, which emerged as a global superpower at the same time that its Jewish population became the largest in the world. However, after decades of oppression and persecution, millions of Jews emigrated from Russia in the late 1980s and early 1990s, coinciding with the dissolution of the Soviet Union. Today, Russia is a shadow of its former self, facing an imminent demographic collapse and isolation from the democratic world.

The United States is no exception to this rule. The US rose to superpower status in the early 20th century when millions of Jews arrived on its shores, where they were granted equal rights and treated with dignity. For the next 100 years, as American Jews thrived, the US reached the pinnacle of its influence and power. Today, as the cancer of antisemitism spreads throughout the nation, America's future is uncertain. What will happen if the US turns against Israel and antisemitism worsens, driving masses of Jews to emigrate?

God promised Abraham: "I will bless those who bless you, and the one who curses you I will curse, and all the families of the earth shall be blessed in you" (Genesis 12:3). Though this verse has become a hackneyed phrase for many Bible believers, history has proven its truth. Will the leaders of the United States remember this verse in time? America's future as the world's most prosperous nation and leading democratic superpower hangs in the balance.[12]

A People Unlike Any Other

Most of all, the October 7 war has shaken the people of Israel. The war of Ishmael and Edom on the people of the Bible forced Israel to grapple with its destiny - a destiny most Jews have worked hard to avoid.

"Are you not like the children of the Cushites to Me, O children of Israel? says the Lord. Did I not bring Israel up from the land of Egypt, and the Philistines from Caphtor and Aram from Kir?" (Amos 9:7). The prophet compares Israel to the people of Cush, the biblical name for Ethiopia. Just as an Ethiopian is always distinguishable by his black skin, even if he is exiled from his land and lives among other peoples, a Jew is always a Jew, even if he tries to assimilate among the other nations. "Did I not bring Israel up from the land of Egypt?" Even though the Israelites lived as slaves in Egypt for many generations, they nevertheless remained a separate and distinct people. The Philistines and Aramites were conquered by other nations and disappeared from history, but the people of Israel cannot avoid their destiny, no matter how hard they try. Like God did with Jonah, so He will do to the people of Israel throughout history. If the Jews forget their identity and lose sight of their mission, God will intervene to remind them, using Israel's enemies as His tool.

For thousands of years, most Jews were not interested in returning to the holy land and reestablishing Jewish sovereignty. Even after the Holocaust made clear that Jews desperately needed their own country, the State of Israel was established in 1948 by a small minority of world Jewry. Of the 11 million Jews who survived World War II, only 600,000 were "crazy" enough to make Israel their home. After the Holocaust, the vast majority of world Jewry opted out of the Jewish national experiment. Nevertheless, God determined that it was time for the Jews to return home - and so Israel was established.

During the 1967 Six-Day War, Israel conquered Judea, Samaria, Gaza and the Golan Heights against its own will, when Egypt, Syria and Jordan threatened Israel with destruction. Other than a small minority of Religious Zionists who yearned to settle Israel's biblical heartland, most Israelis were ready to "return" God's land to the Arab nations that had attacked them, if only there was an Arab nation willing to make peace with Israel. But of course, there was no such nation, and so the people of Israel were forced to hold on to its biblical heartland and discover why God's land is central to its destiny. In the decades since, Israel has repeatedly tried to give away this land - only to learn, over and over again, that giving God's land to terrorists leads only to disaster. God's will cannot be denied.[13]

For well over a century, most American Jews just wanted to fit in. They abandoned their Jewish heritage with hardly a second thought, delighted to live in a country that embraced them and gave them an opportunity to comfortably assimilate. But God had other plans.

The explosive rise of antisemitism since October 7, primarily from the left but also from the right, has forced millions of diaspora Jews to awaken and grapple with their identity. Since the start of the war, Aliyah applications have surged, with a 300% increase from France, a 150% jump from Canada, a 100% rise from the United States, and a 40% increase from the United Kingdom.[14] Has another great ingathering begun?

"You will rise, You will have mercy on Zion for there is a time to favor it, for the appointed season has arrived. For Your servants desired its stones and favored its dust" (Psalm 102:14-15). "This means that Jerusalem will only be rebuilt when the children of Israel yearn for it to such an extent that they embrace her stones and her dust."[15] Every day, more Jews turn their eyes to the holy land, for "when there is a great war in the world, the power of redemption is awakened... The world is renewed with a new spirit... and the seeking of redemption increases."[16]

The war has also brought the people of Israel back to Jerusalem. Walking around the holy city during wartime, you will see evacuees from Israel's war-ridden north and south visiting the Western Wall, groups of IDF reservists who completed their service and have come with their families to give thanks, students and teachers, and solidarity missions from the diaspora.[17] Many had forgotten the power of Jerusalem; still others, secular from birth, had never before stepped foot in God's city. Today, they are drawn to Jerusalem by a magnetic force they cannot explain in words.

"We, the Jewish people, are stronger than the spirit of the times; we are the strongest nation in the world."[18] More than anything else, the war revealed the greatness and strength of the people of Israel. On Saturday morning, October 7, everyday Israelis left their synagogues to take up arms, often without waiting for instructions from the government or the military. Instead of running away, thousands of citizens picked up their guns and ran towards the fire to save their fellow Jews. Many of them did not come home.

Jews are accustomed to telling stories of holy rabbis and heroic figures of the past. Every year, on Israel's Memorial Day and Independence Day, we tell stories about the early generations of pioneers who drained the swamps and brought life back to the holy land. But since that fateful morning, the only stories we tell are our *own* stories, about the heroes of today - the 19-year-olds who courageously ran into booby-trapped buildings, the 40-year-old fathers who voluntarily reenlisted, and the hundreds of thousands who put their lives and businesses on hold, at great personal cost, to defend our country.

The heroism extends beyond the soldiers, to their families and friends. Galit Waldman, mother of Ariel Ben Moses, a soldier who heroically fell on October 7, told an Israeli newspaper: "I'm happy to see people hanging out in cafes, laughing, working, happy. This is what they are fighting for in Gaza, and they must keep fighting until we are victorious. I don't have time to cry; we have to *win*. I have merited to have sons who are fighting in the holiest and most just war that has ever been fought. When do I cry? At night… I get up in the morning and I put on a lot of makeup. I have to give strength to my other boys, and send them back to the army, to university, to their studies. I have to carry the torch for the family, and I can't allow myself to fall."[19]

Iris Haim's son Yotam was taken hostage and later shot dead in error by IDF troops in northern Gaza, who mistakenly identified him as a threat. Iris sent a message to the soldiers of Unit 7828, the unit responsible for the tragic mistake. She said, "I am Yotam's mother. I wanted to tell you that I love you very much, and I hug you here from afar. I know that everything that happened is absolutely not your fault, and nobody's fault except that of Hamas, may their name be wiped out and their memory erased from the earth. I want you to look after yourselves and to think all the time that you are doing the best thing in the world, the best thing that could happen, that could help us. Because all the people of Israel and all of us need you to be healthy… And don't hesitate for a second if you see a terrorist. Don't think that you killed a hostage deliberately. You have to look after yourselves because only that way can you look after us… At the first opportunity, you are invited to come to us, whoever wants to. And we want to see you with our own eyes and hug you and tell you that what you did — however hard it is to say this, and sad — it was apparently the right thing in that moment. And nobody's going to judge you or be angry. Not me, and not my husband Raviv. Not my daughter Noya. And not Yotam, may his memory be blessed. And not Tuval, Yotam's brother. We love you very much. And that is all."[20]

In the words of a popular new Israeli song: "Sure, everyone here looks normal, but we are a nation of superheroes. Inside every one of us there is always a soldier hiding, ready to save the entire world."[21] These are the people of Israel. If the world refuses to see their greatness, it is only because they are deaf and blind.

From Hatred to Blessing

Why do the children of Ishmael and Esau hate Jews with such passion?

"Until the time of the final redemption, Israel's influence on the world has come through the teaching of obligations, morality and justice of the true

God. The world does not want to accept obligations, and if they do accept these obligations, they do so with resentment in their hearts towards those who taught them, for these obligations do not allow the barbaric soul to satisfy its desires."[22]

Ever since Israel was anointed as a "nation of priests" at Mount Sinai, Ishmael and Esau have held a grudge against their erstwhile teachers. The very presence of the people of the Bible among them is an unwelcome reminder of God's expectations of mankind, expectations that do not allow them the guiltless pleasures they desperately seek. "Let us break their bands and cast off their cords from us" (Psalm 2:3).

But the day will come when even Ishmael and Esau will learn to appreciate Israel and the Bible. As Rabbi Abraham Isaac Kook wrote, "When the time comes for the light of the world to be revealed, it will become known to humanity that we have shared the path of life, of true pleasure, without which life is lacking all meaning. Every man can appreciate pleasure and happiness, and they will come to honor and treasure the people who are its source. And therefore, 'In those days, ten men of all the languages of the nations shall take hold of the shirt of a Jewish man, saying, 'Let us go with you, for we have heard that God is with you' (Zechariah 8:23)."[23]

The Book of Genesis alludes to a happier future in which Ishmael and Esau learn to appreciate Israel. When Jacob died, Joseph and his brothers brought their father back to the holy land for burial in Hebron. "And they came to the threshing floor of the thorn bushes, which is on the other side of the Jordan, and there they conducted a very great and impressive eulogy, and he made for his father a mourning of seven days" (Genesis 50:10). The sages explain that something remarkable happened at this moment. "They surrounded Jacob's coffin with crowns like a threshing floor which is surrounded with a hedge of brambles, because the sons of Esau and of Ishmael… also came… They came to wage war [against the Israelites]; but when they saw Joseph's crown hanging upon Jacob's coffin, they all took their crowns and hung them upon his coffin."[24]

By nature, Ishmael and Esau come to wage war against Jacob and his children. But they, too, will one day be forced to acknowledge the greatness of Israel. "And their seed shall be known among the nations, and their offspring among the peoples; all who see them shall recognize them that they are seed that the Lord blessed" (Isaiah 61:9).

When Jacob struggled with the guardian angel of Esau,[25] he refused to let the angel go until he received his blessing. "And he (the angel) said, "Let me go, for dawn is breaking," but he (Jacob) said, "I will not let you go unless you have blessed me" (Genesis 32:27). What was the blessing Jacob wanted so badly from the angel? Jacob demanded, "Acknowledge for me the blessings with which my father blessed me, which Esau is contesting."[26] Jacob could not, and would not, declare victory until Esau acknowledged that he was worthy of Isaac's blessings.

When the angel said "Your name shall no longer be called Jacob, but Israel" (Genesis 32:29), he acknowledged Israel's rightful status as God's chosen nation. "'It shall no longer be said that the blessings came to you through trickery (*akvah*, from the same root as *Yaakov* / Jacob) and deceit, but with nobility and openness, and ultimately, the Holy One, blessed be He, will reveal Himself to you in Beth-el and change your name, and there He will bless you, and I will be there.' The angel then acknowledged the blessings belonged to Jacob."[27]

"And he blessed him there" (Genesis 32:30). According to the sages, "The angel blessed Jacob that his children should merit to serve their Creator in Jerusalem."[28] Ultimately, Ishmael and Esau will understand the centrality of Jerusalem and the blessing it bestows on them. The day will come when they recognize that Israel was chosen by God to bring blessing and joy to the world. "And kings shall be your nursing fathers and their princesses your wet nurses; they shall prostrate themselves to you with their face on the ground, and they shall lick the dust of your feet, and you shall know that I am the Lord, for those who wait for Me shall not be ashamed" (Isaiah 49:23).

"On that day, I will raise up the fallen Tabernacle of David, and I will close up their breaches, and I will raise up its ruins, and build it up as in the days of yore. In order that they inherit the remnant of Edom and all the nations because My Name is called upon them, says the Lord Who does this" (Amos 9:11-12). While most of the children of Edom will fall in the war of Gog and Magog, the remaining remnant will recognize the name of God alongside all other nations when the Messiah arrives.[29] The day will come when Ishmael and Esau will realize that their doomed war against the God of the Bible was prophesied in the Bible itself.

That time is not yet here. The war is not yet won, and the day when Esau, Ishmael and the nations "will know the name of God" remains an inheritance for the Messiah. But even now, even as we must stand and fight the enemies of God and the Bible, there are glimmers of light.

In February 2024, Rabbi Oury Cherki, a leading Religious Zionist thinker in Israel, was invited to the United Arab Emirates for an open religious dialogue on Judaism and Islam. Throughout the three-day trip, the Emiratis made clear that they strongly oppose all Islamist movements, including ISIS, the Muslim

Brotherhood, Hamas and Iran. Incredibly, Israel's war against Hamas didn't even come up. The Emiratis rejected as a fabrication the Islamist division of the world into *Dar al-Islam*, territories under Islamic control, and *Dar al-Harb*,[30] territories not yet under Islamic control which must be conquered by force. They explained that al-Aqsa Mosque is not of central importance in Islam and agreed that all anti-Israel content must be removed from Muslim textbooks.

Encouragingly, the Emiratis are promoting a new form of Islam that can live at peace together with all of the children of Abraham. Though the UAE does not represent the majority of Muslims, they do represent hope for a future in which Muslims can live in peace alongside Jews and Christians. As Rabbi Cherki writes, "I came away with the impression that, at least in the unique country of the UAE, the process of the repentance of the sons of Ishmael has begun."[31]

On the southeastern frontier of Judea, among the hills and caves where David wrote psalms while hiding from the jealous King Saul, there is a small Jewish retreat center called Arugot Farm. Founded by Ari Abramowitz and Jeremy Gimpel, idealistic American immigrants, together with a few native Israelis, it is a Garden of Eden-like oasis on the edge of the Judean Desert.

Sadly, the farm has been a consistent target of extremist left-wing activists who believe Jews have no right to live in Judea, and its founders have been shamefully dragged into Israel's supreme court by Edomite European nations seeking to undermine their right to live in Israel's biblical heartland. But there are also many inspiring moments - and one in particular that offers hope for the future.

As Ari described it: "Then there was the day that the Germans arrived. They told us that they were artisans and craftsmen, many of them children and grandchildren of Nazis. They had come, in their own words, to repent. While their forebears had brought curses and destruction upon the Jewish people, their goal was to bring blessings and to build. When I asked why they chose Arugot Farm from all the other settlements and mountaintops, they explained that we are the furthest settlement in Judea – where the world stands most against us. And if this is where the world stands against us, they explained, then this is where they wanted to stand with us. I'll never forget the moment when I witnessed our Arab workers, descendants of Ishmael, harmoniously working together with our German volunteers, descendants of Esau, to build a synagogue for Jews in Judea. That was a moment in which a great evil of our history became a great blessing. That, too, was a moment of redemption."[32]

"It shall be a divided kingdom... iron mixed with clay (Daniel 2:41). Daniel prophesied that before the final redemption, the Edomites of "iron" and the Ishmaelites of "clay" would join together to destroy God's people. But in the end, this evil alliance will not hold. "They will not cleave to one another, just as iron cannot be mixed with clay" (Daniel 2:43). Standing in unity with other Bible believers across the world, the people of Israel will prevail - from the bloody streets of Gaza to the campuses of Columbia University in New York. The people of Israel will awaken and return home, and the remnant of Ishmael and Esau will repent.

"Be strong and don't be afraid! The light of redemption is shining, peeking out from behind every crack and crevice. From the darkness of evil and heresy… will come a lofty light that will elevate the honor and glory of those who know God and shine a light upon all those who dwell in darkness."[33] "The shofar of the Messiah has begun to blow."[34]

"It is happening; now, now, soon, soon, soon!"

The stone the builders
rejected has become the
cornerstone

PSALM 118:22

ENDNOTES

ACKNOWLEDGEMENTS:

1. Yehoshua November, *Professor*, www.chabad.org/multimedia/video_cdo/aid/1550138/jewish/Professor.htm
2. John Adams, *Discourse on Davila*, Discourse II
3. Rabbi Nachman of Breslov, *Sichos HaRan*, 47
4. Rabbi Abraham Isaac Kook, *Midot HaRa'aya*, Pride #23
5. Joseph Epstein, *The Middle of My Tether*, 24-35

CHAPTER 1:

1. Feast of Tabernacles
2. *Poll: Most young Americans think Israel should be 'ended and given to Hamas'*, www.timesofisrael.com/poll-most-young-americans-back-ending-israel-many-find-jewish-genocide-calls-okay/
3. Craig McCarthy, *Pro-Palestinian protesters, one carrying swastika, swarm Midtown in bid to derail Rockefeller Center Christmas tree lighting*, www.nypost.com/2023/11/29/metro/pro-palestinian-protesters-swarm-nyc-to-derail-rockefeller-center-christmas-tree-lighting/
4. Adam Eiyahu Berkowitz, *PA: "On Saturday, we murder the Jews; On Sunday, we*

murder the Christians," https://israel365news.com/380752/pa-on-saturday-we-murder-the-jews-on-sunday-we-murder-the-christians/

5   Bari Weiss, *You Are the Last Line of Defense*, www.thefp.com/p/you-are-the-last-line-of-defense

6   Esau is the father of the nation of Edom. "And these are the generations of Esau the progenitor of Edom, on Mount Seir" (Genesis 36:9).

7   Rabbi Meir Wisser, Psalm 83:4

8   Rashi, Psalm 83:6

9   Rashi, Numbers 35:10

10 Babylonian Talmud, *Berachot* 10a

11 Rabbi David Kimche, Psalm 83:4

12 Jerry Bowyer, *Is the Bible Dangerous?*, www.forbes.com/sites/jerrybowyer/2017/11/03/is-the-bible-dangerous/?sh=5106c3dd27d2

13 Congressman Jared Huffman, https://twitter.com/RepHuffman/status/1717255196433100969

14 Congressman Jamie Raskin, https://twitter.com/jamie_raskin/status/1717228301842792701

15 Joseph A. Wulfsohn, *Bill Maher compares Speaker Mike Johnson to Maine shooter: Their differences are 'thinner than you'd think'*, www.foxnews.com/media/bill-maher-compares-speaker-mike-johnson-maine-shooter

16 Thomas Sowell, *The Quest for Cosmic Justice*, 146

17 Koran, 98:6

18 Koran, 33:26

19 Koran, 2:191

20 Danielle Greyman-Kennard, *Israel is only the first target, warns Hamas commander*, www.jpost.com/middle-east/article-765304

21 Roee Nahmias, *Geert Wilders: Change Jordan's name to Palestine*, www.ynetnews.com/articles/0,7340,L-3907722,00.html

22 In Romans 1:16, Paul wrote "I am not ashamed of the gospel, for it is the power of God unto salvation for everyone who believes, to the Jew first and also to the Greek." Many Christians understand this verse as a call to bring the gospel to the Jewish people, though others interpret the verse differently.

23 For more on Christian evangelizing to Jews, see Elie Mischel *An Unusual Dinner at ETC Steakhouse*, https://jewishlink.news/an-unusual-dinner-at-etc-steakhouse/

24 Rabbi Meir Soloveitchik, *What Jews Mean to America*, www.nationalreview.com/magazine/2024/04/what-jews-mean-to-america/

25 Eric Cohen, cited in Rabbi Meir Soloveitchik, *What Jews Mean to America*, www.nationalreview.com/magazine/2024/04/what-jews-mean-to-america/

26 Babylonian Talmud, *Sanhedrin* 98b

27 Rabbi Simcha of Vitri, *Machzor Vitri*, section 259

28 Rabbi Meir Bar Ilan, *From Volozhin to Jerusalem*, 367

29 Rabbi Isaac Nissenbaum, *HaMizrachi*, 7 Av, 1921

30 Rabbi Isaac Nissenbaum, *HaMizrachi*, 19 Elul, 1921

31 Babylonian Talmud, *Sotah* 49b

32 Rabbi Haim of Volozhin, cited in Rabbi Moshe Avigdor Amiel, *Hegyonot el Ami*, 405-406

33 These churches joined Bonhoeffer in establishing the Confessing Church, a movement within German Protestantism that arose in opposition to government-sponsored efforts to unify all of the Protestant churches into a single pro-Nazi German Evangelical Church.

34 Abigail Adams, Letter to John Adams, 16 October 1774, https://founders.archives.gov/documents/Adams/04-01-02-0116

35 Rabbi Shlomo Aviner, *A Dual Crisis*, Nekudah, volume 14, August 15, 1980

36 Jewish Prayer Book, *Amidah, Sim Shalom prayer*

CHAPTER 2:

1 Rabbi Pinchas Polonsky, *Religious Zionism of Rav Kook*, 31

2 Adolf von Harnack, *Marcion: The Gospel of the Alien God*

3 Cited in Eric Metaxas, *Bonhoeffer: Pastor, Martyr, Prophet, Spy*, 172

4 Mary Solberg, *A Church Undone: Documents from the German Christian Faith Movement, 1932-1940*, 174

5   Cited in Erik Switzer, *Coveting Relationships Over Association: The Church's Response to the Millennial's Exodus*, https://digitalcommons.liberty.edu/cgi/viewcontent.cgi?article=6138&context=doctoral, page 60

6   R. Kendall Soulen, *The God of Israel and Christian Theology*, 31-33

7   Marilynne Robinson, *The Fate of Ideas: Moses*, in *When I was a Child I Read Books*, 96

8   Rabbi Abraham Joshua Heschel, *Protestant Renewal: A Jewish View*, in *The Insecurity of Freedom*, 169

9   R. Kendall Soulen, *The God of Israel and Christian Theology*, 34

10 Cited in Ronald R. Stockton, *Christian Zionism: Prophecy and Public Opinion*, Middle East Journal 41, www.jstor.org/stable/4327538.

11 L.P. Hartley, *The Go-Between*

12 Babylonian Talmud, *Megillah* 14a

13 Rabbi Zvi Yehuda Kook, *Behaalotecha*

14 Rashi, Deuteronomy 32:7

15 Targum Yonatan, Deuteronomy 32:7

16 "We are obligated to deepen our understanding of the unique implications of our history… To accomplish this, a strong partnership between two kinds of scholars is necessary: on the one hand, those who are experts in faith [which derives from the Bible]; and on the other hand, those with the skill to properly understand the events of our time - the historians, sociologists and philosophers. We have not seen this kind of cooperation thus far, but it is necessary to restore to our people the strength it needs to fulfill its mission." Rabbi Judah Leon Ashkenazi, *A Eulogy for the Messiah?*, 174

17 Cited in Eric Metaxas, *Bonhoeffer: Pastor, Martyr, Prophet, Spy*, 136-137

18 Rabbi Moshe Zvi Neria, *Sayings*

19 Maimonides, *Laws of Kings*, 12:2

20 Babylonian Talmud, *Taanit* 30b

21 Rabbi Abraham Isaac Kook, *Orot*, chapter 6

22 Rabbi Hanan Porat, *The Messiah of David, the Messiah of Joseph and the Secret of their Combination*, 53

23 Rabbi Menachem Kasher, *HaTekufah HaGedolah*, 224

24 Nachmanides, cited in Rabbi Zvi Yehuda Kook, *HaTorah v'HaGeulah*, HaTzofeh, 13 Tevet, 1944

25 Rabbi Meir Wisser, Daniel 12:4

26 Rabbi Joseph B Soloveitchik, *The Return to Zion: Addresses on Religious Zionism and American Orthodoxy*, 113

27 Rabbi Joseph B Soloveitchik, Ibid., 115-116

28 Midrash Tanchuma, Exodus 15

29 Babylonian Talmud, *Shabbat* 31a

30 Rabbi Leo Jung served as Rabbi and as Rabbi Emeritus of The Jewish Center for 65 years, until his death in 1987 at the age of 95. This teaching was shared with the author by Rabbi Jacob J. Schacter, who became the Rabbi of the Jewish Center in 1981 and had the opportunity to learn directly from Rabbi Jung during Rabbi Jung's final years.

31 Rabbi Yaakov Ariel, *Tanach for Our Generation*, https://jewishaction.com/cover-story/tanach-for-our-generation/

32 Terry Teachout, *Henrik Ibsen Part 2*, www.commentary.org/articles/terry-teachout/henrik-ibsen-part-2/

33 Gersonides, I Samuel 3:1

34 Rabbi Meir Wisser, Exodus 18:21

35 G.K. Chesterton, *Orthodoxy*, chapter 2

36 Babylonian Talmud, *Yoma* 75a

37 Rabbi Israel Meir Kagan, cited by Rabbi Menachem Kasher, *HaTekufa HaGedolah*, 20

38 Rabbi Haim David HaLevi, *Aseh Lecha Rav*, 30

39 Rabbi Abraham Isaac Kook, *Letters*, 363

40 Rabbi Meir Wisser, Amos 8:11

41 Rabbi Dr. Sholom Gold, *Viewpoint*, Fall 2005, 45

42 G.K. Chesterton, *Orthodoxy*, The Ethics of Elfland

43 G.K. Chesterton, *Appreciations and Criticisms of the Works of Charles Dickens*

44 Rabbi Abraham Isaac Kook, *Orot HaMilchama*, 1

45 Babylonian Talmud, *Shabbat* 31a

46 Rabbi Haim Isaiah Hadari, *Kol B'hadar*, 142

47 Ethics of the Fathers, 5:22
48 Rabbi Abraham Isaac Kook, *Letters*, 274
49 Rabbi Meir Wisser, Isaiah 63:15
50 Rabbi Abraham Isaac Kook, *Orot: Yisrael U'Techiyato*, Chapter 20
51 George Eliot, *Daniel Deronda*
52 Rabbi Hanan Porat, *The Messiah of David, the Messiah of Joseph and the Secret of their Combination*, 141
53 Rabbi Abraham Isaac Kook, *Ma'amarei Ra'aya*, 257
54 Daily *Amidah* prayer, Nusach Sefard
55 Rabbi Abraham Isaac Kook, *Olat Ra'aya*, 1:279-280
56 Rabbi Abraham ibn Ezra, Isaiah 62:1
57 Rabbi Meir Wisser, Isaiah 62:1
58 Babylonian Talmud, *Ketubot* 111a
59 Rabbi Abraham Isaac Kook, *Orot HaKodesh* 3:71
60 Leviticus Rabba, Emor 27

CHAPTER 3:

1   Midrash Tanchuma, Terumah 6
2   Abraham Ibn Ezra, cited in Nachmanides, *Sefer HaGeulah*, Gate 3, 238
3   This will be explained below
4   Rabbi Saadia Gaon, Daniel 2:41
5   Midrash Tehillim 6
6   Yalkut Shimoni, Genesis #74
7   Midrash cited by Rabbi Menachem Mendel Kasher, *Torah Sheleimah*, Genesis 15:12, note 130
8   Maimonides, *Epistle to the Jews of Yemen*, 1172
9   Rabbi Meir Wisser, Ezekiel 38:2
10 Rabbi Meir WIsser, Daniel 2:41

11 After listing the 70 descendants of Noah, the Bible relates the story of the Tower of Babel: "Now the entire earth was of one language and uniform words … And they said, 'Come, let us build ourselves a city and a tower with its top in the heavens'… And God said, "Lo! [they are] one people, and they all have one language… Come, let us descend and confuse their language, so that one will not understand the language of his companion." And God scattered them from there upon the face of the entire earth, and they ceased building the city (Genesis 11:1,3-4,6-7). The implication is that each of Noah's 70 descendants fathered a different clan, each of which spoke its own language.

12 Rabbi Abraham Abele Gombiner, *Zayit Raanan*, Beshalach 139

13 Rabbi Judah Loew of Prague, *Netzach Yisrael*, chapter 26

14 Fergus Millar, *Hagar, Ishmael, Josephus, and the origins of Islam, in Rome, the Greek World and the East*, Vol. 3, 351 377

15 Rashi, Genesis 21:17; see also Rashi, Genesis 37:25

16 *Ishmael in Islam*, www.newworldencyclopedia.org/entry/Ishmael#Ishmael_in_Islam

17 Rabbi Meir Wisser, Obadiah 1:1

18 Dr. Malka Z. Simkovich, *Esau the Ancestor of Rome*, www.thetorah.com/article/esau-the-ancestor-of-rome

19 Genesis Rabba 65:21

20 Jerusalem Talmud, *Ta'anit* 4:8

21 Gerson D. Cohen, *Esau as Symbol in Early Medieval Thought*, in Studies in the Varieties of Rabbinic Cultures (Philadelphia: Jewish Publication Society, 1991), 243–269

22 Midrash Tanchuma, Genesis 7. In this passage, the sages blend together the events of the Great Rebellion against Rome, resulting in the Temple's destruction in 70 C.E., with the Bar Kochba Rebellion that occurred sixty years later. As a result, they attribute the role of Temple destroyer not to Vespasian or Titus, but to Hadrian.

23 Rashi, Genesis 25:22

24 Rashi, Genesis 25:34

25 Rabbi Meir Soloveitchik, *What Jews Mean to America*, www.nationalreview.com/magazine/2024/04/what-jews-mean-to-america/

26 Nachmanides, Leviticus 26:16
27 Rabbi Bahya ben Asher Deuteronomy 30:7
28 Konrad Heiden, *A History of National Socialism*
29 Rashi, Genesis 11:1
30 Raymond J. de Souza, *Why secular progressives are prone to Jew hatred*, https://nationalpost.com/opinion/raymond-j-de-souza-why-secular-progressives-are-prone-to-jew-hatred
31 In Islam, a hadith refers to a narrative attributed to Prophet Muhammad, recounting his statements and deeds. It serves as the primary source for understanding his authoritative example.
32 Hamas Charter, Article 7, The Covenant Of The Islamic Resistance Movement – Hamas, www.memri.org/reports/covenant-islamic-resistance-movement-%E2%80%93-hamas
33 Preamble to Hamas Charter
34 Hamas Charter, Article 13
35 Ummah denotes a collective of faithful individuals united by their shared adherence to Islam
36 Ismaeel Haniyeh, January 9, 2024, cited in *Hamas in its Own Words*, www.adl.org/resources/blog/hamas-its-own-words
37 Rabbi Meir Wisser, Ezekiel 38:2
38 Rabbi Meir Wisser, Isaiah 60:2
39 Zohar, Genesis 119
40 Rabbi Moshe Cordovero, *Zohar Or Yakar*, 119
41 Rabbi David Kimche, Joel 4:19
42 Rabbi Yaakov Moshe Charlop, *Mei Marom*, Mima'ayanei Ha'Yeshua
43 Rashi, Daniel 2:44

CHAPTER 4:

1 *2 men executed in West Bank for allegedly spying for Israel, as mob cheers*, www.timesofisrael.com/2-men-executed-in-west-bank-for-allegedly-spying-

for-israel-as-mob-cheers/

2 Captain Gary Kosak, *For Zion's Sake I Will Not Keep Silent*

3 *Fogel Family Murderer gets Five Life Sentences*, www.ynetnews.com/articles/0,7340,L-4121856,00.html

4 Jennifer Rubin, *Palestinians celebrate and then reluctantly denounce Itamar murders*, www.washingtonpost.com/blogs/right-turn/post/palestinians-celebrate-and-then-reluctantly-denounce-itamar-murders/2011/03/04/ABN-ZlOV_blog.html

5 https://twitter.com/StandWithUs/status/1569000547214057473?lang=en

6 Rabbi David Altschuler, Psalm 120:5

7 Rabbi Meir Wisser, Psalm 120:7

8 Surah Al-Baqara 2:185, https://quran.com/2?startingVerse=185

9 Statement to Channel 12 News, cited in *IDF: Ramadan flare-up could lead to multi-front or even regional war*, www.jns.org/idf-ramadan-flare-up-could-lead-to-multi-front-or-even-regionalwar/

10 Rabbi Ben Tzion Kook, cited in www.kikar.co.il/_amp/haredim-news/373287

11 Rashi, Genesis 22:3

12 Babylonian Talmud, *Yevamot* 62a

13 Rashi, Genesis 16:12

14 Nachmanides, Genesis 16:12

15 Abraham Ibn Ezra, Genesis 16:12

16 Targum Onkelos, Genesis 16:12

17 Rabbi Samson Raphael Hirsch, Genesis 16:12

18 Cited in Rabbi Mordechai Mozeson, *Pardes Yisrael*

19 Rabbi Israel Meir Kagan, *Chafetz Chaim al HaTorah*

20 Rashi, Genesis 25:9

21 The sages here refer to *zuhama*, the spiritual defilement that the snake brought upon Eve and all mankind when it seduced her to sin.

22 Babylonian Talmud, *Shabbat* 146a

23 Rabbi Shmuel Bornsztain: "As is known, Ishmael draws his essence from

the right side, the side of *chessed*," Shem Mishmuel, Ekev
24 Rabbi Zadok ha-Kohen Rabinowitz of Lublin, *Pri Tzadik, Vayishach*
25 Midrash Shocher Tov, Psalm 110
26 Genesis 18:2
27 Rabbi Shlomo Aviner, *Commentary to Orot HaTechiya*, chapter 9, footnote 466
28 Rabbi Samson Raphael Hirsch, Genesis 16:12-14
29 Zohar, end of Vaera
30 *Zohar*, Exodus 22a
31 Maimonides, *Guide for the Perplexed* 3:49
32 Rabbi Jonathan Sacks, *The Circumcision of Desire*, rabbisacks.org/covenant-conversation/tazria/the-circumcision-of-desire/
33 Pirkei de-Rabbi Eliezer, Chapter 32
34 Rabbi Chaim Vital, *Etz HaDaat Tov*, Psalm 124
35 *Zohar*, Exodus 17a
36 Maimonides, *Epistle to the Jews of Yemen*, 1173
37 Genesis Rabba, 53:11
38 Rashi, Genesis 21:10
39 Individual gentiles who accept Jewish sovereignty over the entirety of the land of Israel and reject terrorism can certainly live in the land as a non-Jewish citizen of Israel. "If your brother becomes destitute and his hand falters beside you, you shall support him whether a convert or a resident, so that he can live with you" (Leviticus 25:35). The sages ask, "What is a 'resident'? Any non-Jew who has accepted upon himself not to worship idols, but eats carrion (i.e., non-kosher food) (Rashi, Leviticus 25:35). Maimonides writes that these people are called "residents," as they are permitted to reside permanently in the land of Israel (Maimonides, *Laws of Idolatry*, 10:6).
40 Genesis Rabba 47:5
41 Rabbi Jacob Ben Asher, *Ba'al HaTurim*, Commentary to Genesis 25:18

CHAPTER 5:

1 *Angela Merkel says "Wir schaffen das" on accepting refugees*, www.history.com/this-day-in-history/angela-merkel-says-wir-schaffen-das-on-accepting-refugees

2 Tuvia Tenenbom, *Hello Refugees*, 113-114

3 Tuvia Tenenbom, *Hello Refugees*, 139

4 Spyridon Mitsotakis, *Refugees And German Politics. Book Review: 'Hello, Refugees!' By Tuvia Tenenbom*, www.dailywire.com/news/refugees-and-german-politics-book-review-hello-spyridon-mitsotakis

5 Emanuel Fabian, *'I captured one!' — IDF recordings show more UNRWA staffers bragging of Oct. 7 crimes*, www.timesofisrael.com/i-captured-one-idf-recordings-show-more-unrwa-staffers-bragging-of-oct-7-crimes/

6 Zina Rakhamilova, *UNRWA complicit in indoctrinating Gazans with antisemitism*, www.jpost.com/opinion/article-783398

7 Zohar, Toldot

8 Genesis Rabba 65:5

9 Aviva Gottlieb Zornberg, *The Beginning of Desire*, 160

10 Rabbi Kalonymus Kalman Shapira, *A Student's Obligation*, Chapter 9

11 Rashi, Genesis 25:29. "But why lentils? Because they are [round as] a wheel, for mourning is like a wheel revolving in the world. Also, just as lentils have no mouth [no crack], as other beans have, so does the mourner have no mouth, for he is prohibited from speaking. It is therefore the custom to feed the mourner eggs at the beginning of his meal, since they are round, and have no mouth. So too does a mourner have no mouth… "A mourner, for the entire first three days, may not respond to anyone's greeting, and may surely not initiate a greeting. From the third day to the seventh, he may respond, but may not greet" (Babylonian Talmud, *Moed Katan* 21b).

12 Genesis Rabba, 63:16

13 Leviticus Rabba 28:1

14 Aviva Gottlieb Zornberg, *The Beginning of Desire*, 160

15 Shakespeare, *Macbeth*

16 Aviva Gottleib Zornberg, *The Beginning of Desire*, 160
17 Babylonian Talmud, *Bava Batra* 16b
18 Rashi, Genesis 25:27
19 Rabbi Bahya ben Asher, Genesis 25:27
20 "And the first one emerged ruddy (*admoni*, from the root word *edom*); he was completely like a coat of hair, and they named him Esau" (Genesis 25:25).
21 Ecclesiastes Rabba, 1:21
22 Genesis Rabba 63:12
23 Alberto Jori, professor of ancient philosophy at the University of Ferrara in Italy, cited in Silvia Marchetti, *Lying down and vomiting between courses: This is how Ancient Romans would feast*, edition.cnn.com/style/how-ancient-romans-feasted/index.html
24 Tanchuma, Terumah 3
25 T. Kasser, K.L. Rosenblum, A.J. Sameroff, *et al. Changes in materialism, changes in psychological well-being: Evidence from three longitudinal studies and an intervention experiment*, Motivation and Emotion 38, 1–22, https://doi.org/10.1007/s11031-013-9371-4
26 Rashi, Genesis 25:25
27 David Goldman, *Horror and Humiliation in Gaza*, www.tabletmag.com/sections/israel-middle-east/articles/horror-humiliation-gaza
28 Edmund Wilson, *Thoughts at Sixty*, 217
29 Rashi, Genesis 27:33
30 Genesis Rabba 63:10
31 Tanchuma, Toledot 8
32 Rabbi Moshe Avigdor Amiel, *Hegyonot El Ami: Genesis*, 270-271
33 Babylonian Talmud, *Shabbat* 104a
34 Sifrei, Beha'alotecha 69
35 *Zohar*, Vayishlach
36 Don Isaac Abarbanel, I Samuel 21:8
37 Don Isaac Abarbanel, I Samuel 21:8
38 Rashi, I Samuel 21:8

39 Rabbi David Altchuler, I Samuel 21:8
40 Rabbi David Kimche, I Samuel 21:8
41 "So Saul died for his transgression which he committed against the Lord" (I Chronicles 10:13).
42 Leviticus Rabba 26
43 Babylonian Talmud, *Sanhedrin* 106b
44 Abraham Ibn Ezra, Psalm 50:16
45 Babylonian Talmud, *Sanhedrin* 106b
46 Rabbi Yehuda Aryeh Leib Alter, *Sefat Emet*, Deuteronomy 5677
47 Rabbi Meir Wisser, Isaiah 63:1
48 Rashi, Genesis 26:34
49 Rabbi Yehuda Aryeh Leib Alter, *Sefat Emet*, Deuteronomy 5677
50 Rabbi Isaac Nissenbaum, *Hamizrachi* #17, 1920
51 Andrew Lapin, *US university professors retract blaming Israel for Hamas massacre after censure*, www.timesofisrael.com/us-university-professors-retract-blaming-israel-for-hamas-massacre-after-censure/
52 Phylis McGinley, *The Angry Man*
53 Ryan King, *Chaos erupts as pro-Palestinian protesters demand ceasefire at the Capitol; at least 3 allegedly assault cops*, https://nypost.com/2023/10/18/chaos-erupts-as-pro-palestinian-protesters-take-to-the-capitol-at-least-three-arrested/amp/
54 Jeremy Carl, *Phylis McGinley and the Left's War on Motherhood*, www.nationalreview.com/2018/05/mothers-day-writer-phyllis-mcginley-reminder-importance-of-motherhood/
55 Rabbi Moshe Avigdor Amiel, *Hegyonot El Ami: Genesis*, 266
56 *Secretary-General's remarks to the press on the situation in the Middle East*, October 9, 2023, www.un.org/sg/en/content/sg/speeches/2023-10-09/secretary-generals-remarks-the-press-the-situation-the-middle-east
57 John Spencer, *Israel Implemented More Measures to Prevent Civilian Casualties Than Any Other Nation in History*, www.newsweek.com/israel-implemented-more-measures-prevent-civilian-casualties-any-other-nation-history-opinion-1865613

58 Genesis 36:20-22
59 Rashi, Genesis 36:12, citing Tanchuma, Vayeshev
60 Midrash Tanchuma 9
61 *Zohar*, Mishpatim 108
62 Sifrei, Beha'alotecha 69
63 Cited by Bernard Schumacher, *The Dictatorship of the Conscience*, Nova et vetera, vol. 15 no. 2, 2017, p. 547-578. Project MUSE, https://doi.org/10.1353/nov.2017.0026.
64 Timothy Snyder, *Hitler's World*, https://www.nybooks.com/articles/2015/09/24/hitlers-world/
65 Daniel Greenfield, *The Redemption of Israel*, www.danielgreenfield.org/2017/04/the-redemption-of-israel.html
66 Genesis Rabba 76:3
67 G.K. Chesterton, *Don't*, Daily News, May 7, 1910
68 Caesaria, a city on Israel's Mediterranean coast, was the Roman Empire's administrative center in Israel.
69 Babylonian Talmud, *Megillah* 6a

CHAPTER 6:

1 Rabbi Zvi Yehuda Kook, *Sichot Rav Tzvi Yehuda, Ishim*, 68
2 Genesis Rabba 76:1
3 Song of Songs Rabba 4:1
4 Babylonian Talmud, *Taanit* 5b
5 Babylonian Talmud, *Brachot* 13a
6 Rabbi Abraham Isaac Kook, *Ein Aya*, Brachot 1:172
7 Genesis Rabba 63:8
8 The sages say that this was the guardian angel of Esau (Genesis Rabba 77:3, 78:3)
9 Rabbi Pinchas Polonsky, *Bible Dynamics*, Genesis 34

10 Rabbi Jonathan Sacks, *The Struggle of Faith*, https://aish.com/the-jewish-journey/

11 Ibid.

12 Olivia Land, *Israeli hostage Rimon Kirsht, who was hailed for 'death stare,' gave Hamas an ultimatum*, https://nypost.com/2023/11/30/news/israeli-hostage-rimon-kirsht-who-was-hailed-for-death-stare-gave-hamas-an-ultimatum/

13 Rabbi Menachem Kasher, *HaTekufah HaGedolah*, 116

14 Moses Mendelssohn, *Gesammelte Schriften*, ed. G.B. Mendelssohn, 5:493-494, cited in Ravitsky, *Messianism, Zionism, and Jewish Religious Radicalism*, 11

15 Rashi, Leviticus 26:37

16 Rabbi Abraham Isaac Kook, *Ikvei Tzon*, 21

17 Rabbi Moshe Avigdor Amiel, *Ezer el Ami*

18 Rabbi Isaac Nissenbaum, *Days of Self-Reflection and Judgment*, in *Hamizrachi* #37, 1921.

19 Rabbi Moshe Avigdor Amiel, *Hegyonot el Ami*, 46. See *A Religious Revival? Mordecai, Esther and the Lion Within*

20 Rabbi Abraham Isaac Kook, *Iggrot HaRaaya*, #378

21 Danielle Wallace, *Columbia rabbi tells Jewish students to leave campus, warns that school, NYPD 'cannot guarantee your safety'*, www.foxnews.com/us/columbia-rabbi-tells-jewish-students-leave-campus-warns-school-nypd-cannot-guarantee-your-safety

22 Paula Fredriksen, *Secundum Carnem: History and Israel in the Theology of St. Augustine*, in *Essays on Late Antique Thought and Culture in Honor of R. A. Markus*, 41

23 Rabbi Joseph B. Soloveitchik, *The Return to Zion: Addresses on Religious Zionism and American Orthodoxy*, 171-172

24 Babylonian Talmud, *Shabbat* 30b

25 Rabbi Yehudah Aryeh Leib Alter, *Sefat Emet, Bo, Hachodesh Hazeh Lachem*

26 Rabbi Abraham Isaac Kook, *Orot, Yisrael U'Techiyao*, chapter 29

27 Mark Twain, *Concerning the Jews*, Harper's Magazine (1898)

28 So fundamental is this first national commandment that Rashi cites his father, Rabbi Isaac, who said "It was not necessary to begin the Bible

except from 'This month shall be unto you' (Exodus 12:2), which is the first commandment that the Israelites were commanded" (Rashi, Genesis 1:1). Rashi goes on to say that the only reason the Bible begins with the story of the creation of the world in Genesis is to justify God's decision to give the land of Israel to the people of Israel. "For if the nations of the world should say to Israel, 'You are robbers, for you conquered by force the lands of the seven nations [of Canaan],' they will reply, 'The entire earth belongs to the Holy One, blessed be He; He created it and gave it to whomever He deemed proper. When He wished, He gave it to the other nations, and when He wished, He took it away from them and gave it to Israel.'"

29 Pesikta D'Rav Kahana, 12:6
30 Rabbi Abraham Isaac Kook, *Orot Yisrael* 1:15
31 Rabbi Abraham Isaac Kook, *Orot HaTechiya*, chapter 5
32 Jared Sorhaindo, *Did FDR Really Abandon the Jews of Europe?*, https://mosaicmagazine.com/observation/history-ideas/2020/03/did-fdr-really-abandon-the-jews-of-europe/
33 Gal Beckerman, *When They Come for Us, We'll Be Gone: The Epic Struggle to Save Soviet Jewry*, 231-232
34 Rashi, Esther 6:13

CHAPTER 7:

1 Rashi, Zechariah 1:1
2 Rashi, Zechariah 9:1
3 Rashi, Zechariah 9:9
4 National Covenant of the Palestine Liberation Organization, www.gov.il/en/pages/11-national-covenant-of-the-palestine-liberation-organization-28-may-1964
5 Rabbi Elijah of Vilna, Commentary to Habakuk
6 Rabbi Zvi Tau, *L'Emunat Itenu*, 1:125
7 Tzvi Joffre, *Palestinians largely support October 7 massacre, deny atrocities*, www.jpost.com/israel-hamas-war/article-777918
8 Rashi, Isaiah 11:14

9 Rabbi Meir Wisser, Zephaniah 2:7

10 *'We will repeat October 7 again and again'* - Hamas official, www.jpost.com/arab-israeli-conflict/article-771199

11 Rashi, Zechariah 9:8

12 Rashi, Zechariah 9:12

13 Jon Levine, *Majority of Americans 18-24 think Israel should 'be ended and given to Hamas'*, https://nypost.com/2023/12/16/news/majority-of-americans-18-24-think-israel-should-be-ended-and-given-to-hamas/

14 Rabbi Abraham Isaac Kook, *Orot HaTechiyah* 1

CHAPTER 8:

1 Rabbi Meir Wisser, Ezekiel 38:17

2 *Targum Yonatan*

3 Rabbi Yehoshua Pfeffer, *Prophecies and Providence: A Biblical Approach to Modern Jewish History*

4 Daniel chapter 2

5 See chapter 3, *The Fourth Kingdom: Edom and Ishmael Unite*

6 According to Rabbi Loew, though the Arab nations are formidable, they are not counted separately among the four exiling kingdoms described in the Book of Daniel. The rationale behind this omission lies in the assertion that the four empires considered in the count actively seized kingship and authority from Israel. Consequently, these nations could postpone the redemption, as long as they held sway, preventing the restoration of the nation of Israel's dominion. Unlike Babylonia, Persia, Greece and Rome, the Arab nations never seized authority from Israel, and so they are not counted as one of the four kingdoms.

7 Rabbi Meir Wisser simply interprets Persia as "the armies of Ishmael", Ezekiel 38:5

8 Rabbi Judah Loew of Prague, *Netzach Yisrael*, chapter 21

9 Rabbi Judah Loew of Prague, *Gevurot Hashem*, chapter 72

10 Rabbi Judah Loew of Prague, *Ner Mitzvah*, 11b

11 Babylonian Talmud, *Avodah Zara* 2b
12 Pesikta Rabbati 36
13 Rabbi Chiya HaRofeh, *Ma'aseh Chiya*, cited in Rabbi Menachem Kasher, *HaTekufah HaGedolah*, 233
14 Rabbi Meir Wisser, Isaiah 66:8
15 Rabbi Meir Wisser, Ezekiel 38:17
16 Rabbi Meir Wisser, Ezekiel 39:1
17 Rabbi David Kimchi, Ezekiel 38:9
18 Rabbi Meir Wisser, Ezekiel 38:11
19 Rabbi Meir Wiisser, Ezekiel 38:20
20 Rabbi Meir Wisser, Ezekiel 38:12
21 Rabbi Abraham Isaac Kook, *Ein Ayah, Brachot* I, 173
22 'Oct. 7 was just a rehearsal,' warns Sinwar, www.jns.org/oct-7-was-just-a-rehearsal-warns-sinwar
23 Rabbi David Kimche, Isaiah 66:22
24 Don Isaac Abarbanel, Ezekiel 38:21
25 Rabbi Meir Wisser, Ezekiel 29:21
26 Rabbi Meir Wisser, Ezekiel 38:7
27 Don Isaac Abarbanel, Ezekiel 38:21
28 Rabbi David Kimche, Isaiah 54:15
29 Rabbi David Kimche, Isaiah 66:17
30 Rabbi Meir Wisser, Isaiah 66:16
31 Rabbi David Kimche, Isaiah 61:2
32 Rabbi Meir Wisser, Ezekiel 39:21
33 Rabbi David Kimche, Isaiah 66:24
34 Rabbi David Kimche, Isaiah 25:3
35 Rabbi Meir Wisser, Isaiah 66:9

CHAPTER 9:

1. *Our Narrative: Operation Al-Aqsa Flood*, www.palestinechronicle.com/wp-content/uploads/2024/01/PDF.pdf
2. https://www.instagram.com/ritainspired/p/C3GOWL9rs2x/, citing Babylonian Talmud, Tractate *Sukkah* 41a
3. Cynthia Ozick, *My Hero: George Eliot*, www.theguardian.com/books/2012/apr/20/my-hero-george-eliot-cynthia-ozick
4. Maimonides, *Laws of the Chosen House*, 6:16
5. In the Hebrew Bible, Zion is used over 150 times to refer to Jerusalem. *Encyclopedia Talmudit, Jerusalem*, 1:6
6. Rabbi Abraham Joshua Heschel, *No Religion is an Island*, 260-261
7. Shmuel Agnon, *Speech at the Nobel Banquet at the City Hall in Stockholm*, December 10, 1966, cited in Nobel Lectures, Literature 1901-1967
8. Rabbi Shlomo Carlebach, *Chayei HaLev*, 377
9. Rabbi Judah HaLevi, *Kuzari*, Conclusion
10. Rabbi David Kimche, Isaiah 66:11
11. Abd al-Hamid as-Sa'ih, Radio Amman, Sept. 23, 1967, cited in Middle East Record, 3:294.
12. Ricky Hollander, *Backgrounder: The Battle Over Jerusalem and the Temple Mount*, www.camera.org/article/updated-the-battle-over-jerusalem-and-the-temple-mount/
13. Daniel Pipes, *Nothing Abides: Perspectives on the Middle East and Islam*, 28
14. https://www.israeltoday.co.il/read/clarity-on-the-temple-mount/
15. Zachi Dvira, *Relics in Rubble: The Temple Mount Sifting Project* https://library.biblicalarchaeology.org/article/relics-in-rubble-the-temple-mount-sifting-project/
16. Lt. Col. (Res) Maurice Hirsch, *What is the Temple Mount 'Status Quo'?*, www.israeltoday.co.il/read/what-is-the-temple-mount-status-quo/
17. R.J. Zwi Werblowsky, *The Meaning of Jerusalem to Jews, Christians and Muslims*, 2
18. Daniel Pipes, *The Muslim Claim to Jerusalem*, www.meforum.org/490/the-muslim-claim-to-jerusalem

19 Koran, Sura 17:1
20 R.J. Zwi Werblowsky, *The Meaning of Jerusalem to Jews, Christians and Muslims*, 3
21 George Sandys, *Relation of a Journey*
22 Mark Twain, *Innocents Abroad*, Chapter 56
23 Targum, cited by Rashi, Genesis 22:14
24 Isma'il Raji al-Faruqi, Islamic Book Trust Kuala Lumpur/American Trust Publishers, 24-25
25 Daniel Pipes, *The Muslim Claim to Jerusalem*, www.meforum.org/490/the-muslim-claim-to-jerusalem
26 Rabbi Menachem Kasher, *HaTekufah HaGedolah*, 43
27 Rabbi Menachem Kasher, *HaTekufah HaGedolah*, 44
28 *We have Risen and been Encouraged*, Olam Katan #946, 2 Iyar, 11
29 Sarah Chlala, *Jerusalem march unites thousands of Christians from 90 countries*, www.i24news.tv/en/news/israel/society/1696450965-jerusalem-march-unites-thousands-of-christians-from-90-countries
30 Babylonian Talmud, *Sanhedrin* 20b

CHAPTER 10:

1 Rabbi Meir Wisser, Obadiah 1:1
2 Babylonian Talmud, *Sanhedrin* 39b
3 Babylonian Talmud, *Sanhedrin* 39b
4 Midrash Tanchuma, Exodus 1:6
5 Rabbi Meir Wisser, Obadiah 1:1. Incredibly, Rabbi Wisser wrote these prophetic words in the 19th century, when the Arab nations were weak and the Ottoman Empire was known as the "Sick man of Europe."
6 Peter Smith and Lucas Webber, *The Israel-Hamas War and Resurgent Jihadist Threats to Europe and the United States*, www.lawfaremedia.org/article/the-israel-hamas-war-and-resurgent-jihadist-threats-to-europe-and-the-united-states

7   Rabbi David Altschuler, Daniel 11:40

8   Adam Eliyahu Berkowitz, *PA: "On Saturday, we murder the Jews; On Sunday, we murder the Christians,"* https://israel365news.com/380752/pa-on-saturday-we-murder-the-jews-on-sunday-we-murder-the-christians/

9   Rabbi Meir Kahane, *Never Again*, 246-247. Rabbi Kahane was murdered by an Arab terrorist in 1990 at the New York Marriott East Side hotel in Manhattan, New York City.

10 Rabbi Meir Wisser, Obadiah 1:5

11 Abdullah Asiran, *Dutch Muslims worried about Islamophobic Wilders' election victory*, https://www.aa.com.tr/en/europe/dutch-muslims-worried-about-islamophobic-wilders-election-victory/3064647

12 Soeren Kern, *Germany's Woke Government Wavers as Islamists Declare Holy War*, www.nationalreview.com/2024/05/germanys-woke-government-wavers-as-islamists-declare-holy-war/

13 *A Proclamation on Transgender Day of Visibility*, 2024, www.whitehouse.gov/briefing-room/presidential-actions/2024/03/29/a-proclamation-on-transgender-day-of-visibility-2024/

14 *Hamas' Exploitation of Humanitarian Aid*, www.idf.il/en/mini-sites/the-hamas-terrorist-organization/hamas-exploitation-of-humanitarian-aid/

15 George Phillips, *Iran Deal: $150 Billion to Fund Obama's War*, www.gatestoneinstitute.org/6225/iran-150-billion-dollars

16 Barak Ravid, *U.S. condemns Israeli ultranationalist ministers' call to push Palestinians out of Gaza*, www.axios.com/2024/01/02/us-condemns-israeli-ultranationalist-smotrich-ben-gvir-gaza

17 *Remarks by President Biden and President Abbas of the Palestinian National Authority in Joint Press Statement*, www.whitehouse.gov/briefing-room/speeches-remarks/2022/07/15/remarks-by-president-biden-and-president-abbas-of-the-palestinian-national-authority-in-joint-press-statement-bethlehem-west-bank/

18 Yuval Barnea, *Simon Wiesenthal Center condemns Palestinian Authority leader Mahmoud Abbas' remarks*, www.jpost.com/diaspora/antisemitism/article-758258

19 *Palestinian 'Pay for Slay' Keeps Growing*, www.wsj.com/articles/palestinian-pay-for-slay-hamas-oct-7-israel-gaza-antony-blinken-ramallah-2dce9a22

20 Rabbi Meir Wisser, Isaiah 25:12

21 *UN Secretary-General Blames Israel For Hamas Attack; Jews Respond*, www.israel365news.com/377716/un-secretary-general-blames-israel-for-hamas-attack-jews-respond/

22 "If you want to do it as an application of law, I believe that they'll find that it is genocide, and they have ample evidence to do so," Warren said at the Islamic Center of Boston in response to a question from an audience member on whether she thinks "Israel is committing a genocide." *US Sen. Warren: World Court has 'ample evidence' to find Israel guilty of genocide*, www.timesofisrael.com/us-sen-warren-world-court-has-ample-evidence-to-find-israel-guilty-of-genocide/

23 Rabbi David Altschuler, Obadiah 1:15

24 Jonathan S. Tobin, *Biden's double game on Hamas should fool no one*, www.jns.org/bidens-double-game-on-hamas-should-fool-no-one/

25 Clarence Thomas, *My Grandfather's Son*

26 G.K. Chesterton, *The American Ideal*, SIdelights

27 G.K. Chesterton, *The Mad Official*, A Miscellany of Men

CHAPTER 11:

1 *Biden: '2-state solution only way to guarantee long-term security of Israelis, Palestinians'*, www.ynetnews.com/article/hyo7an11hp

2 Rabbi Meir Wisser, Joel 3:1

3 Noah Browning, *Abbas wants 'not a single Israeli' in future Palestinian state*, www.reuters.com/article/idUSBRE96T009/

4 Rabbi Abraham Isaac Kook, *Chazon HaGeulah* 171-173

5 Rabbi David Kimche, Joel 4:2

6 "Now Sarai, Abram's wife, had not borne to him, and she had an Egyptian handmaid named Hagar" (Genesis 16:1).

7 "And his mother took him a wife out of the land of Egypt" (Genesis 21:21).

8 *Av HaRachamim* Prayer

9 Ibn Ezra, Joel 3:1

CHAPTER 12:

1. Lazar Berman, *After walling itself in, Israel learns to hazard the jungle beyond*, www.timesofisrael.com/after-walling-itself-in-israel-learns-to-hazard-the-jungle-beyond/amp/
2. Rabbi David Kimche, Isaiah 60:22
3. Rabbi Isaac Nissenbaum, *Chomer L'Drush*, 93
4. Rabbenu Chananel ben Chushiel
5. Genesis Rabba 91:10
6. Rabbi Moshe Chaim Luzzato, *Da'at Tevunot* 146
7. Rabbi Israel of Koznitz, cited in Rabbi Hanoch of Alexander, *Chashvah L'Tovah*, 10
8. Babylonian Talmud, *Sanhedrin* 98b
9. Rabbi David Kimche, Isaiah 59:19-20
10. Rabbi Meir Wisser, Habakkuk 3:16
11. Babylonian Talmud, *Sanhedrin* 98b
12. Babylonian Talmud, *Megillah* 17b
13. Rabbi Hillel Rivlin of Shklov, *Kol HaTor*, 127
14. *Soldier who lost both legs implores Netanyahu: 'Don't let our sacrifice be in vain'*, https://worldisraelnews.com/soldier-who-lost-both-legs-implores-netanyahu-dont-let-our-sacrifice-be-in-vain/
15. Rabbi David Kimche, Isaiah 26:8
16. Pesikta D'Rav Kahane #5
17. Rabbi Abraham Isaac Kook, *Chazon HaGeulah*, 177
18. Rabbi David Kimche, Isaiah 26:20
19. Abigail Adams, Letter to John Quincy Adams, January 19, 1780, https://founders.archives.gov/documents/Adams/04-03-02-0207
20. Mary McCarthy, *Memories of a Catholic Girlhood*, 16-17
21. Rabbi Reuven Sasson, *A War for God: Essays of Encouragement during a Time of War for Soldiers and Citizens*, 28-30
22. Rabbi Joseph B. Soloveitchik, *The Return to Zion: Addresses on Religious Zionism and American Orthodoxy*

23 Rabbi Joshua Bachrach, *Machar Chodesh*, 78
24 Rabbi Moshe Avigdor Amiel, *Hegyonot el Ami*, 407
25 Rabbi Abraham Isaac Kook, *Orot HaKodesh*, 2:561
26 Rabbi David Kimche, Isaiah 54:7
27 Rabbi Meir Wisser, Malachi 1:2
28 *Ahava Rabba*, Morning Prayer Service
29 Genesis Rabba 89:1

CHAPTER 13:

1 Jerusalem Talmud, *Berachot* 4b
2 Rabbi Meir Wisser, Isaiah 49:12. Rabbi Wisser wrote this prophetic commentary in the late 19th century, years before Theodor Herzl launched the modern Zionist movement.
3 Rabbi Meir Wisser, Micah 4:8
4 Jewish tradition requires men to cover their heads as a gesture of reverence and respect towards God during prayer, Torah study, blessing recitation, and synagogue attendance. The custom traces back to biblical times, when priests in the Temple were directed to keep their heads covered. As a longstanding tradition, Jewish males, regardless of age, typically don the *kippah* as a constant reminder of their acknowledgment and submission to a divine authority.
5 Rabbi Abraham Isaac Kook, *Shuvu L'Vitzaron*, in *Ma'amarei Ra'ayah*, 362
6 Rabbi Haim Isaiah Hadari, *Kol B'Hadar*, 213
7 Rabbi Yechiel Michel Tucazinsky, *Sefer HaShemitta*, 318
8 Rabbi Hanan Porat, *The Messiah of David, the Messiah of Joseph and the Secret of their Combination*, 443
9 Rabbi Abraham Isaac Kook, *Olat Reiyah*, 2:287
10 Rabbi Alex Israel, *Chipazon - Rapid Redemption*, https://etzion.org.il/en/holidays/pesach/chipazon-rapid-redemption
11 Rashi, Exodus 15:22

12 Babylonian Talmud, *Pesachim* 87a

13 Rabbi Judah Loew of Prague, *Netzach Yisrael*, 47

14 Rabbi Zvi Yehudah Kook, *The State as the Fulfillment of the Vision of Redemption*, *L'Netivot Yisrael*, Volume I

15 According to Rabbi Moses Hayyim Luzzato, before a soul descends to earth, it is forced to eat the "bread of shame," for it has not earned the pleasure it receives in the upper worlds. Only by descending to this earth, where human beings can choose between good and evil, can the soul be freed from its shame. See *Da'at Tevunot*, 18.

16 Rabbi Hanan Porat, *Kima Kima*, in *Yom Ha'atzmaut v'Yom Shichrur Yerushalayim*, Be'er Miriam, *Sidra l'Chagim*

17 Rabbi Abraham Isaac Kook, *Letters*, 3:20

18 Rabbi Hillel Rivlin of Shklov, *Kol HaTor* 6:2

19 Rabbi Gedaliyah Schorr, *Or Gedalyahu*, *Vayera* 5

20 Rabbi Abraham Isaac Kook, *Orot HaTechiya*, 29

21 Rabbi Judah Leon Ashkenazi, *A Eulogy for the Messiah?*, 74

22 Rabbi Shlomo Aviner, *There are Difficulties in Redemption*, http://shlomo-aviner.net/index.php?title=(מאמר)_יש_קשיים_בגאולה

23 Rabbi Yaakov Moshe Charlop, *Mei Marom* 6, Chapter 31

24 Rabbi Zvi Yehuda Kook, cited by Dr. Moshe Herskowitz, *Bless the State of Israel, the Beginning of our Redemption*, Olam Katan, #946, 2 Iyar, 2024

25 This is not meant as a criticism of Jews living in exile who wish to move to Israel but have not yet done so because of familial responsibilities or financial concerns, but rather of those Jews who believe they are meant to remain in exile until God brings them to the holy land through open miracles.

26 Rabbi Menachem Kasher, *HaTekufah HaGedolah*, 222

27 Song of Songs Rabba 8:9

28 Maimonides, *Laws of Kings and Wars*, 11:1

29 Rabbi Hayim Druckman, *Kima Kima*, 25

30 The *Bnei Menashe*, descendants of Menasseh, one of the ten lost tribes of Israel exiled by the Assyrian Empire over 27 centuries ago, migrated through Central Asia and the Far East before settling in present-day north-

eastern India, near the borders of Burma and Bangladesh. Through the centuries, they maintained Jewish traditions such as observing the Sabbath, adhering to kosher dietary laws, celebrating festivals, and observing laws of family purity, while nurturing the hope of eventually returning to their ancestral homeland.

31 Babylonian Talmud, *Sanhedrin* 98a
32 Rabbi Elijah of Vilna, cited in *Kol HaTor*
33 Rabbi Hanan Porat, *The Messiah of David, the Messiah of Joseph and the Secret of their Combination*, 486
34 Among this group were Rabbis Haim Druckman, Eliezer Waldman, Moshe Levinger, Shlomo Aviner and others
35 Haggai Segal, *Dear Brothers: The West Bank Jewish Underground*, 21-22
36 G.K. Chesterton, *Orthodoxy*, chapter 5
37 Rabbi Shlomo Aviner, *Commentary to Orot*, footnote 2119
38 Midrash Shocher Tov, 72:3

CHAPTER 14:

1 Amit Segal, *The Story of Israeli Politics*
2 Dr. Pinchas Polonsky, *The Messianic Process of Modern Israel: The 3 Stages of Shaul, David and Shlomo*, mizrachi.org/hamizrachi/the-messianic-process-of-modern-israel/
3 Rabbi Haim ibn Attar, *Or HaChaim*, Numbers 24:17
4 Ethiopian Jews descend from the tribe of Dan, while about 5,000 *Bnei Menashe* (Children of Manasseh) have returned to Israel from their communities on the Indian-Burmese border.
5 Rabbi Yehuda Leon Ashkenazi, *A Eulogy for the Messiah?*
6 Interestingly, Sharon named his son 'Omri,' after the wicked king who nonetheless is praised for building up the land of Israel - though unlike Sharon, the wicked King Omri did not destroy what he built.
7 *Garinim Torani'im: The Religious Zionist idealists transforming communities throughout Israel*, mizrachi.org/hamizrachi/garinim-toraniim-the-religious-zionist-idealists-transforming-communities-throughout-israel/

8. Eliran Aharon, *'IDF shouldn't fight half its soldiers'*, www.israelnationalnews.com/news/247302
9. Caroline Glick, *It's Not about Democracy*, www.jns.org/its-not-about-democracy/
10. See chapter 15, *Fight Like David: The Biblical Response to Terror*
11. Babylonian Talmud, *Zevachim* 54b
12. Attributed to Rabbi Zvi Yehuda Kook, cited by Meir Vaknin, *The Holiness of Man and Time*, https://ladaat.co/archives/74201
13. Babylonian Talmud, *Sanhedrin* 102a
14. *Ethics of our Fathers*, 5:16
15. Rabbi Tzadok Hakohen of Lublin, *Poked Ikkarim*, 1:33

CHAPTER 15:

1. The traditional seven day mourning period observed by immediate relatives for their loved ones.
2. Traditional *Avinu Malkeinu* (Our Father, Our King) Prayer
3. Rabbi Joseph Soloveitchik, *Kol Dodi Dofek*, www.sefaria.org.il/Kol_Dodi_Dofek%2C_Six_Knocks?lang=bi
4. Micah Bar, *Red Lines in the Israeli Deterrence Strategy*, Ma'arachot, 1990, 92
5. Eric Metaxas, *Bonhoeffer: Pastor, Martyr, Prophet, Spy*, 314
6. "And they married Moabite women, one named Orpah, and the other named Ruth…" (Ruth 1:4).
7. Numbers Rabba 14:1
8. Itamar Segal, *Time To Awaken*, Olam Katan, March 15, 2024, https://olam-katan.co.il/archives/12618
9. Babylonian Talmud, *Yevamot* 79a
10. Menachem Begin, *The Revolt*, 36
11. Jewish Prayer Book, The *Amidah* Prayer

CHAPTER 16:

1. Eric Metaxas, *Bonhoeffer: Pastor, Martyr, Prophet, Spy*, 249-250
2. Daniel Goldhagen, *Hitler's Willing Executioners: Ordinary Germans and the Holocaust*
3. *Poll shows Palestinians back Oct. 7 attack on Israel, support for Hamas rises*, www.reuters.com/world/middle-east/poll-shows-palestinians-back-oct-7-attack-israel-support-hamas-rises-2023-12-14/
4. *Poll: 72% of Palestinians support forming more armed groups in West Bank*, www.timesofisrael.com/poll-72-of-palestinians-support-forming-more-armed-groups-in-west-bank/
5. Andrew Tobin, *'Just as Cruel as the Terrorists': Many Ordinary Palestinians Joined in Hamas's Atrocities Against Israel*, https://freebeacon.com/national-security/just-as-cruel-as-the-terrorists-many-ordinary-palestinians-joined-in-hamass-atrocities-against-israel/
6. Ibid.
7. Dov Fischer, *The "innocent" civilians of Gaza*, www.israelnationalnews.com/news/382016
8. https://twitter.com/EinatWilf/status/1716227100716237132
9. Daniel Greenfield, *The Redemption of Israel*, www.danielgreenfield.org/2017/04/the-redemption-of-israel.html
10. Rabbi Joseph B. Soloveitchik, *Kol Dodi Dofek*, 78-79
11. See *Esau: The Deceptive Pig*
12. Babylonian Talmud, *Megillah* 13a

CHAPTER 17:

1. Bari Weiss, *Bibi's Back: A Conversation with Israel's New Prime Minister*, www.thefp.com/p/bibis-back-a-conversation-with-israels
2. Yossi Klein HaLevi, *The Fall of Benjamin Netanyahu*, www.latimes.com/opinion/story/2023-03-27/israel-protests-benjamin-netanyahu-judicial-legislation

3 Aviel Schneider, *Hamas is Amalek – and Israel is obliged to destroy them*, www.israeltoday.co.il/read/hamas-is-amalek-and-israel-is-obliged-to-destroy-them/

4 See chapter 16, *Jews Who Refuse to See: From Nazi Germany to Gaza*

5 Rabbi Meir Wisser, I Samuel 15:9

6 Elie Mischel, *Bibi's Brother-in-Law: The 3 Sins that Led to October 7th*, https://israel365news.com/379075/bibis-brother-in-law-the-3-sins-that-led-to-october-7th/

7 Babylonian Talmud, *Gittin* 45a

8 Rabbi Yehuda Leon Ashkenazi, *A Eulogy for the Messiah?*, 72

9 *Statement by PM Netanyahu*, www.gov.il/en/departments/news/statement-by-pm-netanyahu-10-jam-2024

CHAPTER 18:

1 Yael Ingel, *We Shall Return: The Spirit of Kibbutz Nirim Will Prevail*, https://blog.nli.org.il/en/hoi_nirim/

2 Miryam Zakheim, *What Is the Meaning of "Um-Shmum"? David Ben-Gurion vs. the World*, https://blog.nli.org.il/en/hoi_um_shmum_ben_gurion/

3 Rabbi Meir Wisser, Zephaniah 3:11

4 Nancy A. Youssef & Jared Malsin, *U.S. Delays Sending Precision Weapons to Israel*, www.wsj.com/world/middle-east/u-s-delays-sending-precision-weapons-to-israel-253f12f0

5 Natan Ehrenreich, *Menachem Begin Warned Us about Joe Biden*, www.nationalreview.com/corner/menachem-begin-warned-us-about-joe-biden/

6 Rabbi Moshe Avigdor Amiel, *Hegyonot el Ami*, 203

7 Rabbi Moshe Avigdor Amiel, *Hegyonot El Ami*, Genesis, 350

8 Lahav Harkov, *Justice Minister Levin: Washington aiding Israel's protesters against judicial reform*, www.jpost.com/israel-news/article-741759

9 Rabbi Yaakov Moshe Charlop, *Mei Marom* 6:61

10 Rabbi Abraham Isaac Kook, *Letters*, #644

11 Jonathan Silver, *The Return of Paganism and the Desecration of Self-Govern-*

ment, https://mosaicmagazine.com/observation/politics-current-affairs/2021/01/the-rise-of-paganism-in-america-and-the-desecration-of-self-government/

12 Christopher Cann, *The young are now most unhappy people in the United States, new report shows*, www.usatoday.com/story/news/nation/2024/03/21/world-happiness-report-young-people-u-s/73051010007/

13 Jacob Laznik, *Israelis are fifth happiest in the world despite ongoing war, report finds*, https://m.jpost.com/israel-news/article-792821

14 Paul Moreland, *The riddle of modern Israel's remarkably high birth rates*, www.thejc.com/lets-talk/the-riddle-of-modern-israels-remarkably-high-birth-rates-rcfo0j6c

15 *Israel's Rightward Shift*, www.csis.org/analysis/israels-rightward-shift

16 Anita Singh, *Israelis rush home to volunteer in fight against Hamas: 'I'll do whatever I can'*, www.independent.co.uk/news/world/middle-east/israel-gaza-hamas-war-india-us-b2428451.html

17 *Israeli cabinet unanimously opposes unilateral recognition of Palestinian state*, www.i24news.tv/en/news/israel/politics/1708253348-netanyahu-proposes-gov-t-measure-rejecting-unilateral-recognition-of-palestinian-state

18 Babylonian Talmud, *Shabbat* 151b

19 Rabbi Pesach Wolicki, *The possible Rafah invasion and the status of US-Israel relations*, www.jpost.com/opinion/article-790615

20 Alex Kane, *The New Debate Over Aid to Israel*, https://jewishcurrents.org/the-new-debate-over-aid-to-israel

21 Dov Fischer, *The message of defeating Hamas in Rafah without Biden*, www.israelnationalnews.com/news/389727

CHAPTER 19:

1 Emma Lazarus, *The Banner of the Jew* (1882)

2 Josh Hasten, *New York radio talk-show host Sid Rosenberg visits Israel for first time*, www.jns.org/ny-radio-talk-show-host-sid-rosenberg-visits-israel-for-the-first-time/

3 www.youtube.com/watch?v=tODy1TCcDmg

4 The fringes or tassels worn on four cornered garments by Jewish men, per Numbers 15:37–41 and Deuteronomy 22:12.

5 Rabbi Abraham Isaac Kook, *Orot HaTechiyah* 1

6 Andrea Samuels, *October 7 has ignited the Jewish spark*, www.jpost.com/opinion/article-779096

7 Moshe New, *Amid War, Terror and Antisemitism, Survey Reports Spiritual Awakening of American Jewry*, www.chabad.org/news/article_cdo/aid/6166742/jewish/Amid-War-Terror-and-Antisemitism-Survey-Reports-Spiritual-Awakening-of-American-Jewry.htm

8 Rabbi Abraham Isaac Kook, *Chadarav*, 207

9 Rabbi Yaakov Moshe Charlop, *Mei Marom*, Volume 6

10 *Poll: Most young Americans think Israel should be 'ended and given to Hamas'*, www.timesofisrael.com/poll-most-young-americans-back-ending-israel-many-find-jewish-genocide-calls-okay/

11 Babylonian Talmud, *Megillah* 12a

12 The Men of the Great Assembly, known in Hebrew as *Anshei Knesset HaGedolah*, were a distinctive group of Jewish leaders who took charge of Jewish affairs between 410 BCE and 310 BCE. This era began after the destruction of the First Temple and extended into the early years of the Second Temple period, culminating with the invasion of the Greeks under the leadership of Alexander the Great.

13 Rabbi Benjamin Lau, *Shivat Zion*, 153-155

14 Babylonian Talmud, *Megillah* 13b

15 Babylonian Talmud, *Taanit* 23a

16 Rabbi Yosef Hayyim of Bagdad, *Ben Yehoyada*, *Megillah* 13b

17 Rabbi Meir Kahane, cited by Lenny Goldberg, *The Wit and Wisdom of Meir Kahane*, 149-150

18 *On Israel, Progressive Jews Feel Abandoned by Their Left-Wing Allies*, www.nytimes.com/2023/10/20/us/politics/progressive-jews-united-states.html

19 Babylonian Talmud, *Megillah* 14a

20 Babylonian Talmud, *Shavuot* 39a

21 Rabbi Judah Halevi, *Kuzari*, 2:24

22 Justin Wise, *Protesters chant 'Go home, Jacob' after Minneapolis mayor refus-*

es to commit to defunding police, https://thehill.com/homenews/state-watch/501530-protestors-boo-chant-go-home-jacob-after-minneapolis-mayor-says-he/

23 Cited by D Yudelovitz, *The Legion and the Torn Torah Scroll*, Hamashkif, September 9, 1940
24 Vladimir Jabotinsky, *Jabotinsky's warning to Warsaw Jews, Tisha B'Av 1938*, https://thejerusalemconnection.us/blog/2011/08/08/jabotinsky-warning-to-warsaw-jews-tisha-bav-1938/
25 George Eliot, *Daniel Deronda*
26 Rabbi Abraham Isaac Kook, cited in Avinoam Roznack, *The Dream and Reality: Struggles, Loneliness and Pain*, https://lib.cet.ac.il/pages/item.asp?item=18599
27 Rabbi Isaac Nissenbaum, *Resisim* 13, HaMizrachi #11 (1920)
28 Rabbi Abraham Isaac Kook, *Iggrot Ra'aya*, #555
29 Elie Mischel, *Uncomfortable Truths: Speaking Honestly as Life Turns Upside Down*, https://jewishlink.news/uncomfortable-truths-speaking-honestly-as-life-turns-upside-down-part-one/
30 Hillel Halkin, *Letters to an American Jewish Friend*, 240-241
31 Babylonian Talmud, *Ketubot* 112a
32 *Amidah* Prayer
33 Yael Leibowitz, *Go, and Know...*, https://blogs.timesofisrael.com/go-and-know/
34 Rabbi Shlomo Carlebach, *Return Again*

CHAPTER 20:

1 Cited in Menachem Kampinsky, *Between Two High Priests*, 105-106
2 Rabbi Abraham Isaac Kook, *Orot HaMilchama* 6
3 Gianluca Pacchiani, *Hamas official says group aims to repeat Oct. 7 onslaught many times to destroy Israel*, www.timesofisrael.com/hamas-official-says-group-aims-to-repeat-oct-7-onslaught-many-times-to-destroy-israel/
4 Ohad Merlin, *Qatari official: Jews are murderers of prophets; October 7 is only*

a *'prelude'*, www.jpost.com/middle-east/iran-news/qatari-official-jews-are-murderers-of-prophets-october-7th-is-only-a-prelude-798358

5 *At Emergency Special Session, General Assembly Overwhelmingly Backs Membership of Palestine to United Nations, Urges Security Council Support Bid*, https://press.un.org/en/2024/ga12599.doc.htmhttps://press.un.org/en/2024/ga12599.doc.htm

6 Lawrence Richard, *Columbia University anti-Israel protests: 5 dramatic moments from a week of chaos*, https://nypost.com/2024/04/22/us-news/columbia-university-anti-israel-protesters-5-dramatic-moments-from-a-week-of-chaos/

7 *'Baby killers' – Jewish mom stunned by violent threats against her schoolkids, 5 and 7*, https://worldisraelnews.com/baby-killers-jewish-mom-stunned-by-violent-threats-against-her-school-kids-5-and-7/

8 Lisa Klug, *Super-conservative PragerU aims to arm pro-Israel students for their campus 'wastelands,'* www.timesofisrael.com/super-conservative-prageru-aims-to-arm-pro-israel-students-for-their-campus-wastelands/

9 Dennis Prager, *A Reminder to American Jews: Civilization Is Fragile*, https://jewishjournal.com/commentary/opinion/322560/a-reminder-to-american-jews-civilization-is-fragile/

10 Michael Lee, *'Death to America' rapidly emerging as key slogan of anti-Israel agitators in US*, www.foxnews.com/politics/death-to-america-rapidly-emerging-key-slogan-anti-israel-agitators-us

11 Steven Vago, *Pro-Israel protesters call on 'traitor' Chuck Schumer to resign: 'Chuck the Chuck'*, https://nypost.com/2024/05/10/us-news/pro-israel-protesters-call-on-traitor-chuck-schumer-to-resign-chuck-the-chuck/

12 Reuven Feuerman, *Why the United States is in Existential Danger*, Olam Katan #947 https://olam-katan.co.il/archives/12938

13 Rabbi Yehuda Leon Ashkenazi, *A Eulogy for the Messiah?*, 70-71

14 Etgar Lefkovits, *'Aliyah' applications from Western countries surge since Oct. 7*, www.jns.org/surge-in-aliyah-applications-since-war-began/

15 Rabbi Judah HaLevi, *Kuzari*, Conclusion

16 Rabbi Abraham Isaac Kook, *Orot HaMilchama* 1

17 Sivan Rahav Meir, *Jerusalem Consoles*, www.jewishpress.com/judaism/parsha/sivan-rahav-meir/jerusalem-consoles/2024/03/22/

18 Rabbi Abraham Isaac Kook, *Orot HaTechiya*, chapter 5

19 *We have Risen and been Encouraged*, Olam Katan #946, 2 Iyar, 10

20. *'Not your fault': Mother sends love, support to troops who killed son in tragic error*, www.timesofisrael.com/not-your-fault-mother-sends-love-support-to-troops-who-killed-son-in-tragic-error/
21. HaTikvah 6, *Superheroes*
22. Rabbi Abraham Isaac Kook, *Orot Yisrael* 5:15
23.
24. Babylonian Talmud, *Sotah* 13a
25. Genesis Rabba 77:3
26. Rashi, Genesis 32:27
27. Rashi, Genesis 32:29
28. *Lekach Tov*, cited in Rabbi Menachem Kasher, *Torah Sheleimah* 148
29. Rabbi Meir Wisser, Amos 9:11-12
30. "House of War"
31. Rabbi Oury Cherki, *The Emiratis' Islam of tolerance is the hope of the Muslim world*, www.jpost.com/middle-east/article-790200
32. Ari Abramowitz, *Arugot Farm: Redemption on the Judean Frontier*, https://mizrachi.org/hamizrachi/arugot-farm-redemption-on-the-judean-frontier/
33. Rabbi Abraham Isaac Kook, *Orot*, chapter 14
34. Rabbi Abraham Isaac Kook, *Orot*, chapter 71

IN HONOR OF

Elie & Rebecca

We send much love and wish you mazal tov on the publication of this beautiful sefer!!

You have written with insight and great strength and shown us, in the words of Elie Wiesel, that "in Jewish history, there are no coincidences."

May Hashem bless you with the strength to continue to write and inspire with your words of Torah. We are so proud of you!!

HOWIE & TERRY
MISCHEL

JUDAH & ORA
MISCHEL

ARIEL & YOSEF
GINSBERG

SARAH & ARI
GOLDBERG

IN HONOR OF

*Our wonderful,
loving children
& grandchildren*

Each a blessing from Hashem, and constant
reminders of how truly rewarded we are.

OPA LENNY &
GRANDMA MUSHY FULD

IN HONOR OF

Rabbi Mischel

ALICE & JACOB KLEIN

IN HONOR OF THE

brave soldiers of the Israel Defense Forces

who are protecting our people.

LOUIS AND ELKE CHAPMAN
MICHAEL AND CHANI CHAPMAN

To all the fallen of the nation of Israel

may we bless the generations to come with the strength to overcome the senseless hatred that has shadowed us through the ages.

בַּיּוֹם הַהוּא יִהְיֶה יְהוָה אֶחָד וּשְׁמוֹ אֶחָד

In enduring memory and hope

BENSHUSHAN FAMILY

Mazel Tov Reb Elie!

*May we merit to continue to see
God's miracles in our days as we march closer
to the final redemption.*

RAMI GOLDBERG

Mazel Tov to Reb Elie

*It is an honor to pay tribute to R' Judah and Ora Mischel
A couple who are involved and accomplish so much for Klal Yisroel.
May הקב"ה give them the strength to continue in their עבודת הקדוש.*

With much admiration,

EPHRAIM & CHAYA MILLER

Greetings

FRAN & JERRY WEINBERG

www.ingramcontent.com/pod-product-compliance
Lightning Source LLC
Chambersburg PA
CBHW070326010526
44107CB00004B/428